Public Administration

Public Administration

The Interdisciplinary Study
of Government

Jos C. N. Raadschelders

OXFORD
UNIVERSITY PRESS

OXFORD

UNIVERSITY PRESS

Great Clarendon Street, Oxford OX2 6DP

Oxford University Press is a department of the University of Oxford.
It furthers the University's objective of excellence in research, scholarship,
and education by publishing worldwide in

Oxford New York

Auckland Cape Town Dar es Salaam Hong Kong Karachi
Kuala Lumpur Madrid Melbourne Mexico City Nairobi
New Delhi Shanghai Taipei Toronto

With offices in

Argentina Austria Brazil Chile Czech Republic France Greece
Guatemala Hungary Italy Japan Poland Portugal Singapore
South Korea Switzerland Thailand Turkey Ukraine Vietnam

Oxford is a registered trade mark of Oxford University Press
in the UK and in certain other countries

Published in the United States
by Oxford University Press Inc., New York

© Jos C. N. Raadschelders, 2011

The moral rights of the author have been asserted
Database right Oxford University Press (maker)

First published 2011

All rights reserved. No part of this publication may be reproduced,
stored in a retrieval system, or transmitted, in any form or by any means,
without the prior permission in writing of Oxford University Press,
or as expressly permitted by law, or under terms agreed with the appropriate
reprographics rights organization. Enquiries concerning reproduction
outside the scope of the above should be sent to the Rights Department,
Oxford University Press, at the address above

You must not circulate this book in any other binding or cover
and you must impose the same condition on any acquirer

British Library Cataloguing in Publication Data
Data available

Library of Congress Cataloging in Publication Data
Data available

Typeset by SPI Publisher Services, Pondicherry, India
Printed in Great Britain
on acid-free paper by
MPG Books Group, Bodmin and King's Lynn

ISBN 978-0-19-969389-4

1 3 5 7 9 10 8 6 4 2

Preface

Public administration is the academic study concerned with the internal structure and functioning of government (i.e., its officials and its organizations) and with government's penetration of society and interaction with its citizens. Scholars of public administration seek to capture the complexity of government in society, but how this is done depends upon what is considered the nature of the study: Is it a science, and/or a craft/profession, and/or an art? Some scholars have tried to provide the study with a clear identity by considering it as a science, others have attempted to do so by focusing on the craft and/or profession element (e.g., usable knowledge; medicine, law, engineering, architecture). While many will agree that governing is also an art, so far no public administration scholar has endeavored to develop the study's identity on that basis. It appears there is no agreement about the nature of the study. What public administration scholars implicitly agree upon, as many social scientists do, is that careful attention for methodology (i.e., the study of methods) and appropriate application of methods will result in better knowledge.

Curiously, much less effort is spent on developing an epistemology, that is, an inquiry into the nature and sources of knowledge, in the study of public administration. An epistemology of the study is rooted in an ontology of it, that is, an inquiry into the nature of the phenomenon that public administration studies. This phenomenon, government, constantly changes in response to both natural and social events. Social phenomena cannot be analyzed in the same manner as natural phenomena, because they are not "governed" by universal laws (e.g., gravity, magnetism). Thus, social scientists should reflect upon the nature of the phenomenon they seek to study and how it can be studied. Applying methods and studying methodology without regard for epistemology and ontology is not unlike spanning the cart before the horse. Thus, wondering whether the study is science, or craft/profession, or art, is really not the way toward determining the nature of the study. And so, it continues to suffer, as Waldo observed, "... from so many identity crises that mere adolescence seems idyllic."

Waldo was the first to speak of an identity crisis (1968) but it really started with the acidic exchange between him and Simon in 1952. This identity crisis has not abated one bit. In fact, one might even say that since the 1950s and 1960s, "empiricists" and "interpretivists" have dug their heels deeper in their own sand. The question "What is (the identity of) public administration?" cannot be answered through a top-down approach that either assumes that the study is a science, or a craft/profession, or an art, or presumes the possibility that the study can be unified around a particular methodology and set of methods. The former precludes that public administration can be science, and craft/profession, and art; the latter forces scholars into an unproductive ranking of methods and approaches. Each of these approaches (science, craft/ profession, art; methods) to identifying the nature of the study tells more about their respective advocates than about the nature of the study. It is more profitable to develop conceptual maps of the study's sources, topics, theories, and methods, and debates in all the richness and variety so evident in its many and varied publications. These conceptual maps are building blocks – hence providing a bottom-up approach – for establishing the nature of the study that represent neither a simplistic but inclusive list of the study's diverse sources, concepts, theories, methods, and debates, nor an exclusive list of what is "scientific" and what is not.

One of the challenges confronting any effort at connecting sources of knowledge and theories and concepts-in-use is that attention for government as a social phenomenon is fragmented across the social sciences, that public administration scholars are internally divided about the nature/identity of their study, that the object of the study is not only determined by scholars but also by practitioners, corporate executives, and citizens, and, finally, that sources of knowledge are dispersed across thousands upon thousands of public organizations and societal associations. Can we get beyond the fragmentation of knowledge about government within the study and across the social sciences and somehow map these highly dispersed bodies and sources of knowledge?

The short answer is that public administration's nature is sooner captured by its capacity for building bridges between bodies and sources of knowledge then by a search for disciplinary boundaries. The study of public administration serves as an *intellectual umbrella* for research on government across disciplines and studies. Given that knowledge about government is dispersed across the social sciences, and given public administration's "umbrella" function, a search for boundaries is a dead end. The long answer is presented in the remainder of this book. To date, the study is defined through top-down approaches, with the study organized around a central concept and/or around a specific methodology. In this study a bottom-up approach is used, with conceptual maps as building blocks, focusing on the epistemological foundations of the study by means of mapping its sources of knowledge, its topics, theories, intellectual traditions, and modes of knowledge integration.

The rationale for this book is elaborated in Chapter 1 which will open with a section on why public administration has no boundaries and then explore the emergence of the study against the background of the expanding conception of state (since the sixteenth century) and the growth of public services (since the seventeenth century). This will provide the basis for a discussion of the study's identity crises in comparison to that in political science. Some attention will also be given to the fact that most of the disciplines and studies within the three main branches of knowledge report identity crises simply as a function of differentiation through specialization on the one hand and because of different intellectual schools within each discipline on the other hand. Next, this book's method of conceptual mapping is briefly explored. Finally, the claim is made that the study is mature, and this is substantiated in the remainder of this book.

In Chapter 2 the study of public administration is situated in the three great branches of learning: the natural sciences, the social sciences, and the humanities. This is done, first, by discussing various examples of how scholars (from various disciplinary backgrounds) have attempted to link bodies of knowledge together through conceptual maps of knowledge at large. Following that, second, the three branches of knowledge are compared. This is important because the quality of public administration research has been questioned upon the argument that the study is not even close to the achievements of the natural sciences. But, is such a comparison appropriate and/or fair? Next, challenges and problems of social science research are discussed in connection to some preliminary remarks about the specific nature of the study of public administration.

In Chapter 3, various sources of knowledge for public administration will be mapped and the first figure in that chapter is the first conceptual map specific to the study of public administration. It will be shown that knowledge in public administration about government is not only fragmented within the study itself (i.e., in the study's specializations) and across the social sciences, but also across governmental organizations and across society at large. Indeed, to get a flavor of the extent to which sources of knowledge (and, by extension, organizational memory) in government organizations are fragmented, organizational structures are presented from the most general (federal government) to a very specific (local) level. The examples provided are from American government organizations, but these can easily be replaced by organizational structures in other countries. Also, examples will be provided of how policymaking really draws upon the interaction between and collaboration among various levels of government, which is further evidence of the extensive fragmentation of knowledge sources about government. While the entire book is focused on the nature of the study of public administration, it is in this chapter that the reader may think that the focus shifts to a discussion of government. However, that is not the case. Chapter 3 merely seeks to provide a conceptual map of the fragmentation of knowledge sources that the study has to deal with.

In Chapters 4–7, conceptual maps of various aspects of the study are presented and discussed. In Chapter 4, topics of interest to the study are identified, and several examples are discussed of how various authors have mapped the study. Some authors developed conceptual maps with the aim to frame an introductory textbook, others sought to frame the study as a whole. An example of how large the variety of theories is that are used in the study, is provided in Chapter 5. Use of different theories is indicative of different ideas about what constitutes appropriate and good scholarship and so different schools of thought and intellectual debates in public administration are mapped in Chapter 6. Chapter 7 contains conceptual maps of how knowledge can be integrated, of examples of knowledge integration in public administration, and of public administration's interdisciplinarity. In the final chapter the book's main argument is summarized: public administration is an interdisciplinary, bridging study. Also a variety of chronic intellectual challenges will be identified.

In this book an effort is made to develop conceptual maps for the study of public administration. Chapters 1, 2, 3, and 8 contain mostly new material. The other chapters are partially based upon a series of articles and chapters published between 1999 and 2010, the contents of which have been adapted to avoid overlap. The arguments and thoughts put forward in these earlier publications are somewhat compartmentalized, with each publication focusing on one aspect of public administration's nature. Each of these publications can still be read in and of themselves, but they coalesce into the larger theme of the nature of the study of public administration. Tempting as it is to say that there was a conscious research plan that propelled these publications, there was none. They were born as much from accidental conversations with superb journal editors, from requests to write pieces, from dreams (the reader can take this most literally), as they were from simple thinking. Any effort to apply reconstructive logic to the sequence, the content, and the timing of these earlier publications is artificial.

This book's content primarily aims at scholars and advanced students in the study. It is not likely that it will settle debates between various groups of scholars about the nature of the study. It is, though, the first time that a case is provided for an interdisciplinary study of public administration that includes any conceivable approach (i.e., ranging from science to postmodern approaches). This book fills a significant gap in the public administration literature by exploring at length the epistemological (and to lesser extent the ontological) features of the study. Attention for methodology in and for the study dominates, but there is very little, if at all, attention for the nature of the study and how knowledge claims are justified in the study. It is critical that this issue is addressed, because in the current situation where government and society are heavily intertwined, and thus where "society" expects government to solve collective problems that cannot or will not be solved by the market or by collectives of citizens, it is important to explore the quality of knowledge used by government. Indeed, there is no historical precedent to the size of contemporary government in the Western world however that size is measured (personnel, revenue and expenditure, regulations, organizational differentiation). Consequentially, knowledge about government is increasingly dispersed and we lack so far any framework that links the various elements of the study together. In other words, this book provides the theoretical and conceptual foundation for a holistic view of the study. It provides a generalist's view of the study that has disappeared in the proliferation of specializations and of intellectual traditions and schools. Finally, this book is relevant to scholars and students anywhere in the world. About two-thirds of the references are drawn from American literature but that is a function of the fact that American scholarship (and especially the literature about the nature of the study) has dominated since the Second World War. Also, American scholarship is the most accessible to scholars elsewhere since English has become the *lingua franca* of the academic world.

This book has been written out of a drive to understand the nature of the study of public administration, but it would not have been possible without the engaged interest of others. Richard Box, George Frederickson, Rod Rhodes, Richard Stillman, and Gary Wamsley are the careful and critical friends and editors any scholar could wish for. Their encouragement and patience has been more important than I can describe. Richard Stillman and Kwang-hoon Lee took the trouble of reading the entire manuscript and I am in their debt for their insightful, thoughtful, and straightforward comments. It was humbling to see what one overlooks while writing, and it was humbling that they made the effort to crawl into my thoughts and enlighten me with their comments. Also, between 2003 and 2010, various American, European, and South-East Asian universities offered the opportunity to lecture on the interdisciplinary nature of the study of public administration. I have benefited from the various comments and responses received at these occasions. I would also like to extend my appreciation to David Musson and Emma Lambert from Oxford University Press, and the anonymous reviewers. David Musson not only shepherded the manuscript through the review process but also provided helpful comments upon its contents and upon the reviewers' responses. Emma Lambert, the assistant commissioning editor, patiently responded to any inquiry about reference, bibliography, and indexing styles. The anonymous reviewers graciously provided extensive comments and I hope to have done them justice.

An important part of what makes me tick is my family, and I could not have done this without their support. Julie convinced me that this book was a worthwhile endeavor (and she knows the parts I dreamed about!). My children let "daddy do his thing" and, now being teenagers (in reference to the concluding sentence in the introduction of my 2003-book), they can take less (but still quite a bit) for granted.

Jos C.N. Raadschelders
Norman, Oklahoma, January 2011

Contents

Acknowledgments

- Portions of Chapters 1 and 4 were adapted from an article published earlier as 1999. "A Coherent Framework for the Study of Public Administration," *Journal of Public Administration Research and Theory*, 9(2), 281–303. Used with permission from Oxford University Press.

- Portions of Chapters 2 and 3 were adapted from an article published earlier as 2000. "Understanding Government in Society: We See the Trees, but Could We See the Forest?" *Administrative Theory & Praxis*, 22(2), 192–225. Used with permission from M.E. Sharpe, Inc.

- Portions of 3 and 5 were adapted from an article published earlier as 2005. "Government and Public Administration: Challenges to and Need for Connecting Knowledge," *Administrative Theory & Praxis*, 27(4), 602–27. Used with permission from M.E. Sharpe, Inc.

- Portions of 4 originated in Jos C.N. Raadschelders (2003*b*). *Government. A Public Administration Perspective*. Armonk, NY: M.E. Sharpe. Used with permission from M.E. Sharpe, Inc.

- Parts of Section 4.4 in 4 have been adapted from a chapter published earlier as 2003, "Understanding Government through Differentiated Integration," in M.R. Rutgers (ed.), *Retracing Public Administration*, Amsterdam: JAI Press, 329–56. Used with permission from Elsevier Limited.

- Portions of 5 were adapted from an article published earlier as 2004. "A Model of the Arena of PA-Theory: Bogey Man, Doctor's Bag and/or Artist's Medium," *Administrative Theory & Praxis*, 26(1), 46–78. Used with permission from M.E. Sharpe, Inc.

- Portions of 6 were adapted from an article published earlier as 2008. "Understanding Government: Four Intellectual Traditions in the Study of Public Administration," *Public Administration (UK)*, 86(4), 925–49. Used with permission from Wiley/Blackwell Publishers.

- Portions of Chapters 1 and 7 originated in an article published earlier as 2010. "Identity Without Boundaries: Public Administration's Canon(s) of

Integration," *Administration and Society*, 42(2), 131–59. Used with permission from Sage Publications, Ltd.

- Part of Section 8.3 in 8 drew upon Jos C.N. Raadschelders and Mark R. Rutgers (2001). "Developments and Trends in the Study of Public Administration, 1945–Present," Paper presented at meeting of Research Committee 32 of the International Political Science Association, March 29, 2001, University of Oklahoma.

Although every effort was made to contact the copyright holders of material in this book, in some cases we were unable to do so. If the copyright holders contact the author or publisher, we will be pleased to rectify any omission at the earliest opportunity.

List of Figures

List of Tables

1

Framing the Nature of the Study of Public Administration: Origins, Identity Crises, Maturity, and Conceptual Mapping

'Tis all in peeces, all cohaerence gone. (John Donne, 1611, as quoted in Bellah et al., 1996)

The time has come for public administration to assert itself conceptually and normatively. If the field does not develop its own vision for itself, no one else will. And if it does not, the field's sense of self-worth and image of significance will continue to wane as the new century unfolds. (Goodsell, 2006)

In the past 100–150 years, government has grown to become a complex service-providing and policy-developing institution the size of which has no historical precedent. As a consequence, this social phenomenon has attracted attention from scholars across the social sciences. Among these, it is the study of public administration whose central object of interest is government, but its academic status is unlike that of "traditional disciplines" such as physics, psychology, or English. In fact, its status is debated, and its scholars do not agree on whether it is and ought to be first and foremost a science, or a profession, or a craft, or an art. At this point in time, the study of public administration has grown significantly in Western and non-Western countries as a function of governments' expanded role and position in society.

Much scholarly research has been devoted to describing and analyzing government, and to developing methods adequately capturing government. But, in view of debates about public administration's academic status, it is necessary, useful, and interesting to explore and outline the nature of the study of public administration. But, should its scholars not solve problems in the real world and stop wasting their time on subjects that are peripheral to that main objective? This question is legitimate but reveals a profound bias in favor of a study focused on mapping and solving present challenges for future benefit. This question also displays a remarkable ignorance about why the study suffers from such an identity crisis about its academic status. To say that the identity crisis is the result of the combined effect of lacking boundaries and interdisciplinary eclecticism (the two are not the same) is correct but not the whole story. We can dig a little deeper by dropping the study's characteristic a-temporal perspective and illuminate how the study's identity crisis (Sections 1.3 and 1.4) emerged alongside and/or following expanding conceptions of the state and growing government services (Section 1.2).

After World War II the study of public administration embarked upon an institutional life separate from its "mother disciplines" (law, political science, organization studies in continental Europe; political science in the United Kingdom and the United States) and endeavored to become truly "scientific." Herbert Simon advocated a science of administration and debunked the prewar "proverbs" and principles, while Dwight Waldo recognized that the art of governing an administrative state required a political theory that would capture a concept of state that was very different from earlier times.

To date, scholars in public administration, especially in the United States, are still out on the question of its identity for several reasons. First, public administration scholars disagree over whether the study should establish an identity defined by academic knowledge ideals only or also by the need to develop usable knowledge for problem-solving in the real world. Second, government officials oscillate between manifest pressures for quick fixes with the craft and tools of usable knowledge, and the more latent need for some kind of wisdom about the art of governing which is, inter alia, what we would expect trustees, guardians, or stewards of the common good to have. Third, the study of public administration is fragmented or compartmentalized into several specializations (quite like other "sciences" of nature, of society, and of humanity) and into – at least – three types of "schools" (i.e., traditional public administration, public management, and public policy schools and units) that prohibit a "unified" outlook on the study. Fourth, the study's object of interest, which is the structure and functioning of government in relation to society, has also attracted the attention of scholars in most other social sciences and even in the humanities and, thus, knowledge about government is also fragmented across the academy. It seems the study is without boundaries (Streib et al., 2001: 522), like Poland open to invasion from all sides (Meier, 2005: 659), but, unlike Poland, equally willing to cross boundaries into other disciplines (Waldo, 1968a: 454).

Is it possible, even desirable, to set boundaries for a study that is said to have none so far? Is it possible to go beyond this imagery of being the " . . . Israel of academic disciplines..." that is "...left to feast on the leftovers..." of the mono-disciplines (Rodgers and Rodgers, 2000: 436, 441). All of the solutions offered thus far, including more rigor in general (e.g., Perry and Kraemer, 1986), more rigorous methodological identity specific to the study (e.g., Gill and Meier, 2000), taking professional needs as starting point (e.g., Waldo, 1955, 1968), staying close to disciplinary political science (e.g., Mainzer, 1994), finding a core, unifying concept (Simon, 1947; Wamsley and Zald, 1973; Van Braam and Bemelmans-Videc, 1986; Debbasch, 1989; Raadschelders, 1999; Lan and Anders, 2000), and so forth, have each failed to gather a majority in the scholarly community. This is not surprising. Reconciliation of different viewpoints or theories around one or a few concepts and/or from a core methodology is ludicrous and unproductive, because one can expect that many existing theories and viewpoints are incommensurable. Boundaries, however defined, are not the solution to the challenge of capturing the nature and intellectual identity of the study, because the object of interest – that is, government – is studied in some fashion in every social science. Connecting the wide variety of theories and concepts-in-use in public administration through conceptual maps can help connect knowledge sources relevant to public administration, thus carrying the intellectual identity beyond the customary eclectic listing of topics and theories.

So far, suggestions for resolving the identity crisis have a top-down approach in common, organizing the study around one or a few concepts and then branching out into specializations. This book represents an effort to establish public administration's nature through a bottom-up approach: situating the study among the great branches of learning (Chapter 2), mapping various sources of knowledge (Chapter 3), mapping topics of interest (Chapter 4), mapping theories-in-use (Chapter 5), mapping schools of thought (Chapter 6), and mapping types of knowledge integration (Chapter 7). In the concluding chapter (Chapter 8), this bottom-up approach to constructing the study's nature is summarized. The study emerges then as fundamentally interdisciplinary that bridges knowledge sources from (at least) across the social sciences. The lack of boundaries may prove to be chronic, but is this a threat or an opportunity? The answer to this question will be saved for the final chapter.

In this chapter the rationale for this book is outlined. First, we need to explore why public administration has no boundaries and why, in fact, they are not possible (Section 1.1). This lack of boundaries is partially a function of the unprecedented expansion of state and government in society and requires a discussion about changes in the understanding of the concept of state in the past four centuries (Section 1.2). This is followed by attention for the study's identity crisis as it is traditionally perceived, particularly in the United States where this issue has generated more debate than in Europe. There is, however, not one crisis but there are four interrelated crises (Section 1.3). These crises have partly to do with public administration's origins in other disciplines, and especially in political science. It is interesting to see that the latter study faces the same identity challenges, even when some of its flagship journals tend to lean much more toward empirical research than do several flagship public administration journals (Section 1.4). In fact, an argument can be made that identity crises have become normal in all branches of knowledge (Section 1.5).

When all studies have identity crises, why bother trying to capture public administration's nature? The answer is simple. So far, discussions about the nature of the study have focused on the methodological challenge. Indeed, students are well prepared in the methodological intricacies of empirical research. What the study is missing, though, is attention for its ontology and its epistemology. There is ample literature on this for the social sciences at large and for a variety of different disciplines and studies, but there is dearth of publications that concern public administration (for exceptions, see Rutgers, 2004; Riccucci, 2010). That being so, the nature of the study is captured by developing conceptual maps and the method of conceptual mapping is discussed in Section 1.6. In the final section it is argued that public administration's identity crises only exists when defining and evaluating scholarship from an a-temporal perspective and along the narrow yardstick of objective, impersonal, and a-contextual knowledge so characteristic for the natural sciences. When defining scholarship on a broader basis (see Chapter 2), the identity crisis dissolves and the study appears as mature. That thesis, though, will be explored in Chapters 2–7.

1.1 Why Public Administration has no Boundaries

Establishing boundaries of knowledge concerned initially the demarcation of science from non-science (Popper, 1963) but also became important to understand the demarcation between and within disciplines (Good, 2000: 386). The so-called "boundary-work" is the means by which knowledge in a discipline is restricted, maintained, protected, expanded, and enforced (Good, 2000: 387). This boundary-work, as Gieryn (1983) called it (see also Lamont and Molnár, 2002), has become more and more important in the twentieth century because of the emergence of "mixed" disciplines. Knowledge boundaries have several rationales based on:

1. *ontology*: the nature of the phenomena that researchers wish to study. Can they be encompassed within a discipline or do they spill across disciplinary boundaries? This question concerns the academic character of the study and invites to examine some of the basic assumptions made

about what we study (e.g., the executive as hierarchy versus the more horizontal concept of "policy bureaucracy," see Page and Jenkins, 2005);

2. *epistemology*: how are claims to knowledge justified in the study? This question requires attention for the definition of knowledge, criteria and sources of knowledge, what knowledge is possible, and what the relation is between researcher and object of investigation;

3. *methodology*: what methods of analysis can be used to provide support to knowledge claims. Epistemology is concerned with the philosophy of how we can know, methodology is focused on the practice of how we can know.

Most public administration scholars, like many of their colleagues in the other social sciences, are generally focused on methodological questions and tend to neglect ontological and epistemological questions (for an exception, see Wamsley, 1996). This is probably due to a strong bias in favor of empirical research. In this book an epistemological foundation is developed for the study of public administration.

It is important to recognize that academic disciplines are socially constructed and are the product of retroactively defined "paradigms"[1] and research groups. In other words, boundaries do not necessarily reflect all aspects of the social world and are negotiated. Organizationally, disciplinary boundaries are important because they enable a discipline to secure sufficient financial and human resources vis-à-vis other entities. Status as a discipline also provides the independence and identity that may result in higher student enrollments. Thus, it is clear that boundaries serve important functions. Who defines these boundaries?

In "mature scientific communities," to use Kuhn's phrase (or the "hard sciences" in the vernacular), boundaries, identity, choice of research topics,

---

[1] On purpose, the word paradigm is placed between quotation marks. In Kuhn's description of scientific revolutions, one dominant paradigm is replaced by another and this sequential development represents progress of science (e.g., from the Ptolemean universe, to Newtonian physics, to post-Einstein physics). In such a sequential development of science, paradigms cannot but be incommensurable (i.e., Newton is still valid but under stricter ceteris paribus conditions). In the social sciences the concept of "paradigm" is often used, but then in acknowledgment of the simultaneous existence of multiple paradigms which each provide a particular lens upon social reality that are mutually exclusive (see, e.g., Burrell and Morgan, 1979: 25). Using the paradigm concept, a social science induces expectations about the degree to which these have objective knowledge that is acquired independent of the researcher's biases. That is, it may lead to comparisons between the natural and the social sciences where the latter is (a) judged by standards of the former that are inappropriate to its object of knowledge and (b) forced to debate its knowledge in a natural science framework where it cannot possible compete. With regard to the study of public administration it is very important to recognize that there are multiple ways in which reality is investigated. To avoid confusion about expectations of public administration (and social science) research, the "paradigm" concept can easily be replaced by "theory" or "framework of reference."

and quality of research are almost exclusively determined and evaluated by members of the same scholarly community. By contrast, in the social sciences boundaries, identity, choice of research topics, and quality of research are not solely the province of its scholars but also of other social and political actors. The choice of research problems and the quality of its outputs is not only justified in terms of what colleagues consider important, but also "...in terms of the socio-political importance of achieving a solution" (Kuhn, 1973: 164). If this is so for social sciences in general, it is even more so for an interdisciplinary study such as public administration. Kuhn never writes that the social sciences are less mature, but maturity qua "scientificness" does loom large in the minds of many who consider themselves to be positivists, empiricists, and/or evidence-based researchers. This inappropriate use of the paradigm concept, as Walker noted with respect to political science, "...encourages hyper-specialized tribalism within subfields and furthers the Balkanization of political science as a discipline" (2010: 434). Clearly, the same can be said for the social sciences at large (see Section 1.5).

Boundaries demarcate a discipline from other disciplines by means of concepts, models, and theories specific to that discipline. For instance, Lavoisier's periodic table of elements is specific to chemistry; Einstein's relativity theory is specific to particle physics; the Nash equilibrium is specific to mathematics (and applied by game theorists in various social sciences). Boundaries are useful to scholarly communities that act as trustees and guardians of a particular body of knowledge. Clearly, such disciplinary boundaries and identities have been successfully developed in the natural sciences and resulted in breath-taking theories which, in turn, have led to astonishing empirical discoveries (e.g., who in 1922–3 would not have been awed by Edwin Hubble's discovery that the universe is much larger than the Milky Way?). The natural sciences' success can be attributed to scholars who successfully narrowed their interests to explain some regularities in specific phenomena (Fiske, 1986: 74) the nature of which permit them to specify all relevant conditions and parameters under which certain reactions will occur (Secord, 1986: 208). Thus, natural scientists have been very successful in developing nomological networks, that is, systems of interrelated generalizations (D'Andrade, 1986: 28). In the social sciences it is much more difficult, and perhaps impossible, to restrict research to a particular set of objects and to outline *all* ceteris paribus conditions. Obviously, this is certainly the case for public administration.

The study of public administration does not have the kind of nomological network that reflects shared assumptions concerning rules of logic or "laws of nature" which underlies the natural sciences, but that is not indicative of inferior or even immature scholarship. It has been said that the "scientific" standards of the so-called "hard sciences" have been inappropriately applied to the social sciences (e.g., Kaplan, 1964: 398; D'Andrade, 1986: 39; Secord,

1986: 199; Hall, 1989: 33;), but let us be clear about why this happened. Some social scientists continue both explicitly and implicitly to compare research in their own study or field to that of their natural science colleagues and adopt "language" ("paradigm"[2]) and ideas about theory and method (e.g., "objectivity," "replicability") that do not readily fit the nature of the social sciences including the study of public administration (Henry et al., 2008). That is, they engage in a debate about scientificness of findings that is conducted within the framework of objective knowledge that natural science offers (Flyvbjerg, 2001: 3; Montuschi, 2003: 2). In other words, social scientists do not define "scientificness" on their own terms. It is thus that Shapiro notes that " ... the pervasive influence of logical empiricism [and its belief in objective knowledge, JR] on social scientist's conceptions of what constitutes 'scientific practice' ... " and then contrasting that to the realist position of most natural scientists who believe that theory-neutral observations cannot exist (2005: 39, footnote 41). In this study the scientificness of public administration will be constructed in terms relevant to the study, by mapping its sources of knowledge, its topics, its theories, its intellectual traditions, and its possibilities for knowledge integration.

Social science is a branch of knowledge marked by the instability, variability, and irregularity of its subject-matter (Kaplan, 1964: 348). It is clear that ontological and epistemological demarcation is meaningful and useful to natural scientists, but such demarcation is more problematic for the social sciences and certainly for public administration given its interdisiciplinary nature.

At least four concerns need to be addressed when considering the nature of the study of public administration. First, the scholarly community that studies government consists not only of public administration scholars and political scientists, but includes academics in just about every other social science. Students of public administration could try to define ontological and epistemological boundaries, but they cannot lay exclusive claim to the study of government. Public administration's boundaries are nibbled at by other social sciences making it not so much "an Israel," as Rodgers and Rodgers might say

---

[2] Many critics of Kuhn argued that he had suggested ways to improve "science," by reducing " ... the number of comprehensive theories to one, and to create a normal science that has this one theory as its paradigm" (Lakatos, 1970: 198). Kuhn, however, claims that his description of scientific progress does not at all provide a methodological prescription for how to proceed from a pre-paradigmatic to a paradigmatic stage. During the pre-paradigmatic stage, all of the facts that could lead to the development of a science are equally relevant (Kuhn, 1970*a*: 15). He expects that at some unspecified point other fields will experience that transition to science, and only then " ...does progress become an obvious characteristic of a field.[...] And only then do those prescriptions of mine which my critics decry come into play." (Kuhn, 1970*b*: 245). Kuhn, however, does not indicate how this can be done.

(2000: 436), but rather a " ... Poland, defenseless in the face of other fields with territorial designs" (Meier, 2005: 659).[3]

Also, the boundaries for the study of the public administration are often defined by social and political actors who are recipients (i.e., citizens, corporate executives) or designers (i.e., civil servants, political officeholders, lobbyists, interest groups) of government services and policies, and by a scholarly community that consists not only of academics who consider themselves social scientists but also by applied scholars such as consultants and analysts working in and around the governance process. While social scientists can limit their research to questions of "scientific" interest (e.g., Simon), applied scholars and analysts have no choice but to deal with topics thrust upon them by circumstances of the governance process, and to draw upon whatever sources of knowledge they can in order to provide effective and useful application of available knowledge.

Second, it is likely that the boundaries of the study of public administration vary with the degree of government intervention in society. That is, in a situation of limited government (e.g., a night-watchman state), it is conceivable that the study of public administration focuses mainly on government's role in writing and carrying out the law, and in providing basic services. By contrast, consider the situation of government growth since the 1880s (e.g., the emergence and expansion of welfare services) or the current trend toward contracting-out government services. Both required that the study of public administration expanded to include a much wider variety of actors and substantive interests. Indeed, this is what has happened in the past 150 years and has accelerated to a mind-boggling degree in Europe, North America, Australia and New Zealand, India, Japan, and South Korea in the last century and – more recently – in Chile, China, and Brazil. Also, the social, economic, political, and cultural climate influences the scope of government which in turn influences the substance of the study. In light of such changing "boundaries," any effort to establish and maintain "boundaries" of the study and practice of public administration is futile.

Third, boundaries of public administration will vary with political–administrative culture. For example, the study of public administration in the United States shares features with, but is also clearly different from, the Dutch, English, French, German, Italian, Scandinavian, Spanish, Swiss, and other traditions (Kickert and Stillman, 1999; Kickert, 2008: 2; Painter and Peters,

---

[3] Ken Meier, a former student of Waldo, is not the first to use that metaphor. Forty years ago, Dwight Waldo wrote that "Someone has said of Political Science that it is 'like Poland, open to invasion from every side ... [...].' Public Administration certainly has been 'open to invasion' from every side. But the metaphor obscures as much as it reveals. For not only have the invaders usually been welcomed, but often Public Administrationists have invaded other realms, to enlarge their own boundaries or in search of enrichment" (Waldo, 1968: 454).

2010). In contrast, the boundaries of physics are shared among physicists across the globe. Physicists (and mathematicians, chemists) can communicate with chalk and blackboard even when not knowing each other's national language. While, for instance, physicists might be influenced to a relatively minor degree by national culture or politics (such as the pressure to produce nuclear weapons), their attention and efforts are first and foremost influenced by the current "frontiers of knowledge." Of course, one could say that public administration everywhere studies public bureaucracy and organization, public policy and decision-making, political–administrative relations, intergovernmental relations, and so forth. However, public administration not only investigates the institutional arrangements or structures but also processes in what a given culture and society considers as the public sector or the administrative dimension of governance. It also explores how and why these functions operate as they do in a given culture, the extent to which they define the collective realm, the interplay between structure and function, and whether changes in structure and functioning (i.e., its processes and negotiated nature) are desirable. Thus, both the structure and the functioning of public organizations are highly related and vary according to geographical, cultural, and historical contexts (see, e.g., Hall, 1983; Hofstede and Hofstede, 2005).

Fourth, the subject-matter (Kaplan, 1964: 32, 290) of public administration must be defined in terms of its object of knowledge and its knowledge ideals (Raadschelders and Rutgers, 1989a: 75–6). Before addressing this, a vital semantic confusion between American and European usage of the words "subject" and "object" needs to be clarified first. To an American scholar such as Kaplan, "subject-matter" is synonymous to the topic that is studied. To a European scholar, the "object" of knowledge is that which is observed or studied (which is what Americans call the "subject-matter"), while the "subject" of knowledge is the researcher. Traditionally, it was believed that the object of study influences the subject. With regard to social reality this means that the social environment as perceived by humans influences human behavior (cf. the Thomas theorem: If people define situations as real then they are real in their consequences). Immanuel Kant inverted this and argued that it is the constitution (i.e., the sensory capabilities) of the individual (i.e., the subject) that affects the way that objects (i.e., in the social environment) are studied. This was carried one step further with the so-called "linguistic turn"[4] in philosophy that holds that what people perceive as reality is basically an agreement about naming and characterizing what we see. That is, without a

---

[4] This linguistic turn is usually traced to Ludwig Wittgenstein, though elements of it can already be found with the eighteenth-century German philosopher J.G. Hamann (Berlin, 1993: 35, 81), and has influenced theorists such as Richard Rorty, Michel Foucault, and Jacques Derrida (see, i.a., Benton and Craib, 2001: 93; Kurki, 2008: 72–3).

concept, we cannot "see"; there is no pre-theoretical way that we can define and demarcate problems in reality; all observation is theory-laden (Fay, 1996: 76; Shapiro, 2005: 15, 184).[5] John Stuart Mill (Reeves, 2007: 166) and Max Weber arrived at the same conclusion (Weber, 1946: 141–3; Diggins, 1996: 274).

Kant hinted at that by distinguishing a material object of knowledge from a formal object of knowledge: "All our cognition has a *twofold* relation, *first* to the *object*, second to the *subject*. In the former respect it is related to *presentation*, in the latter to *consciousness*..." (Kant, 1988: 37; italics IK). The *material object* of the study of public administration is the ultimate reality of government and governance itself and its interaction with citizens. We cannot, however, know that reality objectively, that is, independent of the observer and his or her context. Therefore, it is through the *formal object*, that is, the specific and formalized way in which the reality about government and its citizens is known and described, that public administration is defined.[6] That formal object includes concepts and their definitions as well as the particular methods with which we study these concepts. To be sure, it is through the formal object (i.e., theories, concepts, etc.) that we try to apprehend, understand, and capture a material object. However, no matter how hard we try, a formal object will never coincide with the fullness of the material object. That is, through our sensory perception and intellectual reasoning, we can only partially grasp reality (see on this basic distinction between material and formal object, e.g., Halder, 1975: 807–8; Maritain, 1979: 59; Cassirer, 2006: 208). It is true that inventors and scholars can and have artificially expanded our sensory capabilities. Consider the "worlds" that were opened up by microscope and telescope. However, these extensions may get us closer to, but never at the material object.

Following Aristotle, Kant argued that we can imagine the specific existence of anything through our senses or faculties (the bodily functions of sight,

---

[5] By way of illustration, as a graduate student I heard about an experiment conducted in the early 1960s by American anthropologists. They had lifted a Papua from New-Guinea and placed him on a busy intersection in Manhattan. Cameras on the four corners of the intersection recorded everything that happened for an hour. At the end of that hour, the researchers asked what the Papua had seen. Answer: "a banana." None of the researchers recalled seeing a banana, but when checking their tapes they noticed that a truck had passed the intersection that had carried an advertisement for bananas. They concluded that the Papua had not seen skyscrapers, cars, trucks, trousers, stores, glass, asphalt, etc., because he had no concepts for them. I recall the story but not its source, so perhaps it is apocryphal. This experiment is reminiscent of Kant, who observes that a savage may be cognizant of a house, but not knowing what it is he cannot cognize about it. See Immanuel Kant (1988: 37–8).

[6] The word "formal" is used as relating to or constituting "...logical, epistemological or ontological forms..." and "...belonging to a formalized system" (Webster's Third International Dictionary, Springfield, Massachusetts, 1993: 893). In the case of the social sciences, theoretical approaches (i.e., from "scientific" to postmodern), concepts, definitions, mathematical models, quantitative-statistical models, etc., are all elements of such a formalized system.

hearing, smell, touch, speech, and taste). The idea that we cannot know anything beyond what we can experience is also found with John Locke and is echoed in the writings of David Hume. With this position, Kant distanced himself from René Descartes who, following Plato, suggested that the sole basis of knowledge can only be self-evident propositions deduced by reason. Hence, to Descartes, rationalism trumps empiricism. To Kant, empiricism is a source of knowledge, but sensory perception does require some type of arrangement based on preexisting categories (cf. a priori knowledge) coded through evolutionary learning (Wuketits, 1990: 82). Going beyond Kant, evolutionary epistemologists such as Wuketits suggest that rationality is as much a function of perception as the senses are (although not of the same nature as the bodily or biological functions) and we can imagine reality only through those senses (ibid.: 185).

The material object of the study of public administration is the internal structure and functioning of government and its interactions with society at large. The question "What is the study's formal object?" is less easy to answer because there are no clear boundaries that demarcate the study from other academic pursuits. Mathematics, physics, chemistry, for instance, have a formal object at the level of their respective disciplines. In the case of public administration, and surely other interdisciplinary studies as well, there is no single formal object at disciplinary level. Perhaps a distinction should be made between a *first order formal object*, that refers to concepts and theories in and relevant to the study of government and governance as a whole, and *second order formal objects*, which concerns theories and concepts in and relevant to the various specializations in the study (e.g., budgeting and finance, implementation, policy process, organization theory, public management, human resource management, etc.). To date there are no first order formal objects in the study, but there are many, many second order formal objects.

The knowledge ideal concerns the methods by which knowledge is captured and includes both the types of knowledge (i.e., description and/or prescription) and the form of knowledge (i.e., quantitative and/or qualitative). The choice of type and form of knowledge depends entirely upon, in European parlance, the formal object of research, and, in American parlance, the subject matter of research. Public administration research uses descriptive and prescriptive approaches as well as quantitative and qualitative methods. That the study of public administration harbors such a large range of object (Europe) or subject (the United States) matters as well as a large range of approaches and methods has to do with the fact that it has systematically broadened its scope since its origins in the seventeenth century.

As will be shown, it was not until the sixteenth and seventeenth centuries that the study of government went beyond the study of polities and politics (that ultimately would become political science) and became the study of public administration emerging in the context of expanding conceptions of state followed by slowly, and later: more rapidly, expanding government services. Where public administration's object of knowledge was highly practical at first, it was the increased role and position of government in society that prompted the study to go beyond its initial rather technocratic and instrumental focus. To understand this process we must consider how the conception of the state expanded in early modern and modern society.

1.2 The Raison d'Être of Public Administration as a Practice and as a Study: From Raison d'État, via Rechtsstaat, to Administrative State

The study of public administration is focused on the structure and functioning of government in relation to the demands and needs of a citizenry living in a state's particular, and, in terms of jurisdictions, well-defined, sovereign territory. As a general concept, "land" can be public or private property but the more specific concept of a country's "territory" is often regarded as a property of the state that cannot be traded or inherited. People can only think of the land they live on in terms of a territory belonging to them when they live there year-round. When population size and density grow, there is a point where members of a community of people no longer know all others. Some anthropologists have suggested that a 150–500 people constitute the threshold (Mann, 1986: 143; Wade, 2006: 72) beyond which some rudimentary arrangements for governing are deemed necessary to augment the more traditional kin- and friendship relations in order to provide for community needs and for conflict resolution mechanisms. When population size and density continue to rise up to another threshold (and to my knowledge the literature provides no suggestion on where that threshold may be), it is government that expands its services to include those hitherto provided by private, generally: religious, organizations.

Up to the middle of the second millennium (Common Era, CE), state and government were very identified in terms of the individual ruler or group of rulers. Small (city-)states could be entirely independent (i.e., ancient Greece) or belong to a larger, distant jurisdiction (territorial state/empire, Trigger, 2003: 272) that allowed a significant degree of autonomy in exchange for annual taxes of some kind. Until the twelfth-, thirteenth-centuries CE, the dominant polities were those of city-state or empire. From that time on regional states emerged in Europe that were larger than city-states, but smaller than empires. These states generally were governed by an individual ruler, and could actually pass from one to the next. Those working for government, worked effectively for an individual in whom government and sovereignty were literally embodied. Louis XIV's (or rather Louis XIII, see Dyson, 1980: 137) *l'état c'est moi* may not quite have reflected the changes in political theory occurring in his time (see next subsection), but certainly reflected the sentiments on the relation between ruler and territory up to the sixteenth and seventeenth centuries. That is, the state was less and less regarded as a personal property of the monarch, and more and more as a rational, secular actor. Louis XIV understood this as well since shortly before his death he observed: *Je m'en vais, mais l'État demeurera toujours* (quoted in Gorski, 2001: 854; see also Poggi, 1978: 68–9; 1990: 47).

There are three necessary conditions to be met before a polity can be called a state. First, where city-state and empire both are characterized by the existence of dispersed and fragmented political powers, in a modern state political power is centralized in an institutional superstructure (usually fragmented in branches of power) and no longer in one individual person or group of persons. In this process of *political centralization*, regional powers are subjected to one central power.

Second, in a fully mature state the link between ruler and territory is severed. The well-being of the political community is no longer perceived as dependent upon the well-being of a ruler who acquired office upon hereditary right or military might, but upon the well-being of the state. Leibniz provided the theoretical foundation distinguishing "sovereign" (i.e., state and government) from "majesty" (i.e., individual officeholder) (Herz, 1976: 106; Dyson, 1980: 33).

Third, city-state and empire rely on a public service that mainly provides the traditional government functions of protecting the order and safety of the territory, such as defense, police, justice, and limited life-support services (granaries, hospital, water supply), and taxation to pay for it. An expanding state will go beyond these traditional services starts providing, for instance, education and health care, hitherto provided by private associations (e.g., usually of a religious nature: church, mosque, temple, synagogue). This process of *administrative centralization* is driven by growing population size and density and prompts a bureaucracy staffed to hire trained laymen instead of clergy (this is part of the reason that universities were established).

Each of these three conditions unfolded over time. In some territories, political and political and administrative centralization occurred early (e.g., Iceland, eleventh century; England and France thirteenth to sixteenth centuries), in others later (Dutch Republic, seventeenth century; Russia, eighteenth century; Germany and Italy, nineteenth century), but the reason was the same everywhere: the regional state emerged because it offered the best possible protection and security to people, and the state system, with sovereignty invested in territorial princes, proved to be a better guarantee of peace than the Holy Roman Emperor (Herz, 1976: 103).

Up to the middle of the nineteenth century, state-making was mainly limited to Europe, which, at the beginning of that century consisted of about twenty-five states. When large parts of Africa, Asia, Australia, and Latin America were colonized, the "mother countries" imposed their institutional infrastructure upon the newly acquired territories. This included the replacement of existing political superstructures or jurisdictions (such as the pre-colonial African empires and states; see Davidson, 1992) and tribal areas by the "state." Decolonization showed how much the "state" had become the dominant political form. Today, most of the earth's territory is part of a geographically defined state (except Antarctica). Political theory had to catch up.

From ancient Greece up to the late seventeenth century, political theory focused on the relation between ruler and ruled. In the context of the emerging state (particularly in twelfth- and thirteenth-century England and France), scholars started to consider and justify the possibility that an unjust ruler could be removed from office without jeopardizing the viability of the polity (Von Borch, 1954). The most extreme step that could be taken, to decapitate a ruler despite the fact that s/he was in office by divine right, illustrated the continuity of political unity through an abstraction that existed by virtue of negotiated right, that is, the state. When Hobbes pondered the choice between absolutism, investing state power in a powerful individual, or anarchy, where all people were subjected to the survival of the fittest, the state was already regarded as the prime unifier of communities of people.

In retrospect, there are two very distinct, yet interdependent, processes that helped turn the state into a unifying force in society. First in time came the conception of the state as a territory, a geographically defined area, whose internal affairs were no one's interest but that of the ruler(s) and his/their subjects. This conception of state, and, by implication, the idea of multiple, co-existing territorial states was affirmed in the 1648 Peace of Westphalia and again confirmed in the 1933 Montevideo conference that defined the state in terms of international law along lines drawn by Max Weber (Tilly, 1975: 27; Dyson, 1980; 1990: 70). Central to the Weberian definition is the Machiavellian idea that the state is the sole actor allowed to use coercion and, if necessary, physical violence in the effort to maintain order and stability in a community. To be more specific, his definition grounds the legitimacy of the state in terms of governments' traditional tasks: to maintain order and stability by means of defense (army, against outside agressors), policy and justice (against inside agressors), some relief against seasonal and economic hardships (e.g., the Egyptian and Roman granaries), some control over vital resources (e.g., irrigation in ancient Egypt and Mesopotamia), and imposing taxes to provide for these functions, tasks, and services. Weber's definition mainly accounts for a state in terms of international law and domestic sovereignty, but implicitly allows the possibility of the welfare state as an enabling and facilitating actor that provides a far wider range of services to help citizens grow to their full potential. That enabling and facilitative modern state is by far more invasive and intrusive than any of its ancient, medieval, and early modern predecessors.

The second process is that the state and its government differentiated from other societal organizations (Badie and Birnbaum, 1983; Birnbaum, 1985). That is, during prehistory and Antiquity the ruler's functions included those of military leader, high priest, supreme judge, and (what we call nowadays) head of state and head of government. These roles slowly separated since the Middle Ages. Also, it was not uncommon that government officials occupied positions in, what is nowadays called, the private sector. For instance, in the early modern age, high-ranking government officials occupied leading positions in (semi-)private corporations, and the various Trade Companies in the sixteenth and seventeenth centuries are a perfect example (e.g., the British and Dutch East and West India Companies). Between the twelfth and the late eighteenth centuries, the state and its government organizations slowly but surely separated from other social organizations, and, in due course, would take over certain functions from, for instance, the Catholic Church (especially in the areas of health care and education).

To understand this change from seeing the state only as one territorial and sovereign unit among others, the definition of which is outward oriented, to the state that is also an enabler and facilitator for citizens' desires, which is inward oriented, one must consider how the concept of state came to be defined by more than "territory."

1.2.1 *At Some Beginning there was the Idea: Raison d'État...*

By the time that Charles I was decapitated (1649), the state as dominant political entity was firmly in place, at least in England. The fate of a land or jurisdiction was no longer to be determined by the health and justness (or lack of these) of a king. The phrase "the king is dead, long live the king" of Arthurian legend had by then been replaced by "the king may die, but the state survives." Charles I was beheaded for a variety of reasons, but deep down he lost his life for *reasons of state*. His taxation without Parliamentary approval, resistance to mounting civil unrest, and his desire to hold on to power cost him his throne. And, as the coming and going of monarchs, presidents, and governing parties or coalitions has shown, the state persisted to be.

This notion of "reason of state," that is, from the French concept of *raison d'état* emerging in the sixteenth century,[7] provides the starting point for

---

[7] Originating from the Italian *ragione di stato* of Francesco Guiciardini (1512), Giovanni Della Casa (1549), and Giovanni Botero (1589) (Meinecke, 1957: 46; Dyson, 1980: 44, note 2).

conceptualizing the state as an abstract entity. Rather than only focusing on territorial boundaries vis-à-vis other states or on regarding the state as a personal property, the term "state" concerns the role and position of state and its government vis-à-vis the population. *Raison d'état* is usually translated as "reason of state" and this term can be understood in, at least, two ways.

First, and most common, is that "motives of state" justify government action in defense of the national interest, even when it violates individual freedom. No state in the past 500 years can claim that it did not justify at one point its actions by sacrificing individual rights for perceived or real collective benefits. Initially, this understanding of *raison d'état* concerned the state's external relations, where the balance of power vis-à-vis other sovereignties was maintained not through "bellicose and bloody-minded" armed confrontation but through the more civilized means of diplomacy (Poggi, 1990: 84). But, one can persuasively argue that *raison d'état* increasingly included the justification of domestic actions. For instance, Abraham Lincoln's suspension of Habeas Corpus, his shutting down of newspapers, and arranging favorable electoral circumstances by creating new states, and George W. Bush's wiretapping and imprisonment of suspected terrorists are just some examples. In both these cases the national unity and/or security was considered more important than individual rights. This is the sense in which *raison d'état* is used in the study of international relations.

Second, the French *raison*, derived from the Latin root "ratio," can also refer to rationality as a state of mind, to the power of reasoning (*raisonnement*). While reason as "motive of state" still allows the possibility that personal (ab) use of power is perceived or presented as legitimate, reason as rationality of state places the state, and then especially the democratic state, beyond anyone's ability to (ab)use power for a prolonged period of time. Think of it in the following manner. If the rationality of the state is best served by an individual officeholder stepping away from power, then that is what officeholders should do. However, so far very few heads of state and/or heads of government have voluntarily stepped away from power. George Washington is the rare exception; as is former French President Charles de Gaulle, but he did so in response to an unfavorable referendum. So, knowing that rulers may not step away from power without some persuasion, modern democracies have constrained the time that elected officeholders can stay in office through election cycles and/or term limits and have severely limited the power and authority of hereditary officeholders. Those who try cling to power no longer have to be decapitated. Reason defined as motive operates at the level of the individual and group: me or us versus you or them. Reason defined as rationality operates at the level of the collective, the imagined community (Anderson, 2006), where reasonable, collective action takes precedence over unreasonable individual action. In the seventeenth and eighteenth centuries, the state came to be regarded as the rational counterweight to the inherent irrationality of the masses.

1.2.2 ... *Then Came the Word:* Rechtsstaat ...

The notion of rationality of state was an idea that emerged in a world still governed by individual rulers, enlightened or not. It was to be, to use Schein's phrase (1985), the "basic underlying value" that provided the basis for efforts to codify the state more explicitly as an institutional arrangement of norms and rules that circumscribe acceptable behavior of public officeholders in the public realm. Enter the German word *Rechtsstaat* which is generally, and poorly, translated as "constitutional state," and better understood as a "state of law and justice." *Rechtsstaat* is a nineteenth-century concept first used by legal philosophers such as Carl Theodor Welcker (the first to use this concept in 1813; see Dyson, 1980: 123), Georg Friedrich Hegel, and Johann Christoph Freiherr van Aretin in the 1810s and early 1820s. The concept gained currency through the work of jurist and public administration scholar Robert von Mohl in the 1830s. It refers to a state whose boundaries are not only defined in terms of territory but also in terms of legitimizing foundation and constraining laws. In the capable hands of Von Mohl, the notion of *Rechtsstaat* changed from being a descriptive category that referred to a politically centralized system that strives to advance civil liberties and justice, to a normative objective where the state is defined by law striving to secure the freedom of the individual (cf. Locke). Doing so might require the state to go beyond its traditional protective functions of police, justice, and military and into the provision of social welfare services. This state is built on rational principles flowing from civil liberties, legal equality (cf. American Declaration of Independence), popular representation and participation of its citizens and is grounded in supremacy of law (Bhat, 2007: 68–9, 89). It is important to observe that this concept of *Rechtsstaat* is the culmination of a process of secularization of law that took centuries, and where the sources of law and justice were increasingly found in the rational faculties and creative imagination of human beings (cf. positive law) rather than in a divine authority (Bhat, 2007: 84). In this sense, *raison d'état* can be contrasted with the interests of the church. Both institutions had been entangled in a fight for domination since the eleventh century that would only be concluded at the end of the eighteenth century in the formal separation of church and state in the world's first constitutions.

The idea of *raison d'état* became word in the concept of *Rechtsstaat*. The world's first constitutions were written at the time of the Atlantic Revolutions (the United States, 1787; France, 1789–91; the Dutch Republic, 1798). The *Rechtsstaat* still represents the codified institutional superstructure of the masses state. Its most visible manifestation, a constitution, has been adopted by most states across the globe as the means through which the *Rechtsstaat* is founded and justified (Grote, 1999). Few states exist that do not have a Constitution, and those that do not generally have a set of constituting documents (e.g., the United Kingdom, New Zealand). Without *raison d'état* and *Rechtsstaat*, it would have been impossible to establish the modern *administrative state*.

1.2.3 ... *That Materialized in Action: the Benevolence of the Administrative State*

The twenty-first century administrative state is not only a regulatory and governing state, but also an enabling and facilitating state that offers a wider range of services to populations at large than any other government in history. It is a state that creates opportunities for individual citizens to advance themselves and even provides/allows instances of co-government (e.g., through corporatist arrangements, citizen participation, collaborative management, public–private partnerships, co-production). The idea that states and their governments should offer services beyond the traditional maintenance of law and order dates back to the eighteenth century. In the middle of that century the German scholar Christian von Wolff sketched the outlines of a welfare state (Rutgers, 2001); by the end of the eighteenth century the Frenchman Condorcet embraced that idea as well. This welfare state was also responsible for the resolution of social problems that could not be resolved through individual effort. Whether because of war and/or social–economic distress, the state expanded its range of activity beyond its traditional services from the early nineteenth century onward. This expansion into new areas called for professionals who were not just experts in governing or knowledgeable about law; it increasingly required training and expertise in a much wider range of disciplines (Carpenter, 2001). Today governments not only hire lawyers, but also anthropologists, ethicists, philosophers, engineers, psychologists, musicians, agriculturalists, meteorologists, physicists, linguists, historians, theologians, medical doctors, nurses, and so on. It will be very difficult to find a profession or study which is not represented in some career position in the civil service.

This vast, invasive, indispensable, administrative state, a concept coined by Dwight Waldo, is where the state acts. It has not replaced politics, as Bloom suggested (1987: 85), but it contains the largest single group of public sector actors (i.e., career civil servants). Its actions are governed, constrained, and encouraged within the institutional arena created by the *Rechtsstaat* (e.g., equality before the law) and, deep down, justified by *raison d'état*. The study of public administration emerged when the state had become a political reality (seventeenth century) whose actions were justified by *raison d'état*; the study sought to develop a holistic view (i.e., grand theory) upon government when the state expanded its services (nineteenth century) as justified by *Rechtsstaat*; and it fragmented into a variety of specializations in response to the rapidly growing government intervention in society (twentieth century). What this meant for the identity of public administration as a study and for government will be further explored in Sections 1.3 and 1.4 where the focus is first on the United States but then broadened to include Europe.

1.3 Public Administration's Identity Crises

Public administration was born within the folds of political science (see Section 1.4) and/or law and quickly developed an interest in principles of organization, management, and leadership in the desire to help solve practical problems. However, what was regarded as scientific up to the late 1930s came under attack in the United States from the late 1940s on. Herbert Simon led the charge on behalf of all those who advocated a more rigorous empirical approach to research that was concerned with facts and blasted prewar public administration as consisting of proverbs. On the opposite side Dwight Waldo observed that in the effort to become scientific (however defined), some public administration scholars forgot about the normative, value-laden side of public administration which, as political theory, had been part and parcel of studying and understanding government since Plato and Aristotle (Sayre, 1958: 104–5). Simon and Waldo "slugged" it out in the *American Political Science Review* in 1952 without arriving at some synthesis. The two sides, that can be called positivist and normativist, were firmly convinced of their own position.

By the time that the behavioral revolution in political science was in full swing, William Siffin wrote that " ... the study of public administration in the United States is characterized by the absence of any fully comprehensive intellectual framework" (1956: 367). A few years later, Thomas Davy observed that the " ... more generalized use of the term public administration does not identify a discrete field of scholarship" (1962: 64). In the same spirit, Waldo observed that public administration was a " ... subject matter in search of a discipline ... " (1968b: 2). In the same chapter he wrote that "Public administration suffers from so many 'crises of identity'[8] that normal adolescence

---

[8] The concept of "identity crisis" was coined by the developmental psychologist Erik H. Erikson (1968) and refers to the period during adolescence when teenagers are in search of their identity. Failure to establish identity will lead to "role confusion." Applied to public administration it might seem that the study suffers from role confusion. However, this is only so when the idea is accepted that there must be one best way to study government.

seems idyllic." (from Rhodes et al., 1995: 1). Had the behavioral revolution bypassed public administration? Not so if we believe Lowi who wrote that "...public administration [had been] transformed by the work of a single, diabolical mind – that of Herbert Simon [...] who lowered the discourse by reducing the entire administrative process to the smallest possible unit, the decision" (Lowi, 1992a: 106). He believed that traditional public administration had been driven out by Simon (1992b: 3). As usual, Simon's response is good reading (1992: 111). Looking back, Waldo observed that there had been "...sometimes bitter encounters..." between behavioralists and others in public administration and political science, and that by the mid-1960s these clashes had become "...too complex, too subtle [with] opinions too tempered, [and with] emotions too exhausted" (1975: 61–2). In the longer run, though, behavioralism had less impact in public administration.

This did not mean that concern about public administration's status had ceased. Vigoda actually believes that the identity crisis has only intensified over the years (2002: 5). Starting with McCurdy and Cleary (1984), a variety of scholars argued in the 1980s that the identity crisis was related to the study's inability to define a theoretical core (Ventriss, 1987: 25) with its own set of methods. V. Ostrom argued that the study suffered from a paradigmatic crisis because of the proliferation of existing theories, experimentation with methodologies, explicit discontent among scholars, extensive philosophical speculation, and unresolved debate about fundamental epistemological issues (1974, 14, 18; see also his exchange with Stillman, 1976, 1978; Ostrom, 1977). He proposed to develop the study as a science of association. In a review of research methodology in the *Public Administration Review*, Perry and Kraemer observed that Fritz Mosher's remark was still relevant:

> The field has not channeled its research efforts; its scope of interest seems unlimited; it has not developed a rigorous methodology; it has been pretty blasé about definitions; it has not agreed on any paradigm or theorems or theoretical systems; it has not settled on any stylized jargon or symbols; with a very few experimental exceptions, the field has not been modeled or mathematized into an "adminimetrics". (1986: 221)

In the same year the political scientist Elmore criticized the study for being a:

> ...collection of discrete and unrelated subjects in search of an intellectual focus, preoccupied with institutional descriptions rather than analysis, and lacking in sufficient rigor to command the respect of other academic disciplines or the public at large. [It has] in the absence of a clear analytic framework [...] tended to teach students descriptive versions of its subject matter – budgeting as "the budgetary process',...personnel as 'personnel systems and structures". (1986: 69)

Since McCurdy and Cleary the crisis of identity has been the subject of various articles (Stallings and Ferris, 1988; Houston and Delevan, 1990, 1994; White, Adams, and Forrester, 1996). Other scholars seemed less concerned, and found identity in subject matter, in multi-theoretical approaches, and in methodological pluralism (e.g., Rhodes, 1979: 7; Morgan, 1983; Goodsell, 1990: 507; Rhodes, 1991: 551). In their view there was every reason to be confident about the state of the discipline.

This identity crisis (or crises? see below) was not limited to the United States. With regard to Britain, Rhodes observed that public administration before 1970 had been a-theoretical, a-historical, and focused on administrative engineering (Rhodes, 1996: 508; see also Ridley, 1972). Since then British scholars fragmented their attention, turning more and more to organization theory, policy analysis, state theory, rational choice, and/or public management. Chevallier reported that in France during the 1960s the legal, managerial, and sociological models were tearing the study apart. While he noted that this period of doubt had come to an end by the late 1980s, thanks to the emerging paradigm (as he called it) of public policy, he concluded that the study would remain wedged between legal dogma, public management theory, and political science. It would, thus, continue to have difficulty staking an exclusive claim to its object of study (1996: 69–70). As for Germany, Seibel mentioned the methodological and theoretical weakness as well, but said that the study's legitimacy was rooted in being a study of and for reform (1996: 78). It seems that German public administration is in this respect quite comparable to what motivated the emergence of American public administration in the 1880–1920 period. In light of the fusion between administrative law and public administration during the nineteenth century, it was specifically difficult in 1960s France, Germany, and Italy to determine whether administrative science should be conceived as an umbrella study for politics, administrative law, history, sociology, and management science or as a study distinguishable from these (Dyson, 1980: 181). In the Scandinavian countries (Beck Jörgenson, 1996) and the Netherlands (Kickert, 1996), an identity crisis existed as well and it was, as everywhere else, related to the multi- and interdisciplinary nature of the study. In the Netherlands, Van Braam observed that the scientific authority of the study would continue to be challenged as long as its scholars could not agree on the core that constitutes the study. While for practical reasons many accept the co-existence of various core concepts, Van Braam argued – and in stronger terms than Perry and Kraemer – that this would not lead to a coherent and theoretically unified study (1998: 49). However, the debate about the discipline's identity has never been as heated in Europe as it was and is in the United States (Bogason, 2008).

So, in both the United States and Western Europe, the study of public administration suffered from the idea that its representatives were not able to gather all research and theory together in a coherent and unified body of knowledge. The debate, if one can call it that, has not lost any of its appeal as recent exchanges between Farmer (1999) and De Zwart (2002) and between Luton (2007) and Meier and O'Toole (2007), and various follow-up pieces (Hummel, 2007; Stivers, 2007; Andrews et al., 2008; Luton, 2008; Lynn et al., 2008; Oswick, 2008) show. But, perhaps Harmon's view is more correct. That is, only when provoked will positivists engage in debate, otherwise they are absent in philosophical discussion. If there is debate, it is between traditional public administration scholars (such as Waldo and his "heirs") and those who advocate phenomenology (Hummel), or critical discourse (Box), or postmodernism (Farmer, Fox, and Miller), or pragmatism (Harmon) as Harmon claims (2006: 34).

Most scholars refer to one identity crisis that centers on the battle between empiricists (Simon, Meier, and O'Toole) who believe in objective knowledge and interpretivists (e.g., Waldo, Stillman) who value the intersubjectivity of knowledge so characteristic of the social sciences. However, the label "identity crisis" is really a generic term that concerns two main types of crises that are relevant to and play out in two very different arenas (Table 1.1).

The *academic (or: epistemic) crises* concern both the study and its object, the practice of public administration or government. This can be seen from many perspectives: the lack of attention for the roots of American government (V. Ostrom, 1974), the theoretical and methodological weakness (Perry and Kraemer, 1986; Seibel, 1996; White et al., 1996; Van Braam, 1998), the controversy about the epistemological status of the study (Chevallier, 1996), the breathless pursuit of fads and fashions in both the study and the practice (Rhodes et al., 1995), the emphasis on practice at the expense of academic inquiry (Haque, 1996: 511), the lack of responsiveness of the study to the needs of practitioners (Denhardt, 2004: 150),

Table 1.1 Existential Crises in the Study of Public Administration and in Government

	Government	The study
Academic crises	How to define government, that is, public administration, and how to distinguish it from private administration and from politics	• Epistemological basis of the study • How to acquire knowledge • Is our knowledge scientific or interpretative?
Existential crises	Lack of moral authority	Discipline among others; subdiscipline within, political science, business administration, law; or interdiscipline

Source: Adapted from Raadschelders (1999: 287) (with permission from Oxford University Press).

and the need for new foundations in governance, in constitutionalism, and in pragmatism (Rosenbloom, 1983; Wamsley et al., 1990; Wamsley and Wolf, 1996; Shields, 2008).

For the purpose of this chapter it is sufficient to roughly outline the differences between Anglo-American and continental-European approaches to the study. While students of government in continental Europe generally appear to favor taxonomy over essay and definition over illustration (Van Braam, 1986; Debbasch, 1989), their Anglo-American counterparts opt for exactly the opposite. Not that definition and taxonomy are unimportant in Britain or the United States, but their starting point of analysis is practical. By way of generalization we could also say that the study in Europe uses theory as starting point, while in Britain and the United States, practice provides the starting point for the organization of the study. This has at least one important consequence for attempts to structure the study. European scholars usually adopt a deductive approach, organizing the study around and developing it from a theory or one or a few core concepts and then position "administrative reality" in it (Van Braam, 1986; Debbasch, 1989). In Anglo-American literature an inductive approach prevails (Stillman, 1997: 334).

The *existential crises* also concern both the practice and the study of government. These are crises in the "lived world" of government officials, citizens, public administration scholars, lobbyists, corporate executives, and so forth. Some believe that the study has achieved moral authority by serving citizens despite the weak scientific authority of the study (Perry, 1991: 15). Haque (1996: 512–13) argues that the existential foundation of government in society remained fairly strong for decades, but that government now faces a different crisis, which influences the legitimacy, ethics, and morale of the public service. He distinguishes between a credibility crisis (i.e., diminishing demand for and unfavorable public attitude toward government), a normative crisis (i.e., gradual displacement of basic public norms of government by market norms of private management), and a confidence crisis (i.e., loss of professional confidence and commitment among scholars of public administration). Haque's analysis certainly strikes a chord, but in the end it does not entirely convince for several reasons. First, since the time that the concept of bureaucracy was coined (mid-1700s), credibility crises have occurred regularly especially during economic recessions. As for the normative crisis, second, suffice it to say that public and market norms compete, and neither can completely displace the other. Furthermore, third, the growing attention to public ethics and public law suggest a normative crisis of quite a different order. Indeed, policymakers and scholars are aware that the market functions better when there is a certain level of government regulation to safeguard the public against greed. Finally, with regard to the confidence crisis, every true scholar will doubt his/her own convictions and the possibility of an identity crisis or multiple crises points to a strength rather than a weakness in and of the study. Waldo said it thus: "My rearing and education disposed me to the soft side; to a humanist approach to social science and to suspicion of all philosophies and methods that offered *Truth*" (1984: xliv).

From an academic point of view the crisis of the practice of government concerns the question: What exactly is public administration? How is government demarcated from the private sector and how is it situated between state and society? What differentiates government from other societal organizations? With respect to the study of public administration, the academic crisis concerns the epistemological basis of the study. How can we acquire knowledge about public organizations? How can we, for instance, relate organizational theories to public organizations? How can we relate our theories about human action to the practice of governing? And the most deadly question of all: to what extent is our knowledge *scientific* or interpretative? The existential crisis in government basically concerns its moral authority, while the existential crisis of the study is about whether it ought to be an independent (inter) discipline (versus political science, business administration, and so forth). In this section (and in the remainder of this book), the focus will be mainly on the academic crisis in the study.

As noted, public administration in Europe had an identity crisis but it was considered less problematic. After Von Stein, the European study was predominantly a legal study (Rutgers, 1997: 290). It was only after the Second World War that other disciplinary perspectives entered the study. The French, the Germans, the Italians, the Dutch, and the Scandinavians developed a conception of public administration with intellectual roots in philosophy, law, sociology, economics, political science, and history. European public administration is rooted in a strong state tradition, making its scholars develop and adopt comprehensive perspectives upon government. By contrast, the study in the United States is embedded in a "weak state" tradition, that makes its scholars avoid such holistic frameworks. However, the contrast between "strong" and "weak states" is by now stereotypical, and the United States today can hardly be called a weak state (Novak, 2008).

There is one question remaining. Public administration scholars chastised their study for its lack of rigor and coherence, especially when eyeing the achievements and methods of the natural sciences. Lacking, though, so far is an exploration of the question whether the study of public administration is unique in having such an identity crisis. This question will first be explored with regard to political science (Section 1.4) and then with regard to other disciplines (Section 1.5).

1.4 Origin in and Bifurcation from Political Science: But, is the Latter's Identity Today Different from Public Administration's Identity?

In part the identity crisis in American public administration is fueled by its origins in and comparison to political science, and further stimulated by the sustained impact of the behavioral revolution in the 1950s and the 1960s. Indeed, just a cursory comparison of the *Public Administration Review* (PAR) and the *American Review of Political Science* (APSR) shows that quantitative-statistical methods and mathematical modeling are much more present in the latter journal. Does this mean that political science has been more successful than public administration in becoming a "real" science? The present relation between public administration and political science and how they compare to each other in terms of "scientificness" can only be understood when going back in time. In Europe and in the United States the origins of modern public administration and political science go back to the second half of the nineteenth century. This section is limited to a discussion of the American situation because it preceded comparable developments in Europe by several decades (Haddow, 1969).

American political science emerged a few decades before public administration, in the 1850s (Farr, 1988: 1175), and it did so at a time that hopes were high that a unifying social science could be created (McCurdy, 1986: 19). Almost five decades later the American Political Science Association (APSA), the "godchild" of the American Historical Association and the American Economic Association (Reeves, 1929), and its journal *American Political Science Review* were created (1903). Public administration was listed as one of its subfields (Somit and Tanenhaus, 1967: 11; Ross, 1991: 282–8; Hill, 1992: 30; Grofman, 2007). So, organizational specialization was generally followed by the establishment of a professional association and followed by the creation of a scholarly journal. It is in that sense that Gunnell could write that in the evolution of the social sciences, disciplines preceded professions (2006: 479, 481).

Public administration emerged as the academic response to the combined effects of industrialization, urbanization, and population growth upon the fabric of society prompting citizens and public professionals to urge for more and better government intervention. To be sure, this only holds true for the United States where disciplines emerged from the middle to late nineteenth century onward. They provided the macro-structure of the academic labor market. In Europe, disciplines did not emerge until after the Second World War; since unto then universities were organized around chair-holders

(Germany, the Netherlands), around patronage groups (France), or around patronage groups of particular colleges (England) (Abbott, 2001: 122–8).

The emergence of independent public administration units occurred in response to the need for practical training that local government managers had been asking for and that departments of political science did not provide. Meeting that need the New York Bureau of Municipal Research (NYBMR) was established in 1906. The Institute of Government Research in Washington DC (which became the Brookings Institution) served the same purpose of training public servants for the improvement of the public service. In 1911 the NYBMR established the Training School for Public Service; both merged in 1922 into the Institute of Public Administration under the leadership of Luther Gulick. During these decades a variety of other training institutes and professional associations were created that gathered under the umbrella of the Public Administration Clearing House at 1313 E. 60th Street in Chicago. Considering the fragmentation of public administration into several organizations, William E. Mosher, Dean of the Maxwell School, called in the 1930s for a society of public administration following the example of the British Institute of Public Administration. The American Society for Public Administration was created on December 27, 1939, during the annual APSA conference (Stone, 1975: 83–4, 90) and was quickly followed by the first issue of *PAR*.

This organizational activity did not pass unnoticed. As early as 1915, NYBMR director Charles Beard advocated that professional education for public servants ought to be organized in a school of public service as a multi-disciplinary organization that represented all units at the university. By way of example he mentioned engineering, accounting, business, political science, medicine, and architecture. Some political scientists supported that idea. Charles Merriam, for instance, believed that the development of political science as "science" could be done side by side with meeting the concerns for public policy and training (Khodr, 2005: 77). Others, like Leonard D. White, believed that the study of administration was not designed to be "applied in action" but meant instead to advance the understanding of the nature of government and its operations (Caldwell, 1965: 55–7). Public administration scholars were confident about their ability to develop the study, while their political science colleagues started to question their study's identity.

In the 1920s, Munro spoke of " . . . the backwardness in what may be called the pure science of politics . . . " (1928: 9). In the mid-1930s it had been described as " . . . a discipline without a clear intellectual identity . . . ," and as a heterogeneous, plural, diverse discipline with little agreement about central concerns, methods, and basic goals (Sorauf, 1965: 20). Political scientists did not think public administration would be particularly useful or helpful in establishing such a focus, yet resisted any move toward an independent public administration (Henry, 1975: 381). Their public administration colleagues increasingly felt that many academic disciplines had relevance to their study (Caldwell, 1965: 58) and that they had to balance academic and practitioner needs. As we have seen, from 1939 on ASPA and APSA went their own ways. Political scientist Roscoe Martin thought this development unfortunate and asked:

> Why should political science and political scientists concern themselves at all with the bothersome problems of public administration? One answer is, to keep from going sterile. Another, to keep in touch with government in action. Another, to take advantage of a wide and inviting road for communication with the other social sciences. Another, to participate in the exciting business of rethinking a field of knowledge. Another still, to profit from the enforced introspection which the process involves. As regards the last, public administration has shown a willingness, indeed eagerness, to search its soul for basic meanings and significances. (1952: 676)

Whether he belonged to a minority of political scientists is hard to say, but public administration scholars felt that the majority of political scientists did not share Martin's views. Consider, for instance, the following two remarks by Van Riper and Waldo respectively:

> There is no hope for public administration in political science and everyone knows it, as far as real support and understanding are concerned. (Van Riper, 1967: 340)

> The truth is that the attitude of political scientists – is at best one of indifference and is often one of undisguised contempt or hostility. (Waldo, 1968b: 8)

Indeed, since 1962, APSA no longer mentions public administration as one of the subfields of political science (Caldwell, 1965: 58; Henry, 1975: 381). Both in Europe and in North America, many political scientists believe that the two studies ought to be connected. Thus, wrote Colomer: " . . . no "geology" – that is, the study of business or public administration – is feasible without solid foundation in "physics" and "chemistry" – that is, in economics and political science" (2007: 137).

Meanwhile, calls for a more rigorous and scientific political science caused that study to shift toward behavioralism and to the individual as the main unit of analysis. This behavioral revolution swept political science in the 1950s and 1960s, but not everyone thought that this was an improvement. Just as Gaus had argued that "A theory of public administration means in our time a theory of politics also" (1950: 168), several political scientists warned that empirical research methods should not crowd out less precise methods (sic) such as history, institutional analysis, and intuition, and should not only consider "what is" but also "what should be" (Redford, 1961: 758), in effect saying that political science still needed philosophy (Schaar and Wolin, 1963: 125). Political scientists should remember that even in the natural sciences the classical interpretation of the scientific method (i.e., fact collection, hypotheses, experimental verification) was at best considered a half-truth (Davidson, 1961: 854; Weinberg, 2001: 85). By the end of the 1960s, Easton reported in his presidential address before the APSA that dissatisfaction with rigorous political science was growing and critiqued that the study had too quickly divorced knowledge from action. It was time that substance would precede technique again (1969: 1051–2, 1059). In the same year, Wolin wrote that political science ought to work with a multiplicity of paradigms (1969: 1063–4). Looking back, Lowi observed that political science had moved too far away from judgmental and evaluative thought (1992a; see also Yankelovich, 1991).

It is interesting that political science in the 1960s found itself back in the situation where it had been in the 1930s (cf. "...we are not sure of our boundaries..."; Redford, 1961: 757), but did not seem to feel the need for introspection, let alone declare an "identity crisis" as Waldo did at the end of the 1960s. It has already been noted in the previous section how the search for identity flared up again in public administration in the 1980s and that this continues to the present day. It was no different in political science. Gabriel Almond (1988) warned that political scientists were sitting at separate tables and that different approaches should interact with one another. But, he believed the chances for that to happen to be limited since scholars seldom challenge or learn from one another (see also Easton, 1991a: 16). Two years later, several political scientists observed that their study lacked a clear core (Monroe), that it was dispersed and pluralistic (Gunnell), that it was eclectic (Shapiro), that there were multiple paradigms (Graham), and that various subspecializations had difficulty communicating with one another (Barber) (see Monroe et al., 1990). In that symposium, Shepsle observed that the discipline was undisciplined and that a core could be developed provided that rational choice would play a significant role in that endeavor. His desire was echoed by Moe several years later (2001). Today, it seems that rational choice theorists have won the day and that political science is internally divided over this "...hegemony of formal theory and methodology" (Lamont, 2009: 95).

So far developments of ideas about public administration's and political science's identity ran parallel and this pattern has not changed in the first decade of the twenty-first century. In fact, it seems that the positions of the "hard science" scholars and of interpretivists have only become more pronounced. In the mid-1980s, Easton wrote that "...there are now so many approaches to political research that political science seems to have lost its purpose" (1985: 143; 1991b: 48). Gunnell wrote that political science had been in an identity crisis since the late 1970s (2002: 340), and Rudolph and Rudolph noted that "Not long ago many political scientists suffered from economics envy" (2010: 747). Mead observed that "At times, virtual civil war has broken out [...] centered on particular research methodologies" (2010: 453). This was further underlined by the small but very vocal Perestroika movement (Barrow, 2008). One of the scholars identifying with that group noted that political scientists had become too obsessed with abstruse mathematical models (Cohn, 1999). Another indicated that this had undermined, if not severed, the relation between academe and practice, two arenas that were much closer related in psychology and economics (Stark, 2002: 578). In another symposium edited by Monroe (2002), Smiley pointed out that "... ranking methodologies is intellectually very difficult, if not impossible, as long as methodological appropriateness follows from, rather than precedes, the nature of the subject matter in question, e.g., politics" (in Monroe et al., 2002: 198) and Monroe herself argued strongly for interdisciplinarity. How strong this call for interdisciplinarity as political science's identity has become is not clear yet (see McGovern, 2010), because voices for a distinct disciplinarity can still be heard as, for instance, in the following observation by Sartori who expressed

> ... some regrets on having fought on the side of science. [and that] ... political science has adopted an unsuited model of science (drawn from the hard, exact sciences) and has failed to establish its own identity (as a soft science) by failing to establish its own, distinctive methodology. (2004: 785)

Sartori's most damning critique was that political science had missed, or even dismissed, its applied side and had become a theory without practice (ibid.: 786; Stark, 2002). Again, intellectual debate in both studies is quite comparable. This is less remarkable then it seems, since social reality cannot be captured in or by one viewpoint only.

So, where is public administration today in political science? Annual reports of the *APSR* still do not list public administration as a subfield even though the number of articles on, for example, bureaucracy has been growing in the past two decades (Meier and Krause, 2003*b*: 293), a significant number of scholars who study bureaucratic institutions and/or public management identify as political scientists (about half of all scholars studying government, Ellwood, 1996: 56), and there is an active public administration section in ASPA with more than 300 members. The relation between public administration and political science may be symbiotic (Fesler, 1988: 892) but remains uneasy. There is no reason to consider public administration as less "scientific" then political science. Qualifying political science as scientific based on what is published in the *APSR* and public administration as less scientific based on what is published in *PAR* is clearly a stereotype. Equally stereotypical is the idea that public administrationists and political scientists cannot see eye to eye, that is, when Mary Ellen Guy proves right when observing that both studies are reconnecting with each other (2003: 652).

By way of contrast, though, consider James March's observation that public administration research used to be cited in major journals in political science, economic, and organization studies, but that this has declined significantly in the past thirty years. At the same time, public administration journals frequently reference articles in other disciplines (March, 2009: 29). This can also be seen in the two tables presented below. Khodr observes that the number of articles and book reviews in the *APSR*, the *Journal of Politics*, the *Political Science Quarterly*, and *PS: Political Science & Politics* that could be labeled as public administration has been steadily declining since the beginning of the past century (Table 1.2).

Khodr also reported that the number of political science articles in three top public administration journals (*Public Administration Review, American Review of Public Administration, Journal of Public Administration Research and Theory*) had increased (Table 1.3).

That the number of political science articles is increasing in these public administration journals is not surprising since the study's range of interest has gone far beyond the initial focus on organizational theory, management principles, and leadership styles. Since the 1970s, a variety of topics and approaches have been "added" such as ethics, gender, law, diversity, non-profit management, public service motivation, network theory, crisis and emergency management, health care, environmental policy, international migration, election administration, political leadership, democracy, and so on. In fact, it is reasonable to argue that the study has adopted various topical areas that were initially identified as political science.

Table 1.2 Articles and Book Reviews on Public Administration in Political Science Journals

Period	Articles	Book reviews
1900–39	75	52
1940–59	40	54
1960–89	8	15 + 38 book notes
1989–2005	14	13

Source: Khodr (2005: 201) (reprinted with permission from the author).

Table 1.3 Articles and Book Reviews on Political Science in Public Administration Journals

Period	Articles	Book reviews
1940–59	0	2
1960–89	2	35
1990–2005	22	19

Source: Khodr (2005: 211) (reprinted with permission from the author).

Both fields have so many different outlets, displaying so many different theoretical and methodological approaches, that we can only come to one of two conclusions. Either both studies are "immature" or both are "mature." Are they the only disciplines/studies that face the question of identity and maturity?

1.5 Identity Crisis as Normal Situation in Most, Perhaps All, Disciplines

When John Donne (1572?–1631) sighed that all coherence was gone, he referred to the emerging split between an earth-centered worldview espoused by Christendom and a sun-centered worldview forced upon society by the discoveries of astronomers such as Galileo Galilei. In other words, he lamented compartmentalization of a religious and a secular/natural worldview and, thus, the loss of a unified worldview. Just as worldviews compartmentalized, so have people fragmented knowledge and they have been doing so since Antiquity. Within the academy compartmentalization of knowledge occurs at two levels: within disciplines and studies through specialization into subfields (see below) and between disciplines and studies through efforts at demarcating bodies of knowledge. A cursory excursion into various other disciplines shows that public administration and political science are not unique in the epistemological challenges confronting them. All three branches of knowledge (natural sciences, social sciences, humanities) face the challenge of dealing with the compartmentalization of knowledge. Specialization has become so extensive that unity of knowledge is further removed than ever. The social sciences face an extra challenge. They emerged in the course of the nineteenth century amid expectations that the systematic study of human society would lead to the discovery of social laws, and propel the social sciences to the heights achieved by the natural sciences. This, however, has not come to pass. Instead, every generation of social scientists has expressed disappointment with the lack of knowledge accumulation and it thus that they are "... periodically beset by intellectual crisis" (Shapiro, 2005: 51).

With regard to the social sciences at large, the methodologist Campbell noted that they harbor a "hodgepodge" of topics and methods and he illustrated this with brief descriptions of anthropology, sociology, psychology, geography, political science, and economics (1969: 329–32). Anthropologists oscillate between symbolic-ethnographic (or: etic) and cultural-materialist (or: emic) approaches (N.B.: the etic–emic distinction was made by Marvin Harris). Those working from an emic-perspective regard anthropology as a study of humanity served best by open boundaries and methodological eclecticism, while "eticists" inch closer to natural science models, especially borrowing from systems ecology and evolutionary biology (Fuller, 1993: 136). In that regard, Trigger notes that balancing rationalists (who believe in cross-cultural regularities of human behavior) and relativists (who emphasize that habits, beliefs, values, arts, etc., are culture specific) poses problems for anthropologists (2003: 11).

Sociologists struggle to balance attention for structure and processes in large social systems with the study of individual actions (Turner, 1991: 74). As a study it is marked by a "healthy diversity of viewpoints and broader perspectives that extends over time and across societies" (ibid.: 80). An entire issue of *Social Forces* (1995: 73(4)) was devoted to exploring sociology's relation to other social sciences and the integrative role it could play within them. While a unifying theoretical paradigm is missing, such is also difficult to imagine (Turner, 1991: 81) in light of the lack of consensus over core concepts and approaches (Levine, 1995: 285; Hodgson, 2001: 202). The "war of paradigms," as Mouzelis called it (2008: 107), raging in the 1960s and 1970s, may be in the past, but the various approaches have not lost any of their vigor.

In the study of international relations (IR) and comparative politics a "great debate" has been raging between traditionalists who favor a descriptive IR and scientists who embrace a positivist approach. Is IR a science or not? A variety of schools have been distinguished such as those of the rationalists, realists, pluralists, structuralists, constructivists, culturalists, and reflectivists (Lichbach and Zuckerman, 1997; Wight, 2002: 22, 28, 33–4). A comparable listing of schools was provided by Sil and Katzenstein: realism, neoliberalism, constructivism, rational choice theory, and historical institutionalism (2010: 413).

Management and business studies are home to a variety of specializations (e.g., supply chain management, marketing, accounting, organizational behavior, information systems, etc.), with its academics belonging to different "warring tribes" (Knights and Willmott, 1997: 10), prompting at least one scholar to observe that it "...remains to be seen whether university business schools created coherent, systematic, clearly bounded body of knowledge" (Khurana, 2007: 91). These functional divisions are increasingly regarded as outmoded, though, and have instigated a drive for more practice-oriented, interdisciplinary studies, at least in the United Kingeom (Knights and Willmott, 1997: 9).

Economics, the social science that is perceived as most successful in emulating the natural science model, is confronted with (neo)classical, Keynesian, and Marxist approaches, each providing a specific angle to the relation between economy and society. Some economists argue that there is no unified discipline of economics and that, when scholars speak of it as if it is a discipline, this is "...often a discursive strategy by one school or another to hegemonize the field of economic discourse" (Amariglio et al., 1993: 150–1;

Hodgson, 2001: 348). This cynical observation points to an externalist approach to what defines science: it is not so much the theories and concepts within a study (an internalist approach) as it is the political (i.e., disciplinary and institutional) dynamics that define a study (Lenoir, 1993: 76). This point is emphasized by Kuhn as well. Some neoclassical economists have recently been criticized for suffering from "physics envy" (Hodgson, 2004: 326). They are not the only scholars looking elsewhere for a pathway to unification.

Psychology is so fragmented that it prompted Henriques' to write that the unified theoretical system of biology leaves " . . . scientifically minded psychologists with feelings of bio-envy" (2004: 1210).

As far as the humanities are concerned, the study of history is torn between humanistic and social scientific approaches. How that will play out will be, according to Tilly, one of four trajectories. First, if it is discovered that reliable knowledge of human action is impossible than both the humanities and the social sciences will collapse. Second, when it can be proven that individual experiences are coherent and intelligible while large social processes are not the social sciences will come to an end. Third, it could also be that proof will come about that subjectivity is never reliable but that recurrent patterns of human action are. That, though, would be the end of the humanities. Fourth, and the most challenging, is the notion that individual experiences can be aggregated in a reliable manner into collective action patterns. That, Tilly argued, would be the desirable route (1991: 114–15), but seems to smack of a methodological individualism that is quite foreign to the study of history. Another historian notes that history has not only moved into a variety of "collateral disciplines" (e.g., anthropology, sociology, psychology, archaeology, geography) but also "threatens" to move into biology, chemistry, and physics (Smith, 1992: 128). Historians of half a century ago will hardly recognize their study today.

Archaeologists suffer from an identity crisis, being torn between explanation and description (Wenke and Olszewski, 2007: 12). History of art scholars debate whether their field should focus on the fine arts (painting, sculpture, architecture) and their masterworks or include anything (objects, images, buildings) produced by human beings (Preziosi, 1993: 216). And this is not all. The various language studies are just as much confronted with questions about identity as a consequence of newer ways to evaluate literary scholarship (see for English: Lamont, 2009: 70–3).

If the plight of the social sciences and the humanities is serious, are the natural sciences better off? Do they enjoy greater unity of knowledge? Even cursory inspection shows that this is not the case. Klein mentions how physics has been called a "federation of disciplines," that geography is "inherently interdisciplinary," and that medicine consists of "loose amalgamations of segments pursuing different objectives in different manners . . . " (Klein,

1993: 197–8). The Physics Survey Committee of the National Science Research Council concluded in 1972 that there was "no definable boundary" between physics and other disciplines (ibid.: 210). With regard to medicine a distinction is made between three main branches: psychiatry, surgery, and medicine. The first is regarded as having few subdivisions, but has still been described as " . . . a field very much in search of itself and increasingly divided along scientific and humanistic lines" (Brendel, 2006: xiii). Should psychiatry embrace the biomedical (natural science) or the psychodynamic approach (humanities)? The former is rapidly replacing the latter (Luhrmann, 2000: chs 4 and 5). "These clashing conceptual approaches have left the science of psychiatry deeply wounded at the start of the new millennium" (Brendel, 2006: xiii). With regard to surgery and medicine, the English Royal Colleges of Medicine and Surgery distinguish between at least seven subdivisions (see Table 1.4).

The evidence in this and the previous section indicates that specialization, whether perceived as rampant or not, has become the normal condition in the natural sciences, the social sciences, and the humanities. Public administration scholars should consider the fact that their epistemic or academic identity crisis is not unique, and merely a function of the proliferation of subfields. They and their political science colleagues should be encouraged by Easton's remark that "The history of inquiry in the natural sciences now seems to reveal that there is no single fixed kind of intellectual product, as classical positivism would have us believe, that can be designated as appropriate and necessary to achieve understanding of any given phenomena" (Easton, 1985: 150). The new unity of science is not expressed in unity within, and certainly not between, disciplines, but in interdisciplinary approaches to understanding and knowing the world (Williams, 2000: 141). This interdisciplinarity turns on problem-driven rather than method-driven research (Shapiro, 2005: 99). An excellent example is provided by the study of the brain that has become increasingly interdisciplinary since the 1960s, connecting

Table 1.4 Subfields of Surgery and of Medicine

System investigated	Surgery	Medicine
Cardiovascular	Cardiac surgery	Cardiology
Respiratory	Thoracic surgery	Chest medicine
Gastrointestinal	Abdominal (general) surgery	Gastroenterology
Nervous	Neurosurgery	Neurology/endocrinology
Locomotor	Orthopedics	Physical medicine/rheumatology
Genitourinary	Urology	Nephrology/Venerology
Skin	Plastic surgery	Dermatology

Source: Armstrong (1993: 236).

molecular biology and neuroscience with the philosophy of the mind and with behaviorist and cognitive psychology (Kandel, 2006: 7).

Considering the present state of knowledge, any attempt at omniscience, which is implied in the desire of unity of knowledge, must be considered stillborn. The remaining question is how a new unity can be established when studies and disciplines are home to scholars who espouse very different approaches. It is not productive to declare a study unified around a particular topic and/or method, because such a top-down approach quickly meets with objections from those who favor a different unifying core or approach. A bottom-up approach by means of conceptual mapping may well be more productive.

1.6 Conceptual Maps

A map is a graphic representation that serves as a frame of reference for its users. The most common are geographical maps that help to determine where one is and help deciding on how best to travel to a particular destination. Once familiar with a specific geographical area, an individual will rely on a mental map that has been acquired over time. The psychologist Tolman developed the concept of cognitive map to help explain how rats found their way through a maze. In his 1937 Presidential Address before the annual conference of the American Psychological Association, he expressed his conviction that "[E]verything important in psychology (except such matters as the building up of a super-ego, that is everything save such matters as involve society and words) can be investigated in essence through the continued experimentation and theoretical analysis of the determiners of rat behavior at a choice point in a maze" (quoted in Henriques, 2004: 1208). He distinguished "strict maps," that simply represent a sequence of choice points, from "broad cognitive maps," that embed these choice points in the larger biological environment (Tolman, 1948: 193; Eden, 1992: 261; Fiol and Huff, 1992: 273). Tolman's cognitive map concerns spatial learning in natural or biological environments.

Just as people use mental maps for locating positions in space (i.e., a building, a city, a country, the globe, the universe), they use mental maps for organizing any type of knowledge imaginable. Conceptual or cognitive maps help an individual to make sense of and organize an otherwise overwhelming – and thus non-sensical – amount of information. A conceptual map is a graphic tool, a template, or a scaffold for organizing and representing knowledge (Novak and Cañas, 2008: 1, 5), and is indispensible as the first element of systematic analysis which Hood called "cartographic work" (2007: 20). Conceptual maps were developed in the early 1970s as part of a research project of biologist and educational scientist Novak and others. They expanded upon the work of Ausubel (1963, 1968), an educational psychologist and practicing psychiatrist, whose theory concerned reception learning in schools. He claimed that learning occurs by assimilating new concepts and propositions (i.e., meaningful statements about links between concepts) into existing conceptual and propositional frameworks.

In natural systems, cognitive or conceptual maps – in this book they are considered as synonyms – refer to features and properties that are more or less stable over time. They represent phenomena that exist and happen independent of human intervention. While cognitive maps of natural systems may vary from researcher to researcher, they generally agree on the basic components and forces of the natural system they study (think of the periodic table of elements in chemistry). In social systems, however, the components and forces of conceptual maps are anything but static. Time and again they are redefined in response to changes in the social, political, cultural, economic, etc., environment. Furthermore, the content of an individual's conceptual map of the social environment is highly determined by an evaluation of what is important *and* by an interpretation and valuation of events. Thus, one can expect that social scientists agree less about the features, properties, forces, and definitions of the phenomena they study than their colleagues in the natural sciences. While natural and social scientists both engage continuously in negotiating the conceptual map(s) of their object of study (Bougon, 1992: 369), this effort is more driven by valuation in the social sciences than in the natural sciences.

Conceptual maps generally share, but do not have to have, two features. First, concepts can be represented in a hierarchical fashion. Linnaeus' taxonomy of flora and fauna is perhaps the best known. An example in organizational theory is the distinction made in population ecology between five levels of analysis: individual, group/unit, organization, population of organizations, communities of (populations of) organizations (Hannan and Freeman, 1978: 136). A different example is the Institutional Analysis and Development (IAD) framework elaborated in the past thirty-plus years by E. Ostrom and associates. Ostrom distinguishes three levels of specificity as essential foundations to the analysis of institutions. Most general are the frameworks that provide a meta-theoretical language that is useful in the comparison of theories and debates. Frameworks contain a great variety of concepts, theories, models, and so forth. Theories are more specific and they allow for the investigation of a certain group of questions on a particular phenomenon. Even more specific, models " . . . make precise assumptions about a limited set of parameters and variables" (Ostrom, 2007: 25–6). Ostrom characterizes the IAD framework as a multitier conceptual map (ibid.: 27).

Second, conceptual maps provide links between concepts, since a concept acquires its true meaning from links to other concepts (Cossette, 2002: 169). Complex maps can break down in clusters that are relatively separated or connected (Eden et al., 1992: 315). A good example of this is the various clusters Hofstede distinguishes when presenting dyadic connections between his five dimensions of societal and organizational culture (1997: 54, 87, 99, 123, 129, 141).

Conceptual maps can be and have been used in various contexts and for various purposes. It is considered a powerful pedagogical tool for it focuses a student's attention and triggers his memory (Novak and Cañas, 2008). It also has been used as an instrument for organizational analysis (Cossette and Audet, 1992: 325; Eden, 1992: 261). At the organizational level it is used to inform and facilitate strategic decision-making (Eden et al., 1992: 321; Fiol and Huff, 1992: 267), to develop decision trees, to situate firms in their competitive environment (Fiol and Huff, 1992: 269), and to identify key actors (cf. Lindblom's "partisan analysis"), events, and processes (Fiol and Huff, 1992: 278). At the individual level it is used to map action and motive frameworks (Cossette and Audet, 1992) and cognitive maps of political elites (Axelrod, 1976; Eden et al., 1992: 309).

In the study of public administration, conceptual maps have been used in two ways. First, they can be used to organize an individual's cognitive map of concepts central and peripheral to an object of research interest. Cossette's cognitive map of Frederick W. Taylor's ideas is an excellent example (2002). Second, one can try and organize scholarly thought for the study as a whole. There are two subtypes of this second type. The first, and most common, subtype is the listing of topics, concepts, or theories, etc. An example is the overview of theories-in-use in public administration by Frederickson and Smith (2003). The second, and less common, subtype is the attempt to structure the study around one or a few concepts (for examples of scholars who structured the study around one concept include, see Chapter 7). Yet another example is Rutgers (2004) who organizes a variety of concepts-in-use around three concept-pairs (public–private, state–society, politics–administration) and places these into – what he calls – "fields of meaning" (Figure 1.1).

Note that in Rutgers' presentation, no effort is made to discern weights or degrees of importance to each concept. His conceptual map does not present the study in a hierarchical fashion, where one or a few central concepts are disaggregated into various components, each of which is further broken down into more detailed concepts. His "fields of meaning" are, though, limited to concepts and topics only. The book before you represents an effort to provide a non-hierarchical conceptual map of the study as a whole that consists of conceptual maps for knowledge sources (Chapter 3), for topics (Chapter 4), for theories (Chapter 5), for school of thought and intellectual debate (Chapter 6),

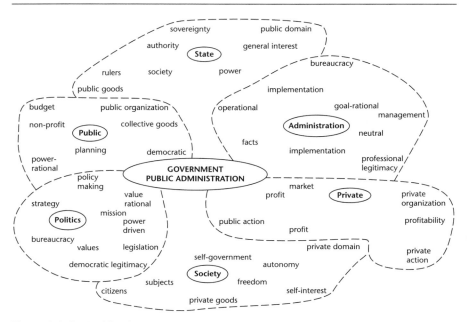

Figure 1.1 Six Fields of Meaning in the Study of Public Administration

Source: Rutgers (2004: 168) (adapted and translated by Raadschelders; published with permission by Coutinho).

and for types of knowledge integration (Chapter 7). Whether this effort con-stitutes "soft science" or "hard art" (Trochim, 1989) is for the reader to decide.

1.7 Maturity through Scholarship as Wissenschaft

Charles Merriam wrote that "It is to be presumed and desired that students of government will play a larger role in the future than in the past in shaping of the types of civic education; but this will not be possible unless a *broader view is taken of the relation of government to the other social sciences, and the function of the political in the social setting*" (1934: 97; emphasis CM). A decade later Simon and Waldo echoed the same sentiment: " . . . the proper training of 'adminis-trators' lies not in the narrow field of administrative theory, but in the broader field of the social sciences generally" (Simon, 1957: 247), and " . . . administra-tive thought must establish a working relationship with every major province in the realm of human learning" (Waldo, 1984: 203). These three comments characterize the study of public administration as one that serves practitioners as well as academics and as one that draws from various knowledge sources in and outside academe in order to advance the understanding of government in society. In the past seventy years, public administration and political science each have, by and large, gone their own way. Political science increasingly addressed academics only, while public administration has continued to try and serve two very different audiences.

The study of public administration has clearly come of age when considering the wide range of generic and specialized journals that were established in the past thirty years, as well as the rapid increase of public administration schools or departments separate from political science (Fry and Raadschelders, 2008: 343). Meier observes that the top twenty-five programs in American public administration are independent, and that of the top fifty only two are situated in a political science department (2007a: 3; based on the 2005-rankings of the US News and World Report)). Henry notes that the most effective public administration programs are freestanding schools and departments that enjoy the fastest rates of student growth (2010: 38). Khodr distinguishes five different organizational patterns. In her thesis she counted a total of 230 programs: 90 independent schools or departments of public administration, 52 programs where public administration was combined with another area (e.g., international affairs, environmental affairs, urban studies), 45 programs where public administration was embedded in a political science department, 30 programs where public administration was linked with a particular policy area, and 13 departments or schools of public administration and political science (2005: 186). In Europe the situation is slightly different. About half of the public administration programs in Finland and the Netherlands are independent. In the other Scandinavian countries, public administration is usually embedded in political science or organization studies, while in Austria, France, Greece, and Spain, it is usually part of a law school. In Belgium, Germany, Italy, Ireland, Portugal, and the United Kingdom, one can find a mixture of independent and embedded programs as in the United States (Verheijen and Connaughton, 1999; Fry and Raadschelders, 2008: 361).

It is the wide range of interests expressed in a rich variety of journals and programs that clearly indicates that the study has, indeed, no boundaries and that it must build bridges between the various knowledge sources and theories and concepts-in-use. The remainder of this book represents one attempt at doing so and is written upon the conviction that maturity is not achieved through attempts at developing public administration as a "science." Instead, maturity already exists when we consider the study in terms of *Wissenschaft*. That argument will be further developed in Chapter 2.

2

Science or *Wissenschaft*? The Study of Public Administration among the Three Branches of Learning

> ...administration is essentially one of the humanities. Administration is, or at least ought to be, wedded to subjects such as philosophy, literature, history, and art, and not merely to engineering, finance, and structure. (Dimock, 1958)

> Would it be intelligent to try to explain how Romeo's love for Juliet enters into his behavior in the same terms as we might want to apply to the rat whose sexual excitement makes him run across an electrically charged grid to reach his mate? Does not Shakespeare do this much better? (Winch, 1986)

Among the three great branches of learning, that is, the natural sciences, the social sciences, and the humanities, a distinction dating back to the seventeenth century, the study of public administration is generally regarded as a social science. This is no doubt correct, but the reasons why it should be considered a social science are not often spelled out. And when they are there is little agreement about the academic status of the study. Is it a science, a craft, a profession, or even an art (see also Chapter 5)? Some public administration scholars appear to aspire meeting the scientific ideals of the natural sciences, while others believe this to be inappropriate and emphasize the increasing theoretical and methodological pluralism in the past century. The contrast between these two amorphous groups of scholars is perhaps best captured in the concepts of *science* and of *Wissenschaft*.

Science, from the Latin root *scientia*, is defined in Webster's *Third New International Dictionary* (1993: 2032) as, inter alia, a "...branch of study that is concerned with observation and classification of facts and esp. with the establishment or strictly with the quantitative formulation of verifiable laws chiefly by induction and hypotheses."[1] This definition fits the natural sciences best. Science in this sense is how knowledge is defined in the Anglo-American world. Continental-European scholars define knowledge in broader terms such as in the German word *Wissenschaft*, which translates best as "branch of knowledge or learning."[2] *Wissenschaft* can be defined as " . . . the systematically organized whole of knowledge and of the rules, regularities, theories, hypotheses, and systems through which further knowledge can be acquired." (Van Dale, 1984: 3402) Note that in this definition the search for knowledge is not limited to "facts" that are captured in some quantitative formulation. Thus understood, *Wissenschaft* represents a broader conception of knowledge and learning and, so, encompasses "science" and other approaches to the acquisition of knowledge (Chapter 6) (Donovan, 2005: 599). Clearly, the German term *Wissenschaft* cannot be satisfactorily translated into the English word "science." The contemporary English word "science" connotes a more limited definition of knowledge and learning than the German concept of *Wissenschaft* that is comparable to the pre-eighteenth century concept of "science." *Scientia*, though, can be understood as a special species of *cognitio* (i.e., to know, study, knowledge) (Stump, 2003: 224). Waldo captured this distinction when observing that science could be defined as " . . . a body of organized knowledge . . . " in general (i.e., *Wissenschaft*) or, more specifically, as " . . . a certain type and quality of knowledge and procedure . . . " (i.e., science) (Waldo, 1984: 182, endnote 50). Discussing the academic status of management sciences, Hood used the same distinction when noting that if public management is a science than it is so largely in terms of *Wissenschaft* rather than in the English sense of " . . . knowledge founded in strict experimental method and rigorous logical reasoning" (Hood, 2007: 19).

This distinction is very important for the effort to determine the academic stature of public administration as a study. Those who embrace the narrow concept of "science" will evaluate the bulk of public administration research as sub-par in comparison to, for example, psychology, economics, or even political science, and certainly underdeveloped in comparison to the natural sciences. This is evidenced in rankings of disciplines according to "scientificness." Those who consider knowledge in the broader concept of *Wissenschaft*

---

[1] The Latin word *scientia*, which refers to "a 'state of knowing' acquired by study," is derived from the verb *scire* (to know; *sciō* = I know, I understand). The Proto-Indo-European root is *skei* (cut, separate, discern); from this the Greek *schizo'* (to split). Until the Enlightenment the word "science" referred to a body of general knowledge and is still used in that meaning in several Romanic languages (French – *science*; Spanish – *sciencia*; Italian – *scienza*).

[2] This is linguistically similar to the Dutch *wetenschap*, the Norwegian *vitenskap*, the Danish *videnskab*, the Swedish *vetenskap*, and the Icelandic *visindi*. The Icelandic word *visindi* is similar to the original word *visindi* in Old Norse which means "knowledge," from *viss* which means "wise, certain" (*vissa* = certainty; *vizka* = wisdom, intelligence). See Buchanan (1933, 39). The German extension *schaft* is possibly derived from the Proto-Indo-European word *(s)kep* which means "to cut, scrape" and could be related to *skei* mentioned in footnote 1.

have less of an inclination to rank different disciplines according to criteria of "science" in the limited Anglo-American sense. The distinction between science and *Wissenschaft* will continue to challenge social scientists. For instance, when discussing the state of the study of international relations, Wight observed that the label "science" was both usurped by logical positivists and conceded by – what he called – traditionalists (2002: 28). "Traditionalists" accepted the positivists' superiority with regard to quality of research and the positivists had no hesitation accepting that designation. One could probably say the same for most if not all the social sciences. If so, could it be that a substantial number of scholars in the social sciences at large do not so much suffer from an inferiority complex but rather from uncertainty about how to weigh the traditional conception of knowledge in the midst of a narrower and more recent conception of knowledge fueled by – what must seem – an avalanche of quantitative-statistical research? When positivists in the study of public administration, such as Meier (2005: 655), suggest that traditionalists suffer from "test-tube" envy, they may actually suffer from "test-tube envy" themselves, that is, from covetously eyeballing the natural sciences with their seemingly more unified theories and methods. The "scientists" in the social sciences must be frustrated with not getting any closer to acquiring the quality of knowledge that is associated with the natural sciences.

Positioning the study of public administration among the three branches of learning raises questions about how knowledge has been organized in general (Section 2.1), about conceptual maps of the various disciplines in these branches of learning (Section 2.2), about differences between the natural sciences on the one hand and the social sciences and humanities on the other (Section 2.3), and about problems of social science research (Section 2.4). What makes it challenging to determine the identity of public administration is that its scholars do not agree upon what constitutes scholarship: science or *Wissenschaft*. This is in part because public administration is an umbrella discipline (Section 2.5). The chapter is concluded with summary comments that provide the first building block in the effort to outline the nature of public administration.

2.1 Compartmentalization of Available Knowledge and its Problems

In Chapter 1, compartmentalization of knowledge within disciplines was briefly discussed as a function of specialization, showing that public administration's plight is not unique. Compartmentalization of knowledge also occurs between disciplines and is then a function of demarcation. The effort to delineate a studies' proper arena of inquiry goes back to Antiquity.

According to Cahill, Ceasar's librarian Varo († 27 BCE) was the first to distinguish between fields of knowledge: grammar, rhetoric, dialectic, arithmetic, geometry, astronomy, music, medicine, and architecture (2008: 193–5). In the Carolingean era (eighth- and ninth-centuries CE), the first seven of these were labeled as the *artes liberales* and they were split into the *trivium* (grammar, rhetoric, and dialectic; i.e., the humanities) and the *quadrivium* (arithmetic, geometry, astronomy, and music; i.e., science). Upon the emergence of universities (since the twelfth century), new studies were added, some of a more practical nature such as medicine and navigation, others of a more theoretical nature such as theology and philosophy, and yet others of a mixed practical and theoretical nature such as law. In the medieval university students had to study the traditional seven liberal arts (compare the "general education" requirements in contemporary American colleges) before they were allowed to venture into areas of learning considered advanced at the time such as medicine, theology, and law. Since then various specializations have been added and this process has not come to an end. In fact, at no time has secession from a "mother" discipline (such as economics and psychology from philosophy, or public administration from political science and/or law) and specialization within disciplines been as substantial as in our own.

This demarcation of branches of learning and of disciplines within each of these challenged the Greek desire for unity of knowledge, the "Ionian chant" as E.O. Wilson called it (1998: 4) in reference to the region of Ionia on the West coast of Turkey that had a large Greek settlement in the fourth- and third-centuries BCE. While the Greeks gave unity of knowledge-wide currency, it originated possibly in the more ancient notion of a reality based upon a large underlying principle of divine origin (Armstrong, 2007: 37). Descartes held that as laws of nature were universal and uniform so there should be universal laws for the social world at large (Nisbet, 1986: 49). Ideas about unified theory thrived in the natural sciences and, in the course of the eighteenth and nineteenth centuries, several attempts were made to develop the same for the social sciences. Analogous to the idea that the discovery of universal laws in natural science dependent upon the replicability of experiments, social scientists believed that comparative research would lead to comparable universal laws for social phenomena. Indeed, some, such as Karl Marx and the English historian Edward A. Freeman, believed in the 1870s that scholars were perhaps a decade away from the discovery of such universal social laws (Richter, 1968/69: 134; Tucker, 1978), truly a belief of "Leonardesque aspirations" (Campbell, 1969: 329). In retrospect, social scientists have not even come close. In fact, specialization only deepened the chasms between the branches of learning and between each of the disciplines in them, simply because it is less and less possible to be cognizant on what knowledge is developed across the social sciences that pertains and is relevant to a particular object of knowledge. This is in part because our cognitive capacities are limited, but also because each discipline or study "wraps" itself in a specific jargon not immediately accessible to others.

Compartmentalization of knowledge is a problem for scholars because they do not understand each other's work unless they take the time to familiarize with the "lingo," that is, the theories, concepts, etc., in another discipline potentially relevant to their own. Koestler pointed to the "...gulf that still separates the Humanities from the Philosophy of Nature" (1986: 9). Familiarization with other bodies of knowledge is usually limited to one or a few disciplines. As far as I know, there are no scholars who have sufficient knowledge of all the social sciences to determine how each of those is or can be relevant to the study of public administration in its effort to provide comprehensive understanding of government. Then, there is a growing gap between scholars/experts and lay people, something that potentially has considerable consequences for public policymaking as the British physicist C.P. Snow pointed out. He was well equipped to contemplate the widening gap between the natural scientists and the literary intellectuals, the two cultures as he called them, for as a scientist he had worked in the British civil service during the Second World War. He had come to conclude that:

> One of the most bizarre features of any advanced industrial society in our time is that the cardinal choices have to be made by a handful of men: in secret, at least in legal form, by men who cannot have a firsthand knowledge of what those choices depend upon or what their results may be. (Snow, 1971: 99)

In a second look at his famous 1959 lecture he wrote how:

> In our society (that is, advanced Western society) we have lost even the pretence of a common culture. Persons educated with the greatest intensity we know can no longer communicate with each other on the plane of their major intellectual concern. This is serious for our creative, intellectual and, above all, our moral life. It is leading us to interpret the past wrongly, to misjudge the present, and to deny our hopes of the future. (Snow, 1971: 51)

The reason that, at least, a limited understanding of the natural science is highly relevant to public servants was driven home in the following phrases:

> It is dangerous to have two cultures which can't or don't communicate. In a time when science is determining much of our destiny, [...] it is dangerous in the most practical terms. Scientists can give bad advice and decision makers can't know whether it is good or bad. On the other hand, scientists in a divided culture provide a knowledge of some potentialities which is theirs alone. All this makes the political process more complex, and in some ways more dangerous, than we should be prepared to tolerate for long, either for the purposes of avoiding

disasters, or for fulfilling – what is waiting as a challenge to our conscience and goodwill – a definable social hope. (Snow, 1971: 76)

At the same time, comparable concerns were voiced in the United States by scientists and politicians alike. Political scientist D.K. Price pointed to problems resulting from a lack of broad-based education:

It is very hard for Americans to admit that practically all policies are based on a mixture of ideas that only scientists can understand with other ideas that most of them do not bother to understand – such as considerations of cost, administrative effectiveness, political feasibility, and competition with other policies. (1965: 275–6)

The physicist Rabinowitz wondered in 1961 about " . . . the capacity of the democratic, representative systems of government to cope with the problems raised by the scientific revolution is in question" (quoted in Price, 1965: 10). In his farewell address, President Eisenhower warned against the possibility that public policy could become the captive of the scientific–technological elite. Alaska U.S. Senator E.L. Bartlett argued in 1963 that " . . . faceless technocrats in long, white coats are making decisions today which rightfully and by law should be made by Congress" (quoted in Price, 1965: 11). Likewise, the economist and political scientist Lindblom observed early on that research of trained experts provides the main foundation for and legitimation of policymaking. He warned that the exclusion of the recipients and beneficiaries of policy would result in less than effective implementation. In his view, scientific knowledge was supplementary to other types of knowledge. Policymakers should make more use of lay knowledge (Dahl and Lindblom, 1953: 79; Lindblom and Cohen, 1979: 90; Lindblom, 1990: 137).

The gap between the public at large and experts has been widening as a function of the enormous prestige that scientific, factual, and technical information enjoys. As type of knowledge it has come to dominate other types of knowledge such as judgment and opinion (Yankelovich, 1991: 3, 184, 197). In an informal hierarchy of knowledge, public judgment finds itself pretty much at the bottom (ibid.: 49). In a society where instrumental rationality thrives, the quality of knowledge is determined by how it was generated (logical, factual, analytical, experimental) and validated (ibid.: 185–7). Commanded by experts this type of knowledge is not easily accessible to the public at large. Consequentially, one can assume that the dissemination of knowledge is a one-way flow from the few with much information to the many that have less information. It is up to the societal leadership of politicians, civil servants, scholars, journalists, and the like, to make expert knowledge accessible to the public at large. In turn, the public should demand the opportunity to participate in public decision-making on the normative, valuing, and ethical side rather than only on the factual and informational side (ibid.: 5; see also Lindblom, 1990).

The concerns of Koestler, Snow, Eisenhower, Lindblom and others are as relevant today as they were fifty years ago. The entomologist E.O. Wilson suggests that public policymaking is influenced by experts from the natural and the medical sciences and that proper assessment of their accomplishments is limited because "Public intellectuals, and trailing closely behind them the media professionals, have been trained almost without exception in the social sciences and the humanities." (Wilson, 1998: 126). Even among societal leaders considerable gaps exist, something that Wilson contributes to the fact that the founders of the social sciences (i.e., Durkheim, Marx, Freud, Weber) ignored the achievements of the natural sciences and were more motivated by political ideology (ibid.: 184). To bridge the gap between the natural and medical sciences on the one hand and the social sciences on the other, Wilson advises to develop core curricula that connect the great branches of learning, and not just the various specializations within one of these branches, because

> Profession-bent students should be helped to understand that in the twenty-first century the world will not be run by those who possess mere information alone. [Knowledge] is destined to become global and democratic [...] We are drowning in information, while starving for wisdom. The world henceforth will be run by synthesizers. (Wilson, 1998: 269)

Wilson appears prophetic (cf. "The world henceforth etc.") but doubts that such synthesizers will emerge since "Each discipline of the social sciences rules comfortably within its own chosen domain of space and time so long as it stays largely oblivious of the others" (Wilson, 1998: 190–1). Are natural scientists more inclined to go outside their chosen domain? Quite frankly, this is doubtful. While efforts to develop interdisciplinary knowledge in the natural sciences (see Bechtel, 1986) and ideas about how to unify the behavioral sciences (see Gintis, 2007, 2009) have been pursued since the 1970s, scholars have neither succeeded in substantive terms nor were they able to dismantle the existing organization of academic disciplines at the university because no unifying concept or theory garnered sufficient enthusiastic support of a majority of scholars. Some scholars even argue that unification of the sciences is not desirable. For instance, in response to Gintis' advocacy, Clarke (2007: 22) argued that unification of the behavioral sciences was undesirable for three reasons. First, they had developed in incompatible ways and unification would require that much work would have to be abandoned. Second, accepting a particular unifying model would limit the possibility of developing new perspectives. Third, the acceptance of one unifying model would stop the development of other unifying models.

It seems that most, and perhaps all, branches of knowledge, will have to live with the "... uneasy compromise between unification and fragmentation" as Henriques observed with regard to psychology (2004: 1207). This subject will be taken up at length in Chapter 7 but let it be said for now that integration of knowledge is not synonymous to unification of knowledge in epistemological terms (which could be called *strong integration*). Instead, integration of knowledge starts with bridging the gap between various disciplines and, more importantly, between experts and laymen. By way of example, the journalist Gary Zukav asked the physicist Finkelstein to describe the accomplishments of twentieth-century physics in everyday terms. The result was a highly readable book (Zukav, 1979). Something like that could be done for other disciplines and studies as well. Making scholarship accessible to others facilitates exchange of knowledge and may result in *weak integration*.

Meanwhile, given that knowledge is fragmented or compartmentalized, and, given the fact that under this circumstance scholars operate with implicit hierarchies of knowledge, we need to look at some of the ways that knowledge has been organized. This is useful for determining where the study of public administration fits among the branches of knowledge.

2.2 Conceptual Maps of Relations between Disciplines: Rankings and Hierarchies of Knowledge

When E.O. Wilson observed that the early social scientists had ignored the natural sciences, he basically suggested that the natural sciences could serve as an example for how the social sciences should have proceeded. Indeed, the natural sciences are often considered as more advanced than the social sciences. When establishing the "scientificness" of a study scholars often use an informal ranking of knowledge that developed in the course of the past three centuries in the Western world (the following based on Yankelovich, 1991: 49–50). Presently, theoretical physics is at the top of this ranking because it combines the virtues of modern science in the limited sense as defined in the introduction of this chapter (i.e., knowledge firmly grounded in experimental validations) with the ancient Greek ideal of explanation that is based on a few unchanging theoretical principles. Experimental sciences come next (e.g., chemistry) and they are followed by disciplines based on observation, description, and taxonomy (e.g., botany, geology). Below these, and in the middle of the hierarchy, comes knowledge based on scholarship (in the broader sense) and on historical investigation. Lower still are the applied sciences and the professions. The status of the social sciences is a matter of debate: to admirers they are close to the more "senior" natural sciences, while critics believe they belong closer to the bottom of the hierarchy. Judgment and opinion, so important to Lindblom's lay probing (see above), are at the bottom of this hierarchy.

In a playful article, Meier argued that this traditional ranking should really be turned upside down when considering the complexity of inquiry as reflected in the degree to which logical, empirical, and design components are included in the analysis. A study that contains all three components is the most difficult, for it not only analyzes phenomena in the real world (through logic and empirical observation) but also tries to develop solutions to real world problems (the design component). In his view, mathematics sits at the bottom of the ranking since it is a pure logical system without empirical or design components. He situates the natural sciences in the middle since they have logical and experimental components, but lack a design element. Finally, the social sciences belong at the top since they have logical, experimental, and design components. He writes that: "Turning a social science into a natural science or worse into a pure logical system is the equivalent of using a hammer to fix your computer software" (2005: 655). Hence, in his view, public administration sits at the top, perhaps not (yet) in terms of methods used, but certainly in terms of the societal complexity it seeks to study and capture.

Benton and Craib also situate the social sciences at the top: social sciences, psychology, physiology/anatomy, organic chemistry/biological chemistry, physical chemistry, and physics. Their rationale, however, is that each level is explicable in terms of the level immediately below it. They also observe, though, that the lower-level science can only explain the constitution of the mechanisms at the higher level; the lower level cannot explain when or with what effects these mechanisms will be used. More importantly, once a higher-level mechanism is formed it influences lower levels. In other words, causality flows up and down (2001: 126–7).

Meier's ranking, which is strongly reminiscent of Comte's theory of knowledge that also uses increased complexity to rank the sciences (Levine, 1995: 164), is an inverted pyramid where complexity of inquiry increases with every level. In a comparable fashion the British sociologist Malcolm Williams conceptualized the hierarchy of knowledge as an inverted triangle, with zoology or botany near the (upturned) base at the top, resting on principles of biology, with chemistry lower still, and physics at the apex. He argued that, superficially, all social behavior rests upon a biological basis, but the big question remains: What is the nature of the relation between the social and the biological realm? One thing, he believes, is clear and that is that the social world has characteristics that are different from the biological or physical world and thus require different kinds of explanations. The social world is constructed and reconstructed by self-aware creatures. Scholars who study this social world generally treat the relationship between the individual and biology as a black box (Williams, 2000: 122–4, 134). We shall see below that it is possible to, at least, conceptualize the link between the natural and social worlds, and that some social scientists do seek to investigate it.

The ranking that Yankelovich discusses is based on the specific and narrow definition of "science" and "scientificness," while the hierarchies of Meier, Benton and Craib, and Williams are based on the complexity of the problems that a study seeks to tackle. What all four have in common is that they are based upon a subjective valuation of what features warrant a higher respectively lower ranking. Yankelovich's ranking is correct when premium value is placed upon the degree to which a study has established an internally consistent and coherent body of knowledge (i.e., in terms of its concepts, theories, and methods), while Meier, Benton, and Craib, and Williams are right when premium value is placed upon the degree of complexity a study seeks to tackle. More importantly, however, is that in the Yankelovich and Meier rankings of knowledge the various "ranks" are neither substantively connected to each other nor influenced or affected by the other "ranks." In the Benton and Craib and Williams's hierarchies, each higher level rests upon principles investigated at the level immediately below it.

Is a more "neutral" (not necessarily objective) hierarchy of knowledge possible that is not based on subjective ranking of what constitutes high respectively low quality science? Several scholars have done so by developing conceptual maps of the disciplines. They organize academic disciplines by using levels of analysis from the smallest to the largest unit in the physical or natural world in connection to using the smallest to the largest unit in the social world. The basic idea is then that what happens at one level of analysis (e.g., the atom or the social group) is affected by both a smaller level (e.g., the quantum or the individual) and by a higher level (e.g., the molecule or the human society) (Knoflacher, 2004: 46), thus establishing a hierarchy of knowledge where the various disciplines are interconnected and interdependent.

In Chapter 1, conceptual maps were described as a way of organizing existing knowledge that helps to assimilate new concepts and propositions. The idea is, of course, that concepts can only be meaningful when they are linked to other concepts. Thus, the form and nature of a "leaf" can only be apprehended when considering it in relation to "higher concepts" such as the leaf on the branch of a tree, and, subsequently, trees, flora, organisms, or the leaf of a book and, subsequently, books, paper, trees, etc. But, the form and nature of the leaf itself is not only understood in terms of higher concepts, that is, in terms of features extrinsic to itself, but also in terms of features intrinsic to itself. In other words, a leaf cannot be understood unless we can explain its existence through extrinsic and intrinsic causes. Aristotle distinguished two constitutive or intrinsic causes, *formal* (i.e., what sort of thing is it?) and *material causes* (i.e., what is it made of?), and two active or extrinsic causes, *efficient* (i.e., how did the thing come into being), and *final or ultimate* (i.e., why did the thing come into being?) *causes* (see, e.g., Kurki, 2008: 220). In the example of the leaf on the branch of a tree: the formal cause is the pattern or blueprint by which we can recognize it (i.e., leaves have different shapes but their similarities are more important than their differences), the material cause is the cells of which the leaf is composed, the efficient cause is that it grew out of a branch, and the final cause is that it exists to produce oxygen out of carbon dioxide. Its form or pattern (the formal cause) and cells (the material cause) are intrinsic to the organism; its growth (the efficient cause) and purpose (the final cause) are extrinsic to the organism (see, e.g., Levine, 1995: 110–1). Building upon Aristotle's idea of a tree of knowledge (see also: Genesis 2, 9), Porphyry (ca. 234 – ca. 305 CE) developed the first tree of knowledge (Sowa, 2006; see also Gibson, 1908: 47). A tree or hierarchy of knowledge is different from a "ranking" since in the former the various layers are mutually dependent upon one another, while in the latter they are not.

By way of example, four knowledge hierarchies will be discussed in this section: those of the Austrian zoologist Riedl, the Austrian psychiatrist and ethologist Medicus, the American psychologist Henriques, and the American chemistry and history of science scholar Small. The first three hierarchies can be used to situate the study of public administration among the various academic disciplines; the hierarchy by Small is very different in nature but could be promising when applied to the study of public administration.

2.2.1 *Riedl's Hierarchy of Knowledge*

Riedl is one of the first scholars to systematically develop a hierarchy of knowledge rooted in the idea that things and concepts exist in interdependent relation to one another. With this in mind he organized the world into twelve layers of increasing complexity: quantum, atom, molecule, biomolecule, ultra-structure, cell, tissue, organ, individual, group, society, civilization (1978/79; 1984*a*). Each layer is a necessary prerequisite for the next (1984*a*: 151; Benton and Craib, 2001). There are few, if any, studies that confine themselves to one level of analysis only. For instance, nuclear physics connects the quantum and atom levels, while physical chemistry connects the atom and molecule levels. There are also disciplines that connect more than two levels of analysis, such as cosmology (quantum, atom, molecule) and neuroscience (e.g., molecular-, cellular-, systems-, behavioral-, and cognitive neuroscience; also computational neuroscience, developmental neurobiology, neuroanatomy, neurochemistry, neuroethology, etc.; see Farmer, 2010: 116). Riedl's unique contribution was to connect these levels of complexity

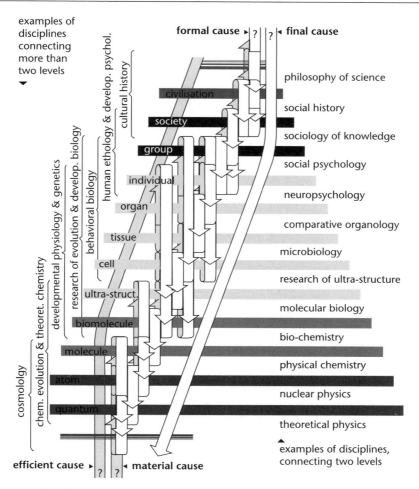

Figure 2.1 Riedl's Stratified Structure of the Real World

Source: Slide 23 in the powerpoint presentation by Gerhard Medicus, accessed 12-17-2008, http://homepage.uibk.ac.at/~c720126/humanethologie/ws/medicus/block1/TheoryHumanSci.ppt Translation of Riedl's model by Medicus (reprinted with permission by Dr. Medicus).

and analysis to Aristotle's four causes (Figure 2.1). It is interesting to read how his insights developed and matured (1984*b*; Medicus, 2008).

Efficient causes (or building blocks) work upward from the lowest level throughout the entire structure, while the final or purposive causes work downward. The cycles of material and formal causes change from layer to layer (Riedl, 1984*a*: 124). Causality is often regarded as a one-way linear chain, but that is not sufficient to explain the structure, functioning, and origins of complex systems. Riedl emphasizes that feedback or network causality captures much better the "reality" of the living world (see also Wuketits, 1990: 24; Benton and Craib, 2001: 127). He visualizes the functional interconnectedness of the four causes by placing them in his model. Understanding and explanation of any phenomenon is impossible without attention for the interplay of the four causes. Efficient causes, that is, the impulse toward change, act from the less to the more complex layers, while the final causes act from the more to the less complex layers (Riedl, 1984*a*: 147).

Using Riedl's hierarchy we can see that the study of public administration encompasses at least three levels (individual, group, society) and possibly four (including civilization) and even five levels (the "organ") of analysis. Simon's research into decision-making is focused on the individual and organ (i.e., brain) levels; Janis's groupthink concerns the group level; some organization theory literature spans the individual to the group/supergroup (i.e., organization) level, while other organization theories explicitly connect the supergroup (organizational) level to its environmental context (contingency theory; population-ecology model). Studies that concern the emergence and development of government over time cannot but include the civilization level (e.g., administrative history).

Obviously, the dominant actors relevant to the study of public administration are human beings whose actions can be goal-directed and goal-intended (Wuketits, 1990: 62–3). *Goal-directed* or *prerational behavior* is characteristic for animals and humans alike and is a response to information gathering by the sense organs processed through the nervous system and serves to help the organism survive. Knowledge acquired through sensory experience is *ratiomorphic* or prerational and concerns only the mesocosm, that is, that part of reality that can be observed unaided through our senses (Wuketits, 1990: 121), and concerns intuitive and instinctive responses to external stimuli (e.g., signs of danger, signs of opportunity to procreate). As far as the social sciences are concerned, this goal-directed behavior can also be influenced by pressure from a peer-group (e.g., groupthink; but consider also Asch's conformity experiment, Milgram's and Zimbardo's obedience experiments). What separates human beings from the rest of the animal kingdom is *goal-intended* or *rational behavior*, that is, our actions in the present as they are influenced by interactions with others, reflections upon the past, and anticipations of the future. The use of concepts such as "preferences" and "calculating citizens" (e.g., rational choice theory), and attention for budget allocation, for policymaking, and so forth, indicate that public administration is very much concerned with goal-intended behavior. However, ratiomorphic or prerational perceptions can not only override rational thought (Wuketits, 1990: 90) as the Asch, Milgram, and Zimbardo experiments showed, but may even precede it (McDermott, 2004: 693).

Another important distinction between animals and human beings is that the former basically act upon the section of reality that they can perceive through their ratiomorphic apparatus (i.e., the sense organs and the nervous system). That is, animals perceive the mesocosm, but human beings can delve into the micro- and macroscosms. They may not be able to see quanta and atoms, or to experience the speed of light, or to visualize the size of the universe, but they can theorize about it. Related to public administration research one could say that data allowing analysis by quantitative-statistical methods enables the scholar to map and/or trace regularities in the microcosm (a particular set of government organizations) or the macrocosm (governments in the world) that are not visible to their sense organs. That is, knowledge gained through inference enables human beings to transcend the mesocosm to which animal perception is generally limited.

Since Riedl other scholars have developed comparable hierarchies. The American mechanical engineer Kline, for instance, developed a hierarchy of thirteen levels based on level of size (from subatomic particles to the universe) and providing examples of biological forms, of human-made systems and objects, of natural physical objects, and of academic disciplines (1995: 107–8). What connects Riedl, Kline, and other scholars who provide conceptual maps of knowledge is that they are profoundly interested in multi- and/or interdisciplinarity (see for the distinction between these two, Chapter 7).

2.2.2 Medicus and the Periodic Table of the Human Sciences

Medicus suggests that Riedl's hierarchy could profit from including the four basic questions and explanations in biology as outlined by the Dutch ethologist Tinbergen. The four basic questions are divided into two groups. The so-called *ultimate (or evolutionary) explanations* concern the evolution of a species and involve two questions. First, when did a species emerge and how has it changed over time (*phylogeny*)? This hints at Aristotle's efficient cause (e.g., mutation or natural selection; environmental influence upon a species' development). Second, why is an organism the way it is (*adaptation* or *function*)? Adaptation or function corresponds to Aristotle's final cause. *Proximate explanations* regard the individual and raise two questions. First, how does an individual organism develop (*ontogeny*)? This relates to Aristotle's material cause. That is, what happens from the first single DNA code through the various stages of life? Second, how does an organism work (*causation* or *mechanism*)? This is reminiscent of Aristotle's formal cause. Combining Riedl's levels of complexity with Tinbergen's four basic questions, Medicus arrives at a periodic table of human sciences (Table 2.1).

Just as Riedl, he argues that many of life's phenomena will be inexplicable if not analyzed in terms of both their ultimate and proximate causes, especially

Table 2.1 Medicus' Periodic Table of Human Sciences

The Periodic Table of Human Sciences

Table 1	Causation	Ontogeny	Adaptation	Phylogeny
Molecule				
Cell				
Organ				
Individual				
Group				
Society				

Source: Medicus (2005: 97) (reprinted with permission from Nova Science Publishers, Inc.).

since the four questions are so closely related. Individual studies seldom, if ever, concern only one of these questions. Consequentially, and in view of his disciplinary background, he argues that behavior and psyche cannot be understood at one level and through one question only and he presents his categories of human knowledge with respect to ethological inquiry (Table 2.2).

Note that Medicus provides a conceptual map of disciplines that study human behavior, while Riedl presents a conceptual map that incorporates all academic disciplines. In the bottom row of Medicus' schema, the social sciences are listed as predominantly concerned with questions about causation, and this especially so with regard to the societal level of analysis. Indeed, it has been said that the natural sciences pay more attention to the ultimate causes, while the social sciences generally investigate the proximate causes (Vanelli, 2001: 53–5). However, one could argue that each of the social sciences has attention for each of the four causes. Taking public administration as example, its scholars are certainly interested in causation (how is individual behavior influenced by the organizational and societal environments and vice versa?), but they are also interested in the development of government and which role the societal (and even natural) environment played in that development (ontogeny), in why government is the way it is (adaptation), and why government developed in specific ways and not differently (phylogeny). Medicus' schema helps to see that public administration scholars are mostly concerned with the "here and now" and with proximate causes and much less with ultimate causes (however, there is, e.g., administrative history). More specifically, scholars who work on the basis of rational choice and behavioral models cannot provide any insight into ultimate causes (Alford and Hibbing, 2004: 718).

Table 2.2 Medicus' Categorization of Human Knowledge

	Questions concerning proximate causes		Questions concerning ultimate causes			
	(1) Causation	(2) Ontogeny	(3) Adaptation			(4) Phylogeny
			(a) Ecological	(b) Intraspecific		
(A) Examples of ethological inquiry and associated disciplines	*How do behavior and psyche "function" on the molecular, physiological, neuroethological, cognitive and social level – and*	*Which developmental steps and which environmental factors play when/which role?* I.e.	*How do specific faculties of perception, subjective internal mentation, learning and behavior benefit the performer? E.g.:* • *Which evolutionary alterations occured in persistent phylogenetically earlier traits, caused by the selective pressure of more recent behavior patterns?* • *What are the costs, what the benefits of a behavior pattern – for example (a/b):*			*Why did structural associations evolve in this manner and not otherwise? Specifically:*
	• What do the relations between the levels look like? • How are genetically programmed behavior patterns (e.g., "instinctive" drives and inhibitions), learning, intellect and culture, as well as ability, volition and conscience entwined with one another and are there differences dependent on the species, age, gender and behavioral realm? • How do perception, subjective internal mentation and behavior correspond with the environment?	• What are the ontogenetic bases of behavior and learning? E.g.: • Which effect have hormones and reafferences for maturing processes and imprinting-like steps? • How are instincts and learning intertwined with one another? • What is learned?	*(a) Ecological:* concerning caloric intake and energy expended?	*(b) Intraspecific:* in relation to familial proximity and social attractiveness?		• Which behavior was a prerequisite of which new form? • What consequences do older traits have for further developments – for example, for synergy and antagonism in hormones and transmitters, neuroanatomical structures and behavioral traits? (space-time-structure) • Which traits are homologous and which analogous?
(B) Examples of behavior	• Endorphine level rise during grooming in enactor and recipient.	• Children recognize themselves in a mirror at 20 months of age. This is one of	• Social bonding is advantageous for	• Friendly behavior helps to develop and maintain		• Parental care and mother–child bond were phylogenetic preconditions

(continued)

Table 2.2 Continued

	Questions concerning proximate causes		Questions concerning ultimate causes		
	(1) Causation	(2) Ontogeny	(3) Adaptation		(4) Phylogeny
			(a) Ecological	(b) Intraspecific	
	• Expression: emotion – enactor – recipient relations. • Friendly behavior patterns are adversaries of aggression, they can be furthered culturally. Unattractive behavior patterns such as wanton aggression can be culturally inhibited	the foundations of social cognition, for example of being able to take another's perspective as a prerequisite for cognitive altruism and cognitive cooperation	- protection against predators, - collective hunting, - building larger structures	bonds as a basis for reciprocal support, for example, during parental care and aggressive interactions	for social bonds. Within this development in addition to their original function, elements of brood behavior became elements of social behavior, for example, kissing and billing, and grooming and preening
(C) Level of inquiry (e.g., atom, molecule, cell, tissue, organ, individual, group, society) with examples of scientific disciplines	*Atom, molecule:* Biochemistry *Cell, organ:* Neurophysiology, Neurobiology *Organ, individual:* Neuroethology, Neuropsychology, Neurology, Behavioral Physiology, B. Genetics, B. Endocrinology, B. Immunology, Chronobiology, Psychiatry, Psychosomatology *Individual group:* Human Ethology, Sociobiology, Behavioral Ecology, Psychology, Pedagogy, Psychotherapeutic Theories, Earliest History *Society:* Sociology, Law, Political Science, Economics, History, Cultural Sciences, Arts	*Organ, individual:* Developmental Neurology, Neurobiology, *Individual group:* Human Ethology, Developmental Psychology, Psychotherapeutic Theories	*Individual group:* Human Ethology, Behavioral Ecology, Sociobiology	*Individual group:* Human Ethology, Sociobiology	*Organ, individual:* Neuroethology, *Organ, individual:* Neuroethology, *Individual group:* Human Ethology

Source: Medicus (2005: 99) (reprinted with permission from Nova Science Publishers, Inc.).

2.2.3 Henriques' Tree of Knowledge

Inspired by E.O. Wilson's 1998-study, but not mentioning Porphyry, and intrigued by the tension between forces of unification (mainly organizational, i.e., departments, journals, association) and those of conceptual fragmentation (i.e., the large variety of concepts and theories), Henriques presents a new (*sic*) approach to unifying psychology (2003: 150; 2004: 1207) based on a description of the evolution of complexity (N.B.: he does not reference Riedl). He distinguishes four main phases in the evolution of complexity between the big bang (almost 15 billion years ago) and the present (Figure 2.2).

The first phase, that of matter, spanned the period of time when the universe came into existence, expanded and cooled, atomic systems emerged, and galaxies and stars formed. Matter concerns a set of material objects and their behaviors through time. Matter emerged out of the Big Bang, as did space and time. These material objects are the focus of the physical sciences such as physics, chemistry, astronomy, geology, etc. Central to understanding this phase are quantum mechanics for the study of microscopic phenomena (e.g., electrons) and general relativity theory for the study of macroscopic

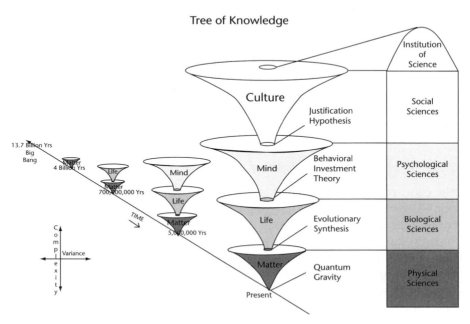

Figure 2.2 Henriques' Tree of Knowledge

Source: G.R. Henriques (2003: 154) (reprinted with permission from the American Psychological Association and Dr. Henriques).

phenomena (such as galaxies). What Henriques calls Quantum Gravity is an imagined merger of these two theories into a unified theory of matter.

In the second phase, between 4 billion and 700 million years ago, life emerged in the shape of self-replicating chemical systems, and evolved into large-scale multicellular organisms. Life concerns the organisms and their behaviors over time and is the object of biology. The central theory is that of natural selection that operates on genetic combinations. This is also known as the Modern Synthesis between natural selection and genetics that was established in the 1930s and 1940s. During the third phase, that of mind, between 700 million and 5 million years ago, animals emerged whose actions were guided by an increasingly complex computational center known as the nervous system. Mind is not synonymous to the capacity for mental experience or rational thought. Henriques proposes that the selection science of behaviorism and the information science of cognitive neuroscience should merge into, what he calls, Behavioral Investment Theory, in order to explain how mind evolved out of life (2003: 158–63).

Finally, from 5 million years ago on, the fourth phase, culture emerged as expressed in the making of tools (since 1.5 million years ago) and the emergence of language (somewhere between 2 million and 50,000 years ago). Culture is understood in terms of human justification systems that span justification of individual action to legitimation of collective behavior through, for example, religious and political schemata. Where matter concerns physical–chemical processes, where life involves biogenetic processes, and where mind involves neuropsychological processes, culture is characterized by sociolinguistic processes and so a justification theory is needed to probe the linkage between mind and culture (2003: 166–75). In Henriques' schema the social sciences are predominantly focused on the fourth phase.

2.2.4 Small's Co-Citation Mapping

The conceptual maps of Riedl, Medicus, and Henriques are a priori classifications, theorizing about how the branches of knowledge can be meaningfully connected. Different from these, Henry Small pioneered a method to map cutting-edge research across the branches of knowledge, but focusing on the natural and the social sciences. He used the method of co-citation mapping that he developed some forty years ago and draws data from, inter alia, the *Current Contents Life Sciences*, the *Genetics Citation Index*, the *Science Citation Index*, the *Social Sciences Citation Index*, and the *Web of Science*. Simply put, co-citation mapping involves tracking pairs of papers cited together in the databases of the Institute for Scientific Information (Small, 1973, 1993, 1997; Small and Garfield, 1985). Already in 1998 this enormous database included almost 20 million articles and 300 million cited references (Garfield, 1998). Through co-citation analysis it is possible to cluster research topics and identify the cutting edge of research (referred to as "emergent fronts"). For a presentation by his colleague Eugene Garfield at a 1998-conference, Small developed a global map of science that consist of a series of five hierarchical maps that, in Garfield's presentation, start with the highest, global level, and then zoom in on areas of interest at four more detailed levels identified on the basis of interest in particular topics in a given year. In Figure 2.3 the global map of science for 1996 is depicted (ibid.: 12).

In his presentation, Garfield argues that a priori classifications systems do not work well since they cannot show that research is constantly in flux and that what is cutting edge (he speaks of research fronts) is changing rapidly. With this in mind it could be argued that the models of Riedl, Medicus, and Henriques are too general and too static. Also, they do not show the relative importance of different fields of study in one moment in time. Small's map captures the relative importance of a field by its "size" defined as the number of people who write about a particular topic in a particular year. For instance,

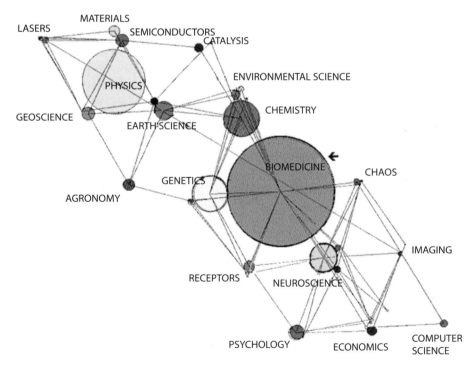

Figure 2.3 Small's Global Map of Science in 1996

Source: http://www.garfield.library.upenn.edu/papers/mapsciworld.html (reprinted with permission from Professors Garfield and Small).

the field of biomedicine was huge in terms of citations in 1996, followed by the field of physics.

A great advantage of the co-citation method is that it is possible to show how the various fields, disciplines, and studies are related to one another. A second advantage is that the global map is based on an analysis of the dominant research themes starting at the author level and then moving up. Small illustrates this, inter alia, by taking the example of economics. The study of economics is situated in the bottom right corner of the global map in Figure 2.3. Zooming in one level the four top major topics are "innovation," "business," "investment," and "stocks." Looking closer at "investing," the three main topics that scholars wrote about in that year were "economic growth," "business cycles," and "stock markets." When looking at the "stock market" only, and we are now at the fourth level, the four main topics studied were "volatility," "futures," "interest rates," and "co-integration." Finally, looking at "co-integration" (a mathematical and statistical tool in economics research) at the fifth level, the most cited core papers and their authors are identified. Then, it is possible at each level to map co-citation links between different fields of research, and thus go from, for instance, economics to physics (ibid. 15; see for other visual maps, Cawkell, 2000). This is considered useful for the development of interdisciplinary programs. The co-citation method is also useful to chronologically map research in a particular area. For instance, Garfield et al. showed which articles led up to and built upon the well-known Watson-Crick article in 1953 on the double helix structure of DNA (2003).

Clearly, Small's map of science has advantages, but there are some limitations as well. First, it is not clear whether a distinction is used between positive and negative references. One could argue that a negative reference can potentially "close off" a particular area of and/or approach to research. Also, it is unclear whether references are substantive and used to built upon through further research or merely used to show that an author knows the relevant literature. Finally, the global map shows the relative importance of various fields of research and topics at one moment in time, but that does not equate to theoretical importance. What is fashionable this year may be completely uninteresting ten years from now.

How is this relevant to public administration? Consider the following. Most scholars agree that cultural and technological development accelerated in the past 50,000 years to a point that it far outpaced the speed of biological development. Cultural and technological developments are the product of a combination of experimentation and experience (ratiomorphic or prerational thought) and of induction and deduction (rational thought). While much public administration research is concerned with rational thought and proximate causes, the continued influence of pre-rational thought upon human behavior cannot be disregarded. The only study available that links the individual, organizational, societal, and ideational levels of analysis for the study of public administration as a whole is that by Raadschelders (2003*b*), but does not provide a systematic analysis of how one level influences another. Meanwhile, various authors have mentioned how important it is to link micro- to macrolevels of research (Merton, 1967; Luhman, 1985; Simon, 1985: 303; Mouzelis, 1991: 106–7). It would be very interesting to see what public administration's map looks like when using Garfield's co-citation method.

2.3 Stereotyping the Social and the Natural Sciences

In Section 2.2, examples were presented of how relations between disciplines have been conceptualized. The rankings of Yankelovich (with which he disagrees) and of Meier are not about substantive but about competitive relations between academic departments. The knowledge structures of Riedl, Medicus, and Henriques represent efforts at mapping all disciplines and studies in their interconnectedness. Attractive as these maps are, they do not show that there are significant differences between the natural sciences on the one hand and social sciences and humanities on the other. Contrasting the latter two with the natural sciences is acceptable since the former studies show natural phenomena while the latter two studies show how humans intentionally interact, organize, and creatively express themselves.

Whatever the concept used, various authors have contrasted the natural sciences from the social sciences and the humanities in different ways (unless stated otherwise the content of this section drawn from Levine, 1995: 195–203; and from Ringer, 2004: 16–28). The most notable and fierce debates were those between German scholars in the late nineteenth and early twentieth centuries and is known as the *Methodenstreit* (battle of the methods) (Diggins, 1996: 114–17). The sociologist Simmel proposed to distinguish *Gesetzwissenschaft* (nomological science, science based on laws) from *Wirklichkeitswissenschaft* (science concerned with concrete realities). The philosopher Windelband argued that a distinction of sciences based on substantive considerations was difficult, because it was not clear where exactly the line between "nature" and "mind" could be drawn. He suggested a contrast based on methodological difference: the nomothetic sciences (*Gesetzwissenschaften*) pursue knowledge in the form of invariant "laws" while ideographic sciences (*Ereigniswissenschaften*) focus on particularizing events or patterns.[3] At the same time the historian, psychologist, sociologist, and philosopher Dilthey

---

[3] Adrian Kay (2006: 19–21) convincingly argues that it is far more productive to think of the ideographic-nomothetic divide as a continuum. Some aspects of human behavior can be better

61

contrasted the *Naturwissenschaften* from the *Geisteswissenschaften* (i.e., sciences of the mind, the spirit) since the latter term emphasized the direct link between human action and observation. The distinction between these two is both useful and unfortunate. It is useful when emphasizing that some sciences study phenomena seemingly outside human control while others study phenomena that are within human control. It is an unfortunate distinction when the pursuit of "objective" knowledge is regarded as nobler and more "scientific" than the study of inter-subjectively interpreted phenomena and the interpretation of subjective experiences. Dilthey considered using the term *Kulturwissenschaften*, but regarded this as too impersonal and abstract. His contemporary Rickert, a philosopher, preferred to speak of *Kulturwissenschaften* since they dealt with more than spirit alone (e.g., Rickert, 1962: xvi, 14; but see Hodgson, 2001: 21–2 for a different opinion).

More recent distinctions between the two branches of knowledge seem to go beyond the descriptive categories used since the late nineteenth century. Whitley (1978) distinguished the restricted sciences that are highly specific in subject and mathematical precision from the configurational sciences (i.e., the social and the life sciences). Pantin (1968) distinguished the restricted from the unrestricted sciences, with the physical sciences being more restricted which is the basis of their success. Biology, for instance, is less restricted since its scholars must be willing to follow their problems into any other science relevant (Becher and Trowler, 2001: 31). Thompson et al. (1969) contrasted highly codified fields such as mathematics and the natural sciences from less codified fields. Lodahl and Gordon distinguished high paradigm sciences, such as physics and chemistry, from low paradigm sciences such as political science (see Thomson and Brewster, 1978). Better known in public administration and political science is Richard Rose who spoke of consensual and nonconsensual fields (1976). Finally, Stephen Toulmin writes about compact disciplines (the natural sciences), would-be disciplines (the behavioral sciences), and nondisciplinary activities (ethics) (1972). For purposes of simplicity, the standard labels of natural science and social science/humanities will be used when discussing differences between natural and socio-cultural phenomena because these are the most neutral labels.

The basic difference between natural and socio-cultural phenomena is that complexity of the former is unorganized while complexity in the latter is organized. Referencing Weaver in his Nobel Prize lecture, Von Hayek observed that the complexity of socio-cultural phenomena is not only a function of the properties of the individual elements and the relative frequency with which

---

explained through nomothetic mechanisms, while others are better captured through an ideographic approach. A comparable argument has been made by Shapiro (2005).

they occur, but also of how the individual elements are connected with each other (Table 2.3). That is, socio-cultural phenomena are artificial, human-made. For most of geological time this difference was irrelevant, but as soon as humankind became self-aware, that is, cognizant of life and death and of past and future, socio-cultural phenomena took on a life of their own. Some scholars date this moment as far back as 50,000 BCE (see, e.g., Henriques above) while others date this as recent as 3,000 BCE (Jaynes, 1990; Snell, 2007: 388–91). This self-awareness makes that "Social practices, institutions and organizations are partially constituted by the beliefs and concepts of [people] . . . ," while "Beliefs about the concepts of physical realities are always secondary to those realities . . . " That is, " . . . the physical world does not require us to have any particular beliefs about it or concepts of it, for it to exist" (MacIntyre, 1998: 57).

Central to evolution is the storage and processing of information in an agent that serves as an unaware (genes) or conscious (memes, cf. Dawkins, 2006: 189) vehicle of change. Socio-cultural evolution accelerates over time because the transmission of information is not left to chance, as in nature, but to selective appreciation of what is useful for survival. In other words, socio-cultural systems are guided by continuous feedback and self-reflection by scholars and by lay people alike.

Given the differences between both groups of phenomena it is easy to see how knowledge claims of the natural sciences on the one hand and of the social sciences and humanities on the other vary (Table 2.4). The natural science ideal is an objective and measurable reality that can be observed independent of the researcher and that, though to varying degrees, can be abstracted from reality. Natural scientists seek knowledge that is applicable to and operative in any time and place, enabling them to develop universal laws through explanation (*Erklären*). They express their insights in universal and formal language (e.g., mathematical and physical models; periodic table of elements). It is important to note, however, that physicists (e.g., Feynman, Heisenberg, Gell-Mann) have re-introduced uncertainty and unknowability in their models, emphasizing the importance of doubt as a method of knowing (Van Gigch, 2001*a*: 209). Especially in the social sciences efforts to achieve preciseness are stymied by the fact that social life is more complex than we can understand (Van Gigch, 2001*b*: 561). Developing such universal laws is con-siderably more difficult for the social sciences (see for a different opinion: Kincaid, 1996) and the humanities given that their object of interest, human behavior and creativity, is not independent from the subject of inter-est (the human being) and focuses on non-homogenous actions as well as on long-term changes that may not be governed by a single law (Fay, 1996: 167–8).

Table 2.3 Characteristics of Natural and of Socio-cultural Phenomena

	Natural phenomena	Sociocultural phenomena
Nature of phenomena (Von Hayek, 1974 after Weaver, 1958; Hacking, 1993: 1996); role of values (Rickert, 1962: 21)	Unorganized complexity; stable, indifferent devoid of value	Organized complexity; unstable, interactive affected with value
Information storage and processing (Dawkins, 2006)	Genes (DNA), genetic	Memes, intellectual
Vehicle of change (Hannan and Freeman, 1978: 140)	Evolution of genetic code through chemical devices	Evolution of cultural code through systems of meaning
Evolutionary pattern (Van Parijs, 1981: 93)	Natural selection through mutation, selection, reproduction	Evolution of cultural code through systems of meaning
Speed of evolution (Wuketits, 1990: 133)	Slow	Fast
Feedback modes (Kline, 1995: 224)	No feedback of any kind in naturally occurring systems	Many kinds of feedback are critical to guiding the system
Learning and self-reflective capacity (Von Mises, 1942/1990; Kline, 1995: 224; MacIntyre, 1998: 57)	None; can be studied from without	Vital among humans at various levels of analysis; comprehension of human action from within
Presence of lay images (Lammers, 1974: 140)	Lay images absent	Lay images present
Origin of culture (E.O. Wilson, 1998: 188)	Product of genetic determination	Product of gene-culture co-evolution

Henriques' "bio-envy" (see Chapter 1) is paralleled by "natural science envy" among social scientists (how many social scientists suffer from natural science envy has never been quantified). Some scholars observe that social scientists are willing to go great lengths in their desire to establish scientific-ness. For instance, Von Hayek suggested that what is treated as important in the social sciences is that " . . . which happens to be accessible to measurement. This is sometimes carried to the point where it is demanded that our theories must be formulated in such terms that they refer only to measurable magnitudes" (1974). The system management scholar Van Gigch observes that contrary to developments in physics, the social sciences appear to try and become more exact through quantification (1997: 386–7; 2001a). The organizational theorist Starbuck makes the same point and also recalls how during a class on mathematical social science, taught by Alan Newell, Herbert Simon advised the doctoral students to always use passive verbs when writing because these indicated sufficient distance between researcher and object. Scientific writing should convey impersonal detachment (2006: 7, 40). Starbuck also observed that social scientists often use general rather than specific nouns (e.g., health care institution instead of Baptist Integris Hospital) and

Table 2.4 Characteristic of Knowledge Claims and Desires

	Natural science	Social science/ humanities
Understanding of truth (E.O. Wilson, 1998, 41: 214; Polanyi, 1964: 14; Gadamer after Heidegger, 1975: 235; Berlin, 2000, 12–13)	Objective, measurable; fore-structure of understanding	Intersubjective (modernity); or relative, personal (postmodern)
Object of knowledge (Gadamer, 1975: 410–1)	Outside the observer and abstracted from reality	The totality of what exists, including the observer
Type of knowledge sought (Winch, 1958/1986: 111; Levine, 1995: 197)	Universal, unity of knowledge, *Erklären* (the distinction between *Erklären* and *Verstehen* from historian Johann Droysen)	Unity of knowledge impossible, understanding desirable, *Verstehen*
Direction of causation (Kline, 1995: 90; Riedl, 1978/79: 1984)	Mostly mono-causal	Usually multi-causal, feedback loops
Type of language (Fay, 1975/80: 13)	Universal, value-free, formal	Interpretation, value-laden, culture-specific

indefinite rather than definite articles (e.g., the environment instead of the environment of Indianapolis) (2006: 34–5), thus suggesting a more generalized argument than the data really allow.

An increasing number of social scientists recognize that a single theoretical framework, a general theory, is impossible in the social sciences. That is, explanatory unification is considered out of reach.[4] But, what is the alternative? Weber distinguished between *Erklären* (explanation) and *Verstehen* (understanding). The first he considered to be more feasible in the natural sciences, while the second was more appropriate for the social sciences. In his words: "For a science focused on the meaning of action an explanation is: the display of how everything was linked together, considering the subjectively intended meaning, in an actual intelligible action" (1985: 4). While explanations in the natural sciences tend to be more mono-causal by nature, those in the social sciences are generally multi-causal and can be functional, structural, classifying, genetic, teleological and/or ideal typical by nature (Raadschelders and Rutgers, 1989b: 23–4).

In light of these knowledge claims and desires, one can expect that characteristics of theory and method are perceived as being different as well (Table 2.5). The main difference between the two is that the social sciences and

---

[4] A discussion of types of explanatory unification (e.g., logical or derivational and ontological unification) is not considered necessary in the context of this chapter. The reader can find more on this in Redhead (1984), Hodgson (2001: 10), Mäki (1999), and Mäki and Marrchionni (2009).

Table 2.5 Characteristics of Theory and Method

	Natural sciences	Social sciences/humanities
Object of research (Bailey, 1992: 50; von Hayek, 1975: 6)	Inanimate objects or controlled subjects; few variables, specific predictions	Animate objects that are infinitely different and constantly changing; many variables, pattern predictions and prescriptions
Paradigm status (Kuhn, 1973: 103, 109; Weinsheimer, 1985: 27)	Substantive differences between succeeding paradigms, as well as differences in method, problem-field, and standard of solution	Pre-paradigmatic (although not in Kuhn's sense); different and competing schools of thought (see also Chapter 6)
Content of paradigm (Starbuck, 2006: 44)	Concerns both substance and method	No agreement on substance and method
Role of theory (Starbuck, 2006: 126–7)	Stabilizing paradigm	Theories raise conflict
Type of model (Raadschelders, 1998b: 65–77)	Formal-causal models specifying agents (e.g., math and physics)	Stage models specifying periods; correlative models
Method of inquiry (Kuhn, 1973; MacDonald and Pettit, 1981; Catton, 1966: 5, 21)	Uniform within a paradigm; explanation only via occurrences prior to the phenomenon being explained	Various methods of inquiry; includes also teleological explanation
Function of mathematics and methodology (Taagepera, 2008: 3, 52)	description, explanation, and prediction	To describe direction of effect, only postdiction achieved
Nature of experiment (Simon, 1957: 250)	Claim that it is independent of consequences for object of experiment	Knowledge that experiment is dependent upon consequence for object of experiment
Relation of scholars to societal environment (Starbuck 206: 104)	Content and method are autonomous and not defined by the environment	Content and method are highly interdependent with the environment
Separate methods courses (MacIntyre, 1998: 61; Weinberg, 2001: 85)	None or very few	Several with emphasis on quantitative methods

humanities do not have a central explanatory theory or a set of consistent theories that can be referred to as a paradigm (or: a first order formal object). Instead, scholars in the social sciences and the humanities are confronted with theoretical and methodological pluralism. Theories raise conflict rather than unite. But, are the differences so great? Most natural scientists acknowledge that their field is as fragmented at least in terms of specializations. Also, Simon argues that the contrast between the two is, as far as experiments are concerned, superficial, since the first developed natural science, that is, astronomy, also " ... never had the advantages of the laboratory in discovering its laws" (1957: 251). While it may be true that the contrast is superficial in some sense, many social scientists have to deal with the rigorous demands placed by Institutional Review Boards upon research proposals that involve human subjects. The Milgram and Zimbardo experiments mentioned earlier would not be allowed today. Thus, as far as experiments are concerned, there is something of a difference.

What is really different between the natural and the social sciences is that the former do not have separate methodology courses in their curricula. In fact, "... most scientists have very little idea of what the scientific method is" (Weinberg, 2001: 85). Graduate degrees in the social sciences, though, cannot be completed without an sequence of introductory, intermediate and advanced (usually "quants") methods courses. The humanities have entirely different conceptions of methods. Whether these methods courses aid in making the social sciences more scientific is up for debate but some, like MacIntyre, consider the function of methods courses to be not much different from "... grease paint, false beards, and costumes in the theater" (1998: 62).

In reference to Tables 2.4 and 2.5, the difference between the natural sciences and the social sciences/humanities with respect to relation between researcher and object of knowledge is possibly less great than initially thought so that the contrast between the natural sciences, on the one hand, and the social sciences and humanities on the other is, by now, more stereotypical than before. This is in part because the question whether the social sciences are inferior to the natural sciences is seldom systematically analyzed (but see Machlup, 1961). Also, in the past 70–80 years, natural scientists have suggested that the interdependence between object and subject is so close that objectivity in their areas of study is a dream. For instance, the Heisenberg principle holds that any attempt at observing and measuring atomic level phenomena must disturb that which is investigated. The physicist Bell provided mathematical proof that the principle of local causes (i.e., what happens in a certain localized area is independent from any intervention of a researcher) is an illusion. In other words, the outcome of an experiment is influenced by the presence of an observer (Zukav, 1979). In relation to the social sciences, and certainly in the case of public administration, it is conceivable that what we observe is determined by the theories and methods used, by demand for usable knowledge, and, possibly, also by background of the researcher (upbringing, early employment experience, intellectual training, etc.).

2.4 Problems with and Challenges of Social Science Research

Researchers are generally quite happy exploring and analyzing their object of interest without too much regard for how their research is interdependent with and/or embedded in other topics and fields. In every specialization one can find many scholars who plow within it and fewer who take a broader view. The study of performance management and measurement (PM) is a case in point. Scholars who take a broad view, such as Behn, Bouckaert, Hood, Lynn, Pollitt, Talbot, and Van de Walle, and who write broad-ranging books, are not as common as those who focus on specific aspects of public management and measurement and report rather through articles. One can have a solid career publishing in any specialization without ever considering (*a*) whether the focus on output (short term) rather than on outcome (long term) measures provides an adequate basis for evaluating public policy and (*b*) how their topic relates to higher and lower levels of analysis. Questions such as "Is what we wish to know measurable?"; "Is what we measure representative of....?"; "Which are the *facts* in evidence of....?" (see Norton, 2004: 80–2) are not considered the best way to get published. Discussion of potential drawbacks and limitations of PM data and research methods is not pursued by advocates of a more "scientific" approach (on social science in general, see, e.g., Dreschler, 2000; specifically on public management, see Ferlie et al., 2007: 724–5). With regard to public administration specifically, Bailey suggested that data most adaptable (i.e., measurable) to a model may also be the most trivial, that data are lifted out of context and can thus not account for variations related to that context, that models eliminate anomalies while – in a Kuhnian perspective – it is the accumulation of anomalies that lead to a new paradigm, and that replication of public administration research is generally impossible because of changes in geographical, political, time, socio-economic contexts and conditions (1992: 50). One of the main challenges of social science research is to find ways in which quantitative and qualitative methods can be fruitfully combined in order to capture reality's complexity adequately (Van Gigch, 2001*b*: 560–1).

A second challenge of social science research concerns the degree to which in the social sciences and the humanities in general, and specifically in public administration, theoretical and methodological pluralism is a fact, and – subsequently – the degree to which knowledge has been compartmentalized between and within the various disciplines in the twentieth century. Such compartmentalization may have been inspired by substantive motives, but was certainly fueled by organizational reasons (autonomy, funding). Indeed, academic disciplines have been defined by Bourdieu as fields of competitive struggle (mentioned in Bechtel, 1986: 26) rather than, more traditionally, consisting of a central problem, of a domain of facts related to that problem, of specific theories and methods, of a set of general explanatory factors and goals, and of having (although not always) concepts, laws, and theories related to that problem (Darden and Maull, 1977: 44). It seems that disciplinary compartmentalization is a human condition rather than a cognitive necessity.

From a cognitive point of view, scholars should be spending some time learning about what is being done on their topic of interest in other disciplines and studies and how their research could benefit from that. However, scholars attempting to cross disciplinary boundaries in order to arrive at more comprehensive understanding face serious criticism. Indeed, objections to interdisciplinarity generally include a charge of shallowness (i.e., can one really be conversant in several areas or specializations?). Also, it is suggested that interdisciplinary researchers underutilize their skills and competence and thus lose their edge, and that interdisciplinarity is nothing but an escape from the rigors of disciplinarity. Finally, interdisciplinarity research lacks applicable standards of evaluation (Bechtel, 1986: 22–3).

Related to the second challenge is, third, the reluctance of scholars with an identified research agenda and an established publication record to cross boundaries. As Bechtel phrases it: "If a group of scientists have accomplished a body of publicly available research in which they argue for a given point of view, theory or interpretation, they may well wish to defend that position from attack and display its value and scope over other positions – even if they are technically able to work from another cognitive or practical orientation. What is involved is a strategy for defending and furthering interests, based on complex calculations about the consequences of various courses of action" (Bechtel, 1986: 24). A fourth challenge of social science research is that each discipline or study is mainly focused on its immediate neighbors and that multi-level analysis is pursued within the specialization and/or discipline but not across disciplines. In reference to the hierarchies of knowledge discussed in Section 2.2, one could say that public administration focuses on the individual up to the societal (and sometimes global and organ) levels, while disregarding the potential relevance of higher and lower levels of analysis. Specifically, scholars of public administration adopt perspectives from political science, economics, psychology, law, and sociology, but are generally less inclined to look at anthropology, history, and philosophy. Interdisciplinarity beyond the horizontal levels (i.e., between closely related disciplines) is truly a challenge, but not only because of cognitive limitations of the researcher.

2.5 Public Administration as Umbrella Discipline

Interdiscisplinarity can and has been defined at various levels. For instance, it can be defined at the level of the individual scholar who strives to combine knowledge sources from two or more disciplines in the hope of developing a more comprehensive understanding of the object of research. In the study of public administration there are numerous scholars whose research interests led them to consider knowledge in other disciplines. Given that the organizational independence of the study did not become widespread until the late 1960s, there are also various public administration scholars whose initial training is in law or political science and some with a background in history, philosophy, psychology, and sociology.

Interdisciplinarity can also be defined at the level of a research project that involves scholars from various disciplines. One example is the project on disciplinary approaches to aging by Indfeld (2002) that includes a volume on public administration and political science. Another example is the project on common pool resource management systems by Nobel prize winner E. Ostrom (1990). Also, it is generally known how public administration and political science have benefitted from economic theories (e.g., Alt et al., 1999) and from insights of cognitive psychologists. With respect to the latter, consider the many publications by Simon and various co-authors about the processes of decision-making in the human brain. Simon's work is an excellent example of research that reaches into a specific component of decision-making at the individual level, the mental processes in the brain.

Finally, interdisciplinarity can also be defined at the level of a study as a whole. Riedl's hierarchy of knowledge provides several examples, such as biochemistry and neuropsychology. In light of these two examples it is clear that public administration is not aligned with a specific discipline but finds relevant knowledge sources (see Chapter 3) in a range of other, generally social science, disciplines. What does this mean for the identity of public administration? For a tentative answer to this question, Whitley's distinction between polytheistic and umbrella disciplines is useful. *Polytheistic disciplines* have a disciplinary identity and work upon a general conception of science. A polytheistic discipline has a variety of specializations but the primary unit of social and scientific identity is that of the discipline as a whole. This is characteristic for the natural sciences. By contrast, research in *umbrella disciplines* is organized at the level of its specializations or research areas. It is perfectly possible, and, in fact, common, that research in one area is and can be conducted without any reference to or influence from the umbrella discipline. The various social sciences are good examples of umbrella disciplines where its scholars do not experience periods of theory consensus with periods of theory pluralism (as Kuhn suggests is the case in the natural sciences). In fact, social scientists in any of their disciplines debate among one another the identity and academic status of their discipline. Whitley notes how such identity debates are especially vitriolic in Anglo-Saxon sociology (1976: 476–85).

In Europe, public administration is one of those umbrella disciplines whose identity is expressed in comprehensive frameworks that are grounded in a sense of interdisciplinarity (Bouckaert and Van de Donk, 2010: 39, 62–4, 101, 153, 196, 267–8) even when such is not often visible in actual research. In the

United States, public administration is an umbrella discipline defined by its specializations rather than by an overall conception of the study. Indeed, the various specializations and research areas within public administration operate quite autonomously from the master discipline (as is observed for the social sciences in general by Bechtel, 1986: 18). But, in both Europe and the United States, it is also an umbrella discipline in a sense not identified by Whitley, and that is that public administration is the only social science that serves as the umbrella for knowledge about government generated in the various social sciences.

2.6 Horizontal and Vertical Interdisciplinarity: Beyond "Splitting the Universe"

Donne lamented the splitting of the universe into two worldviews (see motto Chapter 1). With respect to the secular/natural worldview, knowledge about reality has not only fragmented into three branches of knowledge, but, especially since the nineteenth century, into a wide range of disciplines, studies, and fields. The ancient ideal of unity of knowledge is farther removed than ever. The economist Gintis believes that " . . . from a scientific point of view, [it is] scandalous that this situation [that partial, conflicting, and incompatible models of reality are regarded separately and at face value] was tolerated throughout most of the twentieth century" (2007: 15). No wonder that some scholars tried to salvage some degree of unity at the level of all knowledge, at the level of the behavioral sciences, and at the level of individual disciplines.

At the level of all knowledge, the hierarchies of Riedl, Medicus, and Henriques show how the various disciplines can be substantively connected. Like Aristotle they focus on the interdependence of causes. Western thinking since the seventeenth century has focused increasingly on efficient causes (i.e., how did something come into being?), but that has, in the eyes of some, impoverished understanding of social reality and limited the ability to solve problems arising from multiple, underlying, and inter-related causes (Aaltonen, 2007: 82–4; Kurki, 2008: 12, 220–2). At the level of all knowledge, E.O. Wilson suggested that the branches of knowledge can be theoretically connected through his concept of gene-culture co-evolution.

Wilson's concept of gene-culture co-evolution is, according to Gintis, one of the five analytical tools that can provide a common basis for the behavioral sciences (next to: sociopsychological theory of norms, game theory, the rational actor model, and complexity theory). He acknowledges that there are monumental intellectual challenges in harmonizing these tools but that these " . . . are likely to be dwarfed by the sociological issues surrounding the semi-feudal nature of modern behavioral disciplines" (Gintis, 2007: 16; 2009: 247). While he does not specify what exactly this "semi-feudal nature" entails, he does point out that the behavioral sciences can only advance when analytical and quantitative methods are combined with historical, descriptive and ethnographic evidence (2009: 242).

As it stands, the difference between the natural sciences on the one hand and the social sciences and humanities on the other is generally presented in terms too absolute and too stereotypical. The contrast between the two as discussed in Section 2.3 is illustrative of this, presenting the two as polar extremes and thus obscuring the fact that most research, as Rickert reminds us, is conducted somewhere in between (1962: xii). Indeed, in Rickert's view, unity of science should not be understood in terms of uniformity of all its branches (ibid.: xiii). The world is multifaceted and cannot be captured adequately in one framework, theory, or worldview. Also, some natural sciences do not generate prescriptions, while some social sciences do. For instance, geology and evolutionary biology are both natural sciences challenged with " . . . the contingencies of history that define the subject matter of these fields [and that] render such prediction impossible" (Harmon, 2006, 48). Some social scientists, such as psychologists and economists, have pursued prescriptive knowledge.

Public administration is a social science with clear links to the humanities such as philosophy, history, literature, and art (cf. Dimock, 1958) for it studies the interaction between individuals in the public realm from the individual up to the societal level. While some research has delved into levels beyond the visible, that is, decision-making processes in the brain (i.e., cognitive psychology), most public administration research is focused on the few visible levels and mainly using concepts and theories from neighboring disciplines. Public administration is an umbrella discipline, not just to its various specializations, the content of which is not determined by the discipline as a whole, but also to knowledge about government developed in other sciences or disciplines. The challenge that the study of public administration must face is that of being an inter-discipline and that, in itself, requires much discipline. It requires the discipline to profitably engage with multiple bodies of knowledge relevant to specific research interests (i.e., theories, as well as models and methods) instead of specializing in one body of knowledge only (see, e.g., Farmer, 2010: 225–8). It requires the discipline to develop meta-frameworks for public administration as a whole, guiding scholars to relevant bodies of knowledge. It cannot be any other way. Public administration studies government and its interactions with society. Such a complex social phenomenon cannot satisfactorily be captured in one approach, framework, or model, but requires the application of multiple disciplinary and theoretical angles.

Public administration's standard of quality is not measured solely in terms of rigorous theory and empirical evidence, important though they are. This is not so much because public administration scholars are likely to never agree upon what such a standard should look like. Rather, it is because the standard of quality not only involves the masterful application of appropriate methods, but also the usefulness of findings for solving problems in the real world. Simply proposing a model or a theory that looks "scientific" is not good enough. Public administration need not slide into " ... fashionable pretension masquerading as real science ... " which Braybrooke believed characterizes competition between academics and departments in the social sciences at large (1987: 78).

When determining the nature of a science or study, it also is important to consider the advice of quantum physicist Niels Bohr as that any description of reality is incomplete if it does not include a description of the observer (Reschke, 2005: 9). As far as public administration is concerned, intellectual biographies that pay attention to how environmental circumstances shaped a scholar's theories are few and far between. There is reason enough to believe, though, that life experiences do shape theory development, at least in part (Fry and Raadschelders, 2008: 14, 344; Radkau, 2009; Raadschelders, 2010a). And, of course, biographical histories can be hierarchically nested in cultural (the development of civilization) and natural histories (the development of the human species) so that we can understand better what drives human behavior and decision-making.

To know a scholar's life story and intellectual development is with respect to public administration not enough to determine the study's identity, because its content and interests are not only defined by its scholars but also by users outside academe. Indeed, public administration's sources of knowledge are not only fragmented within the study and scattered across the social sciences but also fragmented across organizations and society. This theme will be explored in Chapter 3.

3

Public Administration and the Fragmentation of its Knowledge Sources: Academic Specialties and Disciplines, Organizational Units, and Societal Organizations

> ... professional 'professions of faith' always tend to be partial faiths. Holistic views of the world are rare among professionals. A generalist philosophy is often missing because professional specialization, by its very nature, induces myopia. (Stillman, 1991)

The American debate about public administration's nature and identity has been cast mainly in the narrow perspective of epistemological unity of knowledge (the positivist ideal), but must also be considered in the larger context of specialization of the social sciences in general, of the proliferation of organizations, and of the fragmentation in society, each of which contributes mightily to the extent that knowledge sources are fragmented. Scholars of public administration are not only confronted by the fragmentation in and across disciplines but also by organizational and societal fragmentation of knowledge sources.

The compartmentalization of knowledge about government is perhaps only a century or so old. In view of government's ever-increased presence in society the compartmentalization of knowledge is a problem when it inhibits a comprehensive understanding of government's role and position in society and when it prohibits decision- and policymaking that is informed by knowledge about the

1. consequences of a decision/policy for/in (non)related areas and organizations,
2. information relevant to a decision/policy in (non)related other areas and organizations,

3. relation between substantive content of a decision/policy (the expert focus) and implementation costs and problems (the administrator focus), and

4. impact and desirability of a decision/policy across various societal groups.

With respect to compartmentalization of knowledge, the study has branched out since the middle of the twentieth century into a variety of specializations (Waldo, 1975: 21–2). Few, if any, public administration scholars will claim to have more than superficial knowledge of theories, models, and methods in each of these specializations. Instead, they are specialists in budgeting and finance, in program evaluation, in policy analysis, in organizational theory, in performance management, in human resource management, etc. In other words, knowledge about government is scattered across the various specializations in the study of public administration, and we cannot assume that scholars in these specializations actively seek exchange of knowledge with colleagues in other specializations.

The fragmentation of knowledge sources within public administration is only the beginning of the challenges for its scholars and practitioners. Given the unprecedented growth of government since the 1880s it is no wonder that it – to varying degree – attracted scholars in other social sciences as well as in the humanities. How many scholars would claim to have insight in all those bodies of knowledge of which the research agenda is partially concerned with government and thus relevant to understanding government?

Knowledge sources are also fragmented across the hundreds of thousands government organizations and their units and across the millions of societal organizations. Survey and census data can only capture part of that knowledge. The challenges involved become especially clear when looking at the extent of horizontal and vertical organizational differentiation (i.e., span of control and hierarchical levels) in the public sector. That is, we should not only think about organizations in terms of whole units, such as the Department of Health and Human Services, or the equivalent state and county departments or units, but regard them as compound organizations that consist of many subunits. Furthermore, these subunits are not only structurally and functionally part of a larger organization at one level of government, but they also interact functionally with organizational units at other levels of government.

In this chapter this compartmentalization of knowledge and its sources about government is described according to a model outlined in Section 3.1 that contains four elements: the specializations within public administration (Section 3.2), the interests across the social sciences and the humanities (Section 3.3), the enormous organizational differentiation of the public sector (Section 3.4), and the fragmentation of Western society at large (Section 3.5). Section 3.4 will be larger than the other sections since the extent of horizontal and vertical organizational differentiation is illustrated with various organizational charts that show the extent to which organizational structures are fragmented and how policy areas at various levels of government are interconnected. In Section 3.6, intellectual, psychological, and organizational problems of fragmented knowledge will be discussed. The chapter is concluded with Section 3.7 on intellectual, pedagogical, and practical reasons why knowledge sources should be connected better than they are thus far.

3.1 Mapping Intellectual, Organizational, and Societal Compartmentalization

The substantive coherence of the study of public administration is inhibited by the fact that its sources of knowledge are dispersed. In Figure 3.1 the academic sources of knowledge are placed in the upper half of the model, while organizational and societal sources of knowledge occupy the lower half.

The shaded part in quadrant A represents the study of public administration and its various sub-specializations. It is here that some level of knowledge integration has occurred, although more so in Europe with its tradition of developing conceptual frameworks that connect dispersed knowledge. The shaded area in quadrant B represents the attention for and knowledge relevant to government in the various social, humanist, and natural sciences. As in quadrant A, cross-fertilization cannot be assumed and is certainly more difficult in quadrant B. In both quadrants A and B, epistemological and substantive compartmentalization are rampant. The area left blank in quadrant B represents the other interests of the various disciplines. The area circumscribed by the dotted lines in quadrants A and B represent, what Polanyi (1958) called, tacit knowledge that generally relies upon experience rather than instruction (see also Kuhn, 1973: 44). This can be personal experience in, for instance, developing, writing, and presenting, as well as the collective memory people implicitly draw upon.

The lower half of the model refers to a slightly different type of compartmentalization. Quadrant C represents government as consisting of thousands upon thousands of organizations that are formally and structurally demarcated from one another while functionally interacting in networks whenever expedient.

Finally, quadrant D depicts society and its various associations as fragmented. Not only do people live nowadays as individuals in imagined

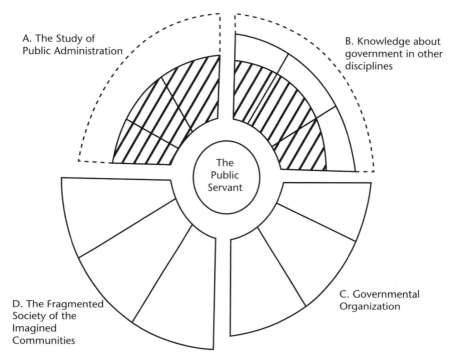

A. The Study of
Public Administration

B. Knowledge about
government in other
disciplines

The
Public
Servant

C. Governmental
Organization

D. The Fragmented
Society of the
Imagined
Communities

Figure 3.1 Conceptual Map 1, Compartmentalization of Knowledge about
Government

communities (Anderson, 2006), but they also identify with a variety of different groups and interests. Given that government policies are supposed to be
representative of citizen needs, this societal fragmentation cannot but present
a challenge with respect to gathering knowledge about what is needed in
society.

3.2 The Fragmented Study of Public Administration in the United States and in Europe

When looking at the table of contents of pre-Second World War handbooks, it
appears that American public administration was focused on organizational
structure and mechanisms, leadership (styles), personnel management, financial management, and several substantive policy areas. There was also attention for intergovernmental relations (both in legal as well as in functional
terms). To contemporary students of public administration, the early study
may come across as somewhat technocratic, as one that regards the

organization as a machine of which the parts can be calibrated so that its performance can be improved. From the 1950s on public administration expanded its attention to the influence of social, cultural, economic, political, technological, and intellectual change upon the structure and functioning of public organizations. As a consequence, the study branched out into a wide range of subject matters and approaches that included, among other things, representative bureaucracy and (more recently) diversity management, public sector ethics, information technology, e-government, gender studies, non-profit organizations, contracting-out and privatization, etc. Also, more than before, public administration scholars started to familiarize themselves with knowledge about government in the studies of law, philosophy and ethics, history, political theory, and theology, to name a few.

In view of this it is reasonable to argue that the range of topics in the study has been steadily expanding and that, consequentially, any hope for epistemological coherence from a formal object point of view was further and further away as time progressed. Within academe the knowledge of government is compartmentalized at two levels: within the study of public administration (this section) and across the social sciences (next section).

Discussing the proliferation of the study since the Second World War, Stillman argued that

> ... the field itself had become captive to its own specialization, subspecialization, and professionalization, fashioning a conceptual heterodoxy fed by diverse university disciplines. [And that] ... postwar American public administration was characterized by a loose heterodoxy of various multidisciplinary university studies. (1991: 126, 134)

For a long time, research was dominated by demands of rigorous empiricism aimed at developing a body of knowledge with law-like generalizations. Specialization was a natural course of action if the study was to outgrow the reflective, contemplative mode of inquiry, so characteristic of political theorizing about government since the Middle Ages, and rise beyond the optimistic pre-war prescriptions that lacked empirical support. This came at a price. Caught between the rock of the *scientific ideal* and the hard place of generating usable knowledge, professionals in academe and practice have lost the bird's eye perspective (see quotation Stillman at the opening of this chapter).

This lack of overall understanding prompted V. Ostrom to speak of *learned ignorance* (1997: 144–5). In the same spirit, referencing studies in economics and political science, E. Ostrom remarked that

> The poverty of our formulations stems, to some extent, from the separation of political economy into two disciplines that have evolved along separate paths. While substantial advantages exist from academic specialization, sweeping

prescriptions based on stylized notions of the institutional arrangements studied by other disciplines are negative fallouts of overspecialization. (1997: 5)

Compartmentalization in the context of public administration is not simply an epistemological concern but certainly also a practical challenge. There is much pressure upon academia to train professionals, so that their problem-solving skills can cater to, in the charging words of Bellah, a consumer mentality and to market orientation (Bellah, 1999). In a nostalgic mood, Bellah et al. recalled a time that students in higher education were required to get some general sense of the world and their place in it. In, what they called, the multiversity, American higher education has become a cafeteria where discrete bodies of information can be digested. Any effort to establish a cross-disciplinary curriculum that is beneficial for training future public servants, quickly turns into a battle between disciplines (Bellah et al., 1996: 279). The cafeteria model of education certainly applies to public administration curricula in the United States. Do public administration students get a general sense of government and its role and position in society, or do they only acquire knowledge and technical skills in a series of disconnected courses (budgeting and finance, policy analysis, intergovernmental relations, public management, and so forth)? Who helps them to connect these specializations and what literature is available to develop such comprehensive views upon government? American handbooks present the study as nothing but a string of specializations. Little has changed since Siffin in the late 1950s wrote that " . . . the study of public administration in the United States is characterized by the absence of any fully comprehensive intellectual framework . . . " (as quoted in Caldwell, 1965: 52).

Is the student in Europe better off? Generally, European public administration curricula are much more organized on, what can be called, a "formal dining room model" where the cook determines what will be served and in what order. That requires thought on the part of cook. However, specialization into various subfields has not been limited to the United States. European handbooks increasingly provide attention to various specializations but generally within a comprehensive overview of the study. The study of public administration, though, is fragmented but then by how it is embedded (e.g., in law as in France and Germany, in organizational studies as in Norway, and in political science or management studies in Britain). Also, there is no European equivalent to American public administration; the various national traditions of governance are reflected in the study. Perhaps a student of public administration should study both in the United States and in Europe.

Meanwhile, specialization can result in " . . . poor preparation for life, especially life in a democracy" (Kiser, 1999: 7). Democracy requires broad

79

knowledge and the " . . . barriers to communication thrown up by specialization enables particular democratic conceptualizations to monopolize public thinking, because people who hold alternative conceptualizations cannot communicate very well with one another" (ibid.: 7). And, as Kiser argued after V. Ostrom (and many before him), democracy requires nothing less than knowledge from all of the sciences and arts of human association (ibid.; V. Ostrom, 1997: 98).

3.3 Compartmentalization of Knowledge about Government Across Disciplines

As noted above, knowledge sources relevant to understanding government are also scattered across the social sciences, and there is both a substantive and an organizational aspect to this.

First, the substantive aspect of compartmentalization of knowledge is a consequence of the fact that government as social phenomenon has become a topic of interest in all of the social sciences. In addition to public administration and political science, major contributions to knowledge about government have been made in economics (e.g., decision-making theory, game theory, rational actor model), cognitive psychology (e.g., decision-making theory, groupthink), sociology (e.g., the function of authority, organizational behavior), and law (e.g., social contract theory, administrative law), as well as by authors who drew from multidisciplinary sources. The understanding of government is also aided by the humanities, such as history (administrative history), philosophy (political theory, epistemology), theology (the nature of authority, Gawthrop, 1998), literature and poetic images of government (Heyen, 1994), and architecture (Nisbet, 1975; Goodsell, 1997, 2001). In today's American multiversity or academic cafeteria – and increasingly in Europe – the discovery and subsequent integration of these various sources of knowledge is left to the student. In the introduction to his study of law as a social science Murphy writes, almost apologetically, that:

> The disciplinary boundaries which have played so important a role in constructing the frameworks through which we know this world are crumbling [. . .] Like many other writes at the present time, I acknowledge the importance of seeking to present difficult and sometimes academically over-elaborated issues in *a more simple format, in order to reach a wider audience*, and in order to try to overcome the constraints of specialization which seem to increase everywhere you look. (1997: ix–x; italics added)

When an experienced scholar such as Murphy recognizes the challenge of providing a cross-disciplinary perspective on law, what must it be like for a student, a practitioner, and a citizen? Simplification is required when an author desires to reach a wider audience, even if his or her study may in parts appear simplistic in the eyes of the specialist.

The contemporary desire for a more rounded education has origins going back to the time when government first started growing. In the view of Woodrow Wilson, candidates for competitive civil service exams should be prepared to display technical knowledge as well as knowledge of the liberal arts. He believed that the disease of specialization led to a fragmented world view. A class of narrow-minded public servants would be "... hateful and harmful to the United States" (Wilson, 1992: 14). A comparative and historical approach to the study of government would serve as counterweight to the danger of technocracy, and he substantiated that by a lengthy study of the history of government (Wilson, 1889–1918: xxxv; see also Wilson, 1970: 291–2). Wilson initially advocated a civil service curriculum with a comprehensive and humanist perspective on mankind that involved the study of language, of literature, and of history. Indeed, leadership education for government service and citizen education were considered important throughout the nineteenth century (Waldo, 1975: 34). Later in his career, though, and in the midst of the Progressive Reforms that increasingly focused on efficiency, Wilson appeared to place more emphasis on specialized education (Saunders, 1998: 26, 32; Raadschelders, 2002).

The challenges of substantive compartmentalization are compounded by organizational demarcation. The social sciences have differentiated into separate organizations. Organizational independence and subsequent growth in size (of faculty, of enrollments, of degrees offered, of publications) is considered a sign of maturity and at least an indication of legitimacy. In the early phase of their career, faculty members are told that research is more important than teaching, and it is not just any research, it is research within the discipline. It is risky to pursue interdisciplinary work as one could find oneself at the fringes of academia and out of the mainstream, with serious consequences. When tenure and promotion are considered, external reviewers may conclude that the candidate has not made a significant contribution to the study or field. Indeed, at the typical university there is very little discussion across disciplines (Kiser, 1999: 1). There is another side to this. Most of the social sciences are organized on the basis of topics or specializations, which is why most of them come across as a hodge-podge (Campbell, 1969: 331–2). Thus, psychology, for instance, is divided into biological psychology, clinical psychology, cognitive psychology, developmental psychology, industrial/organizational psychology, social psychology, personality psychology, and so forth. This "field fixation" on specializations determines how graduate programs are structured, how jobs are advertised, how journals are organized, and how grants are evaluated (Sternberg et al., 2001: 104). Public administration is also organized on the basis of its various specializations and this may well encourage further divisions.

Academic compartmentalization can lead to in-breeding. What is published within the confines of one study and by friends disavows what is produced by "outsiders." Only in theory does academia provide refuge to those who seek freedom of thought. In practice, the organizational fragmentation imposes constraints upon the free pursuit and exchange of knowledge. The Renaissance ideal of the *uomo universalis* can only be looked upon in nostalgia, because there is so much more knowledge than five centuries ago. Can even the knowledge in one discipline be satisfactorily mastered by a single scholar? In view of bounded rationality this seems impossible. It is thus that Campbell writes of the "myth of unidisciplinary competence." If anything, integration and comprehensiveness of knowledge are a collective product, not embodied in one individual scholar (Campbell, 1969: 330, 348). Substantive and organizational compartmentalization of knowledge is a fact of life, and it should stimulate the pursuit of broader understanding. To put this in more dramatic terms: the true scholar develops an open mind to a variety of understandings and approaches, instead of single-mindedly cultivating a specific specialization within a discipline. Likewise, the practitioner is best served by wide-ranging training that provides a context within which s/he can apply the administrative skills and knowledge acquired during the study for a public administration degree.

The compartmentalization of knowledge about government within the study of public administration and across the social sciences is problematic both for students as well as for (future) practitioners. Clearly, students of public administration should be shown how the various specializations inform one another, how knowledge within the study can be further elucidated by research in neighboring studies, and how issues directly relevant to understanding government can be informed by indirectly related knowledge and thus developing a broad understanding of the time and society in which they live. As far as practitioners are concerned, they not only need specific skills (in budgeting, personnel management, program evaluation, performance measurement, etc.) but also develop sensitivity to the organizational and political context in which they work. Possibly, graduates with an advanced degree in public administration have some knowledge about collaborative management and the interplay of politics and administration. Consider, though, that the majority of specialists in government do not have a public administration degree, but had their primary education in medicine, architecture, music, agriculture, engineering, languages, history, law, etc. When they decide to pursue a public administration degree it is to further their careers, but will the public administration curricular cafeteria in the United States or the European dining room model provide the necessary balance between training for skills and education for wisdom? In a society where an instrumental rationality thrives that systematizes, objectifies, and technicalizes social issues and problems, the quality of research and policy proposals is judged by how it is generated and validated (Yankelovich, 1991: 185–7). That type of knowledge is commanded by experts and not easily accessible, if at all, to the public at large. A combination of specific training for skills and knowledge and broad-based education will help specialists to translate what they do in terms that are understandable to the uninitiated. The general public will not be able to participate in public policymaking when its leadership (i.e., politicians, civil servants, scientists, journalists, etc.) does not provide simplified versions of what they believe ought to be done and why. But the public at large is possibly less interested in the factual and informational side as it is and ought to be in the normative, valuing, side of decision- and policymaking. Again, this requires that training and education for practitioners goes beyond technical skills and requires knowledge about the society for which decisions and policies are designed.

The information and knowledge gap between experts or specialists and the citizenry at large was mentioned briefly in Chapter 2, and this gap is real judged by the continued clamoring for more citizen participation and deliberative democracy. But the question is not only whether or not citizens are willing and able to participate, but whether or not experts actively tap into each other's knowledge and into the lay knowledge of the citizenry (Fischer, 2000: 29–46; see also Lindblom, 1990). As far as including lay knowledge or common sense is concerned, policymakers may not go too much beyond the obligatory survey and/or public hearing. To be sure, this is not necessarily their fault or flaw. It could simply be a function of time and budgetary constraints and of the extent to which exchange of knowledge is inhibited by the degree of organizational differentiation.

3.4 Knowledge Sources Across Organizational Units and Policy Subsystems

Knowledge about government is not only generated in academia but also, and probably even more so, in public organizations. Imagine how much knowledge relevant to understanding the structure and functioning of government is acquired by civil servants in the course of a career. They exchange information with one another, but they also withhold information from one another. This is dependent upon what is considered in the best interest of the principal. Who is the principal, though? Is it the organization or employer, the executive, the Constitution, the people, the law, God, the family, self, etc. (Waldo, 1980)? Information in government organizations is sometimes accessible to the public at large, sometimes not. Again, this is dependent upon what is considered sensitive information and what is not. Civil servants work in an organizational environment that is extremely complex and it is that complexity that limits the accessibility of organizations as knowledge sources. Organizational charts best show how complex government really is, and the United States is used by way of example.

There are more than 87,000 units of government in the United States. The federal government is one. There are fifty state governments, more than 4,700 county governments, about 35,000 general purpose local governments (municipality, city, township), and almost 40,000 specific purpose local governments (school boards, and special purpose districts). When looking at the level of federal government, and not considering the political component, there are fifteen departments and almost sixty independent agencies and corporations (see Figure 3.2).

Each of these departments, agencies, and corporations consists of multiple subunits. Look, for instance, at the organizational structure of the Department of Health and Human Services (DHHS) (See Figure 3.3). Not counting the support system for the Secretary and Deputy Secretary, there are twenty-six major subunits. Each of these subunits is further subdivided into smaller units, such as the Administration for Children and Families (ACF) within DHHS (see Figure 3.4). The Assistant Secretary for ACF directly heads thirteen subunits.

Looking at the organizational structure of the Administration on Children, Youth, and Families (ACYF) in more detail (Figure 3.5), we see three major units: the Office of Management Services, the Family and Youth Services Bureau, and the Children's Bureau. The latter is further subdivided into six units. The charts in Figures 3.4 and 3.5 do not show whether other offices are subdivided as well. They could be, they may not be.

Important to note in the ACF structure is the Office of Regional Operations (a federal unit) which supervises the activities of ten regional offices. These regional offices are deconcentrated governments, that is, a regional/local presence of federal government. There are many other examples of federal organizations that operate by means of deconcentrated units (e.g., the Internal Revenue Service, the Federal Emergency Administration, the Federal Bureau of Investigations, etc.). Each of the regional offices has the same organizational structure (Figure 3.6).

The Regional Administrator for Region VI (comprising Arkansas, Louisiana, New Mexico, Oklahoma, Texas) supervises two main offices: that of State and Tribal Programs, and that of Community Programs. Their Website also shows that the Regional Administrator is further supported by a Deputy regional administrator, an Associate Regional Administrator for Administration and Technology, and a Grants officer. This is not all, because Region VI serves a

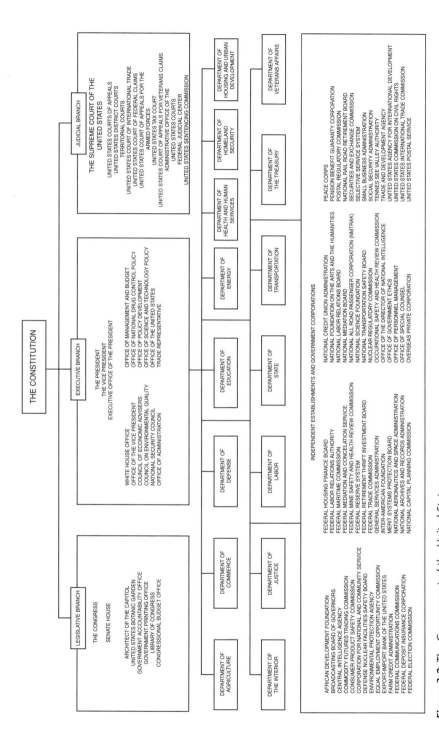

Figure 3.2 The Government of the United States

Source: http://bensguide.gpo.gov/files/gov_chart.pdf (accessed December 14, 2010).

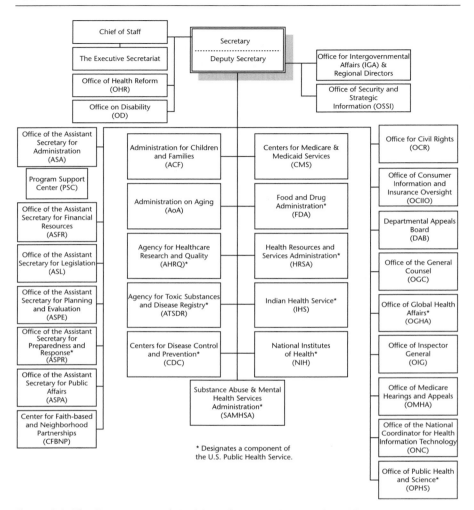

Figure 3.3 The Department of Health and Human Services (DHHS)
Source: http://www.hhs.gov/about/orgchart (accessed December 14, 2010).

total of 68 federally recognized tribes, 176 Head Start Grantees serving 114,647 children, 67 Early Head Start Grantees serving 6,033 pregnant women, infants and toddlers, and 30 Runaway and Homeless Grants. Each of these tribes, (early) head start offices, and grant offices are organizations in themselves.

Moving from the federal to the state level each of the fifty state governments is divided into various departments and offices (Figure 3.7). By way of example, the State of Louisiana has twelve departments answerable directly to the

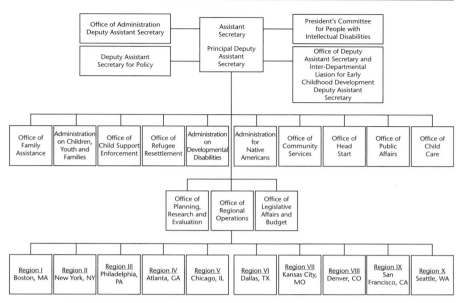

Figure 3.4 Operational Structure of the Administration for Children and Families (ACF), DHHS

Source: http://www.acf.hhs.gov/orgs/opschart (accessed December 14, 2010).

Governor and another nine departments under the authority of elected officials such as the Lieutenant Governor, the Secretary of State and the Treasurer.

Louisiana's Department of Social Services (Figure 3.8) has eight major divisions for statewide policy areas that are subdivided into more than fifty bureaus and programs headed by a Deputy Secretary of Programs (Figure 3.9). One of these, the Child Welfare Section, is subdivided into three large units. Two of these, "Child Protection and Prevention" and "Out of Home Care" are further subdivided into four respectively five units. Several divisions have regional offices across the state, twenty-nine in total, each of which is further subdivided. There are also more than sixty parish offices.

Clearly, government organization is very complex. The proliferation of government organizational units has accelerated in the past 100–150 years. For instance, in 1862 there were seven departments with a total of seventy-five organizational units in the Netherlands; 130 years later this had increased to 2,744 units across thirteen departments (Raadschelders, 1997). One can expect that in the United States these numbers must be much, much larger. One can also expect that cooperation or collaboration between units must have become increasingly difficult. This will certainly be the case between units that share responsibility for particular policies but serve a different jurisdiction and/or have different authority. Collaboration, though, is not

87

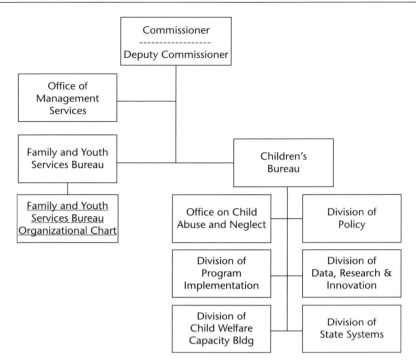

Figure 3.5 Administration on Children, Youth, and Families, ACF, DHHS
Source: http://www.acf.hhs.gov/orgs/charts/acyf.htm (accessed December 14, 2010).

even guaranteed among comparable units. In fact, sharing knowledge and experience between comparable organizations can be counterproductive when the competitor improves its performance and decreases the ranking of one's own unit or organization. Several mid-career professionals told me that the introduction of performance measures and subsequent rankings of productivity had the perverse result that regional units of the same state agency no longer shared best practices with one another for fear of losing their ranking.

Figures 3.1–3.9 only illustrate the extent to which organizations are divided in multiple units, but they do not provide a sense how units in organizations are interconnected with units in other organizations at the same level of government and across levels of government. If ever there was a time that organizations at one level of government could operate somewhat autonomously from one another and from organizations at other levels of government, this is no longer possible. Consider the policy fields map in Figure 3.10 that shows the direct and indirect relationships that the Office of Economic Opportunity (Department of Human Services, State of Minnesota) has with

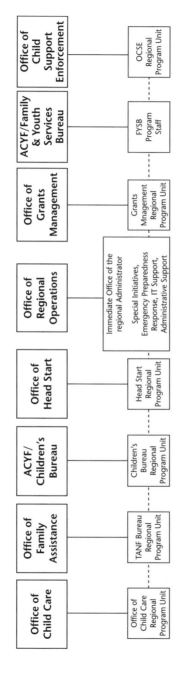

Figure 3.6 Organizational Structure of Region VI, Dallas, of ACF, DHHS

Source: http://www.acf.hhs.gov/orgs/charts/oro.htm (accessed December 14, 2010).

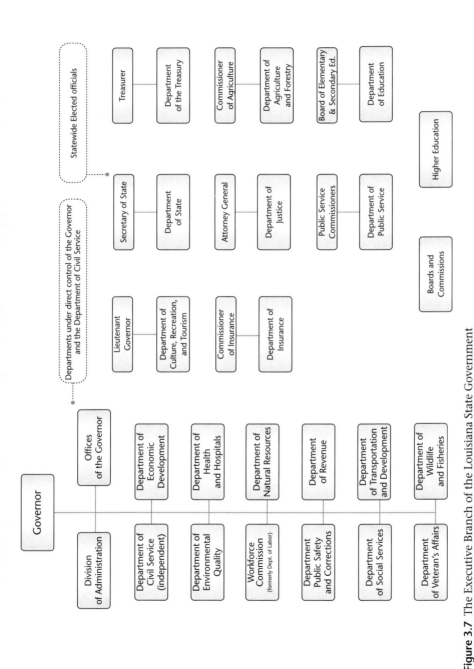

Figure 3.7 The Executive Branch of the Louisiana State Government

Source: http://louisiana.gov/Government/Organization_Chart/Louisiana_State_Orgchart_082008.pdf (accessed December 14, 2010).
(N.B.: the official website listed above speaks of the Department of Children and Family Services, but when clicking on "printable version of this chart," that unit appears as the Department of Social Services).

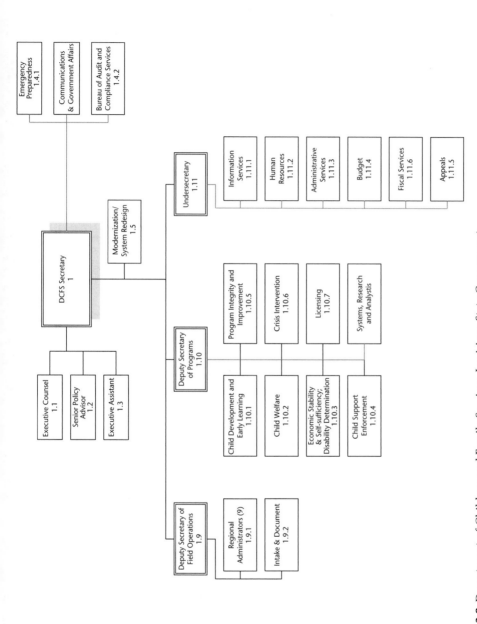

Figure 3.8 Department of Children and Family Services, Louisiana State Government

Source: http://www.dcfs.louisiana.gov/assets/docs/searchable/docs/ManagementFinance/OrgCharts/092310_Secretary.pdf Secretary.pdf (accessed December 14, 2010).

(N.B.: see Figure 3.7).

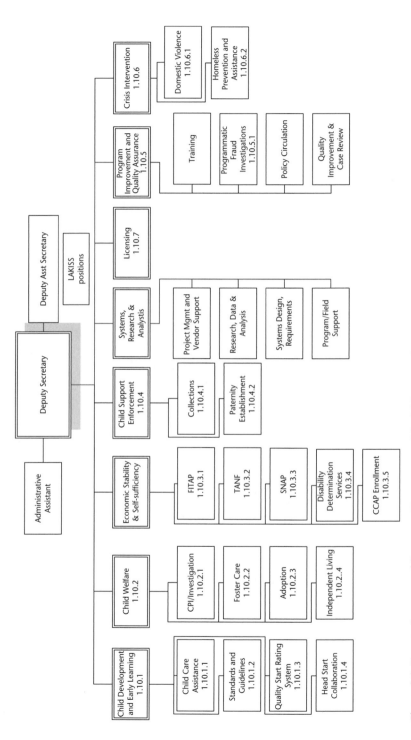

Figure 3.9 Deputy Secretary of Programs, Department of Social Services, Louisiana

Source: Adapted from http://www.dcfs.louisiana.gov/assets/docs/searchable/ManagementFinance/OrgCharts/082010_ProgramsDepSecretary.pdf (accessed December 14, 2010).

(N.B.: see Figure 3.7).

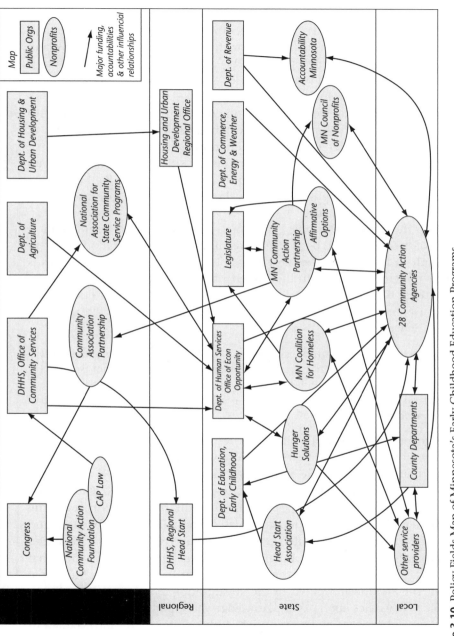

Figure 3.10 Policy Fields Map of Minnesota's Early Childhood Education Programs

Source: Sandford (2010: 640).

various local, state, regional, and federal organizations as well as with non-profit organizations in the area of early childhood education.

Naturally, the intensity of interaction varies. Some organizations and units are in frequent contact with one another, others less frequently. Wamsley and Zald made an effort to visualize this for the 1967 Selective Service System (better known as "the draft") (Figure 3.11). They organized their chart as a solar system: the closer an organization or actor was to the center the more important and/or powerful it/he was.

Wamsley and Zald divided the environment of a specific organization into "allies" and "hostiles." Situated along the dotted vertical line are those who, at the time, were considered neutral or unknown in their opposition to or support of the Selective Service. Goodsell also positions agencies as the hub in a variety of networks (Figure 3.12), and – as Wamsley and Zald implicitly do – emphasizes that the public agency is "first among equals" because of their legal authority and mandate.

What is the point of this brief excursion into organizational fragmentation in light of the topic of this book? First, organizational fragmentation may very well result in loss of overview and a loss of organizational memory. This is perhaps more of a problem in the United States than in Europe, since in the former there is much less a tradition of conserving government documents. Indeed, De Tocqueville expressed his surprise that Americans did not keep records. He wrote:

> Newspapers are the only historical records in the United States. If one number is missing, it is as if the link of time was broken: present and past cannot be joined again. I have no doubt that in fifty years' time it will be harder to collect authentic documents about the details of social life in modern America than about French medieval administration. (1969: 207)

Surely governmental organizations in the United States keep records, and probably more so than 160 years ago. However, this author knows of at least one city manager who, at the end of the year, shreds about 95% of all documents and correspondence between his city and the public. Also, while doing research in another city, it appeared that the bulk of documents regarding developments in that jurisdiction consisted of council minutes, budgets, and reports. By way of contrast, Dutch law requires that *every* document, no matter how insignificant, is kept for a period of five years in the organization that generated or received it. After that period it is to be sent to the Municipal Archive, the Provincial Archive, or the Royal National Archive in The Hague.

Public policy relies upon expert knowledge and input. Consequentially, the highest ranked decision-makers cannot but rely on the quality and accuracy of the information and data provided by policy bureaucrats and upon an impartial analysis of these. A variety of scholars and government officials expressed

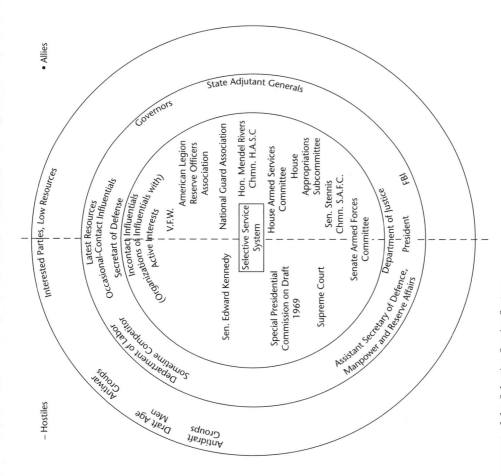

Figure 3.11 The Environment of the Selective Service System

Source: Wamsley and Zald (1973: 29) (reprinted with permission from Professors Wamsley and Zald).

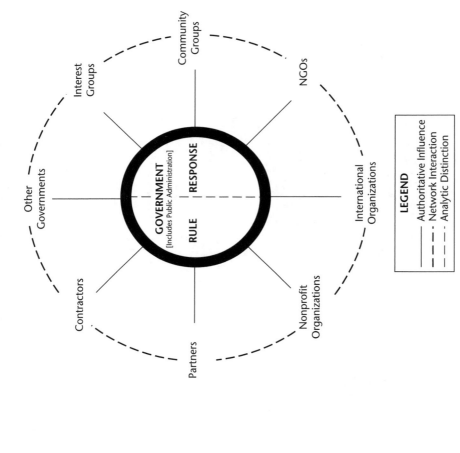

Figure 3.12 The Public Agency as Hub in an Interactive Network

Source: Goodsell (2006: 629) (reprinted with permission from Wiley-Blackwell Publishers).

grave concern with the situation that decision-makers judge and choose upon less than perfect understanding (Chapter 2, Section 2.1). Horizontal and vertical relations between organizations have already been mentioned; indeed, the networks or relationships between one agency and organization at the same level and at other levels of government are very complex. Added to that is that these networks are subject to constant shifts and changes, and not just under the influence of other public organizations. Often networks and relations are maintained upon a formal basis but, as important as they are, one should not overlook how essential informal social networking is for learning, adaptation, and productivity (Barnard, 1968: 223–4). Informal social networking is likely to have increased exponentially with the use of Internet, iPhone, iPad, Facebook, and Twitter.

3.5 Dispersed Societal Interest and Knowledge Sources

In an elegantly brief and intellectually very attractive study, Benedict Anderson (2006) analyzed the fragmentation of modern society into imagined communities. For most of history people lived and worked in one community; in modern society they live in multiple communities and are members of multiple associations that do not necessarily interact. It has been said that what differentiates groups of physical objects such as a mountain range or a forest from people is that the latter may be scattered in space yet simultaneously shared by different groups (MacDonald and Pettit, 1981: 108). In her analysis of the developments of and in the American family in the past two centuries, Coontz argued that "Notions of self-reliance that originally referred to the collective achievements of a community or a class may be reduced to the conceit of the self-made man. The progress of individualism, it turns out, shades easily into fragmentation" (1992: 52). This was possible because the combined forces of urbanization and industrialization had broken the traditional, agricultural communities and prompted people to withdraw in the nuclear family, the "haven in a heartless world" as Lasch aptly called it (1977). The family was the last refuge of love and human decency in a world increasingly dominated by ruthless capitalist competition. This is the context in which government penetrated society beyond the traditional activities of maintenance of public order and safety (Chapter 1, Section 1.3).

Fragmentation of society is not just fed by the triumph of individualism but is embedded in fundamental changes in worldview. In her study on the relation between past and future Hannah Arendt contrasts, the Antiquities' notion of eternal verities, based in particular conceptions of nature and of history, against the modern view of progress which has lost that sense of eternal verities. That being so she argued that humans have lost their relationship to a common world and instead have created a world in which they "live in desperate lonely separation" (as quoted in Luton, 1999: 207).

Fragmentation of society is not only visible in the notion of an imagined community where unity is suggested by means of shared yet rather abstract symbols (e.g., the flag, the National Anthem, the Constitution), in the nature of family life (where extended families are often dispersed in the Western world), and in worldview. It is as much evidenced by the degree to which social or citizen association has proliferated. In a series of publications, Skocpol demonstrated how the chapter-based membership groups of a hundred years ago, geographically dispersed and linked to local community without loss of central direction, has given way to the Washington-based advocacy groups of today. The initial civic associations of members organized in chapters were value-based associations that addressed a variety of different social issues. The advocacy groups in contemporary society are objective-based and address a single social issue (Skocpol et al., 2000: 542; Skocpol, 2003). From this it is a small leap to conclude that civic associations, just as public organizations, build their legitimacy on the basis of specialized knowledge. Contemporary lobbyists do not get their concerns on the political agenda if they are not presented in a focused, compartmentalized fashion.

How many civic and/or nonprofit associations are there? Skocpol mentioned that advocacy groups emerged from the 1960s on. Since then their numbers increased dramatically. The *Statistical Abstracts of the United States 2009* mention that there were about 14.7 million national nonprofit associations in 1980 (table 1245). Their numbers had increased to more than 25 million in 2007. By way of example we could look at three large types of associations. Table 1245 shows that in the United States the number of athletic associations increased from 509,000 to 960,000 between 1980 and 2007. During the same period the number of religious associations increased from 797,000 to a little over 1.2 million. Another example of the growth of associations is the so-called common-interest housing developments (CID's) that are better known as Homeowners Associations (HOA). HOAs are an example of self-governing, self-organizing capacity of citizens. From less than 500 in the United States in 1964, there are now (2005) about 274,000 HOAs (McKenzie, 2005: 29). Less impressive perhaps is the growth of the number of international organizations, increasing from 500 to 5,000 inter- and non-governmental organizations between 1945 and 1995. By 2003 there were nearly 25,000 international organizations, a growth attributed to the increased use of new technologies such as the Internet (*Encarta Online Encyclopedia* 2009).

Society is as much an organized complexity as government is. The few data provided above clearly indicate that the contemporary organizational environment is rapidly becoming more complex. This complexity is not just a function of organizational proliferation but also one of an increasing number and intensity of network interactions. Some scholars have suggested that these interactions may create greater complexity than the organizational structure themselves, and that the traditional top-down, hierarchical style of management will no longer suffice in this interconnected environment (Kapucu, 2003). Hence, traditional analyses are considered to be limited in their usefulness, prompting some scholars to consider the application of new sciences of administration (e.g., Comfort, 1994; Overman, 1996; Morçöl and Dennard, 2000).

3.6 Intellectual, Psychological, and Organizational Problems of Fragmented Knowledge

Government employs specialists and generalists. Academic curricula in public administration are focused on preparing people to be specialists in the application of various techniques in specific areas (budgeting, personnel management, program evaluation, performance measurement, etc.). Academic research is highly specialized in terms of subject area as well as in terms of epistemological and methodological approaches. Specialization is the hallmark of academic institutions, since ideally the search for knowledge is ever more in-depth. Specialization guarantees promotion to higher academic ranks. In government, though, promotion ideally signifies that one is able to shed the specialist's perspective and adopt a more generalist outlook. Entry-level positions usually require some degree of specialization, but one will not get close to the top, and certainly not at the top, if an overall understanding of the managerial, service, and process needs of the organization and its subdivisions is missing. In other words, in academia specialists are perceived as superior, while in government generalists are hierarchically superior to specialists. But, that is perhaps not quite correct, for it has been reported that 53% of the top career executives in American federal government are specialists (Maranto, 2005: 9).

Specialization disperses our knowledge about, and thus understanding of, government. Handbooks of public administration in the United States generally present the study as a range of specializations. Specialization is identified with learning and with in-depth knowledge; the interdisciplinarity that characterizes the generalist is regarded as pseudo-learning and superficial (Mainzer, 1994: 383). The generalist is regarded as a dilettante (Dogan, 1996: 99). Just as historians debate the merits of specialization versus those who pursue comparative studies,[1] scholars of public administration debate specialist and generalist perspectives upon and approaches to knowledge.

With respect to academic specialization there are at least two challenges to overcome. First, there is the challenge of specialized language. Those trained in the formal, positivist approach express their research findings in statistical analysis and/or mathematical formulae. It is a scientific language not easily accessible to those who have not been beneficiaries of education in such an approach. Simon argued that scholars should not dismiss the merits of logical positivism before they acquired " ... sufficient technical skill ... " in its methodology and language. They should meet positivists on their own grounds instead of criticizing them blindly (Simon, 1991). One cannot but agree, but positivists should also take the trouble of acquainting themselves with the merits of other approaches. Are they interested in learning the "language" of, for example, the postmodernist? Patience all around is necessary. The positivist claim that statistical analysis and mathematical modeling result in superior knowledge is as presumptuous as the claim of some postmodernists that everything is relative.

Second, our bounded rationality or limited cognitive abilities make it psychologically attractive to specialize in one language. However, should bounded rationality – which not only assumes that one cannot know everything but implicitly presupposes that one cannot make the claim that some knowledge is superior to other types of knowledge – not invite a childlike curiosity in the perspectives of others? Emphasizing a distinction between science in the narrower and in the broader sense, obscures the fact that both types, in the end, involve extensive interpretation (Goodin and Klingemann, 1996: 12; Kritzer, 1996: 13–15).

Next to these intellectual (i.e., different "languages") and psychological (i.e., familiarity with a specialization) challenges there is the problem of organizational demarcation. In some universities, public administration is an independent school or department, while in others a public administration curriculum is embedded in political science, law, organization studies, or management studies (see Chapter 1). Also, there are schools of public policy, public management, and "traditional" public administration. However public administration is embedded in academe, there does not seem to be much exchange between public administration scholars and, for instance, political scientists nor between specialists within the study. What Cox observed, paraphrasing Almond, with respect to political science is as applicable to public administration: "The end result is a discipline informed not by the vigorous debate

---

[1] Specialists in the study of one country's history are dismissive of comparative approaches that they claim are superficial and comparative historians are dismissive of single case studies holding that those are myopic (Diamond, 2005: 19).

among different perspectives in a pluralistic enterprise, but by [...] sharp sectarian rivalries and obscure cottage industries of research" (1993: 69).

Another major challenge is to develop a generalist's understanding of government and that requires communication between scholars of different persuasion as well as between practitioners and scholars. This does not mean that specialization is abandoned. Specialization is vital to the growth of knowledge and to the quality of decision-making. But, the development of general, comprehensive perspectives on government should neither be sacrificed for the alluring rigor of scientific specialization in academe nor for the seductive appreciation of generalists in the practice of government (Presthus, 1964: 211). Hierarchies of knowledge and of occupational rank prohibit an open mind to the potential merits of other approaches and perspectives. More modest claims about the merits of one's own approach or perspective will facilitate communication.

By way of a side note, advocating the development of a more generalist perspective is especially important for academic education. The question "Why aren't there more scholars [...] who teach students to be generalists, to see the great connections" (Bennis and O'Toole, 2005: 101) may have been raised in connection to business schools but is as relevant to the study of public administration. Is a generalist's perspective important for practitioners? The answer to that question suffers from a lack of knowledge. We know that a slight majority of top civil servants in the United States have a specialist background. What we do not know is whether top career executives have been promoted because of their specialization or because of their increasingly generalist capabilities. It is hard to imagine anyone rising to the top without developing generalist's skills. Such generalist skills would include extensive knowledge of the system of government and of relevant and related policy areas (Cutting and Kouzmin, 2005), knowledge of and experience in various line and staff units of the organization where one is employed, as well as political sensitivity, deep understanding of the nature of interaction between government and society, and the capacity to gauge social trends, atmospheres, and moods.

3.7 Intellectual, Pedagogical, and Practical Reasons for Connecting Knowledge Sources

The study of public administration emerged in the background of the growth of government in the past 100–150 years. The study has expanded beyond its initial interest in organization theory and management. Testimony to the degree of specialization in the American study alone is that there are at least twenty-four sections in the *American Society for Public Administration* and several of these have a journal. The growing public sector has also given rise to increasing numbers of nationally organized professional organizations, many of which also have journals or magazines.

The intellectual reason for connecting knowledge about government in the United States is that comprehensive perspectives upon government are missing. This is especially problematic since, unlike in Europe, there is no tradition of developing conceptual frameworks that enable the practitioner or scholar to connect dispersed knowledge. From a pedagogical point of view it is important to show that knowledge in one specialization is relevant to knowledge in another. It helps students to see how connections can be made. For the practitioner, such overview helps in acquiring the generalist perspective to complement specialist knowledge.

It was mentioned earlier that the content of the study of public administration is not the exclusive playground of academics. Who is to define what the study ought to be about? Is the interest and perspective guiding the civil servants' answer to that question more relevant than that of the political officeholder, or citizen, or scholar? Should the scholar-scientist determine the nature of scientific knowledge? Does the practitioner/civil servant define what "practical experience" ought to be about? Ought the "statesman" and the citizen be interested in defining the study? These questions indicate that coherence will be difficult to achieve in view of the various actors involved. It will also be difficult because of the various substantive areas in the study. An effort at mapping that substantive content of the study is provided in the next chapter.

4

Substantive Topics and Comprehensive Conceptual Maps of Public Administration

> ...public administrationists found disciplines and foci outside political science increasingly relevant to their interests and needs: social psychology, sociology, economics, business administration, and various other sources of data, concepts and techniques. (Waldo, 1984)

The intrinsic function of government is the governance of society and the study of public administration is its umbrella discipline. Government exists because it has the resources to translate citizens' needs into collective action. Whatever area or era, sedentary people had some kind of government. A government will continue to exist for an undetermined period of time as long as it is able to meet the most basic expectations of its population. However, people in Ancient Egypt held different expectations of their government than did citizens in twentieth century democracies. Since the role and position of government in society varies with culture and period, a universal and finite list of topics for the study of public administration can never be developed. When trying to do so, at least four important issues should be considered.

First, what government should be changes over time and so the substance of public administration's object of study changes. The study and the practice will, time and again, have to reexamine their normative foundations and their societal objectives.

Second, what government is varies from country to country. American government is clearly different from that of other countries. The study of public administration first and foremost serves a particular society and its government. Developments in Argentinian, Indian, or Kenyan public administration scholarship and government are not necessarily relevant to the Icelandic or the Philippines government and scholarship. To be sure, the study of public administration all over the world includes attention for bureaucracy and organization, for civil service and personnel systems, for policymaking, for decision-making, for implementation, for budgeting, for intergovernmental relations, etc., but how these actually manifest themselves varies with culture.

Third, what constitutes the study of public administration varies with disciplinary background (Rohrbaugh and Andersen, 1997: 186). Someone trained in political science but working as a public administration scholar may well define the topical content of the study differently than a colleague trained as a cognitive psychologist.

Fourth, what government ought to be also depends upon the position and the perception citizens at large, business elites, political and administrative elites, clerics, and so forth, and its legitimacy rests with the swiftness and adequacy of its response to changing environmental conditions.

What connects these four issues is one basic question: What does *public* and what does *administration* actually mean in the concept of *public administration?* Any attempt to map substantive topics of the study should start with an answer to that question. The concern here is not so much with *the* public, but with what the public domain *is* in terms of collective or general interest. The study of public administration cannot by defined only by its *publicness* or its *administrativeness*. Other concepts have been suggested as well. One is that of self-government, the idea that people are able to associate for and organize collective action on a voluntary basis. Some argue that this is only realistic for small groups (e.g., Olson, 1965; Hardin, 1968) while others argue that self-government is certainly possible in larger groups (V. Ostrom, 1974; E. Ostrom, 1990; cf. G.D.H. Cole, see Dyson, 1980: 194). Indeed, in the eyes of V. Ostrom, public administration should be a science of association. But, a science of association includes all associations (non-governmental organizations (NGOs), homeowners associations, church organizations, labor unions, etc.) and not just public organizations. Hence, public administration as association does not clearly define the study. Other organizing concepts such as power, authority, management, decision-making, communication, and coordination suffer equally from the failure to identify the core of the study of public administration. It might be more fruitful to take the material object, government, of the study as a starting point for mapping its substantive content.

In this chapter the mapping of the study of public administration is continued by looking at changes over time in the attention for specific topics of interest. This will be done through an analysis of the substantive content of *Public Administration Review* (PAR) at eight points in time. We will see that developments in American public administration are quite comparable to developments elsewhere (Section 4.1). Next, attention is paid to some of the ways that scholars initially sought to capture the substantive content of the study as a whole (Sections 4.2 and 4.3). In light of the opening remarks in this chapter as that the study of public administration focuses on government, we should explore whether the study captures government as a whole. With that in mind a meta-framework for the study of government is discussed (Section 4.4). We will see that this has become quite a challenge given that the postwar study had found, as Dwight Waldo indicated, new foci and disciplines that included, but were not limited to, social psychology, economics, sociology, and business administration (see quote at the beginning of this chapter). The discussion in this chapter is neither exhaustive nor definitive. What it provides are some examples of how the content of the study has been defined and/or mapped.

4.1 Topics of Interest over Time: Public Administration as Dynamic Study

Modern public administration emerged in the context of a rapidly growing local government. It was at the local level that the consequences of industrialization, urbanization, and accelerating population growth were felt first. On both sides of the Atlantic, local administrators responded by developing hands-on training programs that focused on specific skills. By contrast, early university-based programs, such as at Johns Hopkins, offered a generalist's education grounded in the idea that the new civil servant needed to be sensitive to trends in society at large (Hoffman, 2002). The post-Civil War reform movement was much more concerned with challenges of morality and righteousness than with efficiency of government (Walker, 1990: 88). Indeed, and following the British model, in the late nineteenth century, Americans regarded higher education as the place where capable and cultivated human beings were nurtured who would regard society and civilization from a comprehensive perspective. As a junior faculty person, Woodrow Wilson supported a liberal arts curriculum that included attention for languages, history, and literature. In later years, as president of Princeton, Wilson emphasized a more scientific, secular, and specialized curriculum (Saunders, 1998: 26, 32).

Wilson's life spans the early reform period that focused on expanding and improving democracy (Karl, 1983: 17) and the late reform period that was much more concerned with the efficiency of government functioning through organizational change and strengthening the federal executive (Arnold, 1995: 409). In the early twentieth century, the American study of public administration was increasingly influenced by ideas and theories in business administration, such as those of Taylor on streamlining production and on defining managerial principles. In general, American public administration in the 1910–40 period was focused on efficiency (more or less equivalent to "performance"; Kelman, 2007), management of and leadership styles

105

in organizations. Less attention was paid to the interaction between organizations and environments.

The traditional and introductory American government course was mostly focused on federal government, and possibly followed by a course in state and local government. The study of public administration was a field of business and as such concerned with scientific management. White (1926) and Willoughby (1927) wrote the first handbooks that focused on the administration of the public sector. White's table of contents displays his focus on the organization and personnel management of bureaucracy, emphasizing that management was more central to government, and thus its study, than law (see also Lynn, 2001: 149). In the third and fifth editions of his 1935 handbook, Pfiffner (1946; with Presthus, 1967) continued to focus on government organization and its staff functions (planning and research, personnel, finance, law, and public relations). In another lesser known prewar textbook, Walker (1937) espoused a functional approach where the various levels of government were presented as if being elements of a living organism. The bulk of the chapters in his book were organized in two main groups. Staff activities included personnel, budgeting, accounting and auditing, purchasing, reporting, and collecting and disbursing revenue. Public services (the line activities) included the protection of life and property, judiciary, health, welfare, education, natural resource conservation, commerce and industry, business and public works.

After the Second World War the study of public administration emerged in other countries as well (European handbooks date from after the Second World War) and proliferated in terms of subject matter, branching out in areas it had not explored before. By way of illustration we can look at the topical development in a number of volumes of *Public Administration Review* to see how the study branched out and how its emphases changed over time (Table 4.1).

For the first five categories articles were published in each of the eight years selected. Striking is the growth of articles on management. Equally striking is the limited number of articles on law. Emerging topics in the past ten years are networks (see also Wachhaus, 2009: 66–7), ethics, accountability, information technology, and e-government (see also Raadschelders and Lee, 2011). The category "other" includes biographical and historical articles, and articles on the nature of the study, on methodology, and on administrative theory. For the years reported these numbers are low, but somewhat increasing.

The value of this table is very limited, since whatever is labeled a "trend" could be a function of the selection of years. Ideally, all PAR issues should have been included to get a sense of the trends. However, making such a table presents huge difficulties (as, indeed, was the experience with making the table below). First, analyzing 289 articles published in PAR during the

Table 4.1 Topics in *Public Administration Review* (PAR) in Eight of its Volumes

	1941	1948	1958	1968	1978	1988	1998	2008
1	7	10	13	8	9	6	6	13
2	11	3	1	16	4	8	5	9
3	3	5	5	6	13	11	3	8
4	2	2	1	2	12	8	6	2
5	2	3	1	1	13	3	6	25
6	–	–	–	1	–	–	4	8
7	–	–	–	1	–	–	2	3
8	1	–	–	4	3	–	3	–
9	–	–	–	4	1	1	1	6
10	2	3	13	4	7	10	9	16
Total	28	26	34	47	62	47	45	90

Legend: 1 = organization theory (including federal, state, local organization); 2 = policy (including federal, state, and local); 3 = personnel; 4 = budgeting and finance; 5 = management; 6 = networks; 7 = ethics; 8 = law; 9 = information technology and e-government; 10 = other.

Note: In 1967, PAR went from four to five issues; in 1968 to six issues. In 2001, PAR went from 90 to 128 pages per issue; in 2006 to 160 pages. The higher number of articles in 1978 is because of two symposia in the fifth issue.

1975–84 period (excluding symposium pieces, review essays, and professional stream essays) Perry and Kraemer did not mention the problem of determining to which category they felt an article belonged (1986: 217) (N.B.: Stallings and Ferrings, 1988, expanded the Perry and Kraemer analyses with a random sample of 176 out of 900 articles published in the 1940–75 period). To illustrate this problem, and using the thirteen categories of Perry and Kraemer, consider whether Lindblom's 1959 article on incrementalism ought to be listed as a policy article or as an administrative theory article? Then, articles on federal, state, and local government can easily be categorized under categories such as, for instance, "public management" or "public policy." Second, Perry and Kraemer picked categories without discussing the logic of their selection (N.B.: Stallings and Ferris only included five categories: policy, management, and local, state, and federal). Why are there no categories for "organization (theory)" and for "decision-making?" To be meaningful, categories have to be broadly defined. But this leads to a third problem, namely that the categories are not sufficiently refined to allow for a nuanced understanding of trends in the study. For instance, studies in ethics could be grouped under "personnel" or "accountability"; studies in public sector motivation were initially part of the organization theory literature (just think of Chester Barnard) but have, since the 1990s, become much more part of the personnel management literature. A fourth problem is that the selection of categories is likely a reflection of particular interests at the time that data were collected.

There is, perhaps, another way that we can get a handle on the proliferation of topics in the study of public administration. Until 1940 there was no American journal specific to public administration. As shown in Table 4.2, Europeans were the first to establish independent public administration

Table 4.2 Year of Origin of Some Public Administration Journals (* = journals related to specific ASPA sections)

1912	*Revue Française d'Administration Publique* (France)
1920	*Die Öffentliche Verwaltung* (Germany)
1920	*Verwaltung: Zeitschrift für Verwaltungswissenschaft* (Germany)
1922	*Public Administration* (UK)
1934	*International Review of Administrative Sciences*
1940	*Public Administration Review*
1941	*Australian Journal of Public Administration* (Australia)
1947	*Bestuurswetenschappen* (Netherlands)
1956	*Administrative Science Quarterly*
1956	*Philippine Journal of Public Administration* (Philippines)
1957	*Canadian Public Administration* (Canada)
1966	*Revista de Administração Pública* (Brazil)
1968	*State and Local Government Review**
1968	*Administration & Society*
1970	*American Review of Public Administration**
1970	*Policy Sciences*
1972	*Policy Studies Journal*
1976	*Public Productivity and Management Review* (since 2000 *Public Performance and Management Review*)*
1976	*Public Administration Quarterly*
1978	*Administrative Theory & Praxis*
1980	*Review of Public Personnel Administration**
1981	*Public Budgeting and Finance**
1981	*Journal of Public Policy*
1981	*Journal of Policy Analysis and Management*
1986	*Beleidswetenechappen* (Netherlands)
1986	*The Korean Journal of Policy Studies* (South Korea)
1988	*Journal of Public Budgeting, Accounting & Financial Management*
1988	*Governance: International Journal of Policy and Administration*
1988	*Azienda Pubblica. Teoria e problemi di management* (Italy)
1991	*Journal of Public Administration Research and Theory*
1993	*Public Voices**
1994	*Journal of Public Administration Education**
1994	*Journal of Public Management and Social Policies**
1997	*International Public Management Journal**
1998	*Public Integrity**
1998	*Revista Iberoamericana de Administratión Pública* (Spain)
2001	*Azienda Pubblica. La Rivista curate dall IPAS* (Italy)
2002	*Estado, Gobierno, Gestión Pública. Revista Chilena de Administración Pública* (Chile)

journals. For almost twenty years, *Public Administration Review* was the only academic journal in the United States that concerned public administration. Since then the number of journals that can be identified as public administration (including management and policy journals) has increased substantially.

If the number of articles since 1988 in Table 4.1 on personnel, budgeting and finance, or policy is considered low, it could well be a function of the range of specialized journals that have emerged since the late 1960s. The listing above only includes American and foreign journals and is not complete. Specialists in the various areas can easily add other titles.

Table 4.3 Number of Normative, Theoretical, and Empirical Articles

	1941	1948	1958	1968	1978	1988	1998	2008
Normative	2	3	3	2	–	–	–	1
Theoretical	5	5	14	13	19	5	10	16
Empirical	22	18	17	32	43	42	35	73

Table 4.4 Number of Practitioner and Academic Authors in PAR

	1941	1948	1958	1968	1978	1988	1998	2008
Practitioners	16	15	18	22	17	12	9	9
Academics	16	12	22	28	58	54	66	149

One issue mentioned by Perry and Kraemer is the domination of empirical articles (see Table 4.3). In the PAR-sample considered for this section, empirical articles dominated every year, but it is interesting to see that normative articles have pretty much disappeared.

There is one more element that may provide some indication about the development of the study and that concerns the number of practitioner respectively academic authors (Table 4.4).

In the first three decades, authorship of articles in PAR was more or less equally divided between practitioners and academics. The number of contributing practitioners declined from then on, while the number of academics increased significantly.[1] The same has happened in other countries. This, however, will not allow for the conclusion that the study is increasingly defined by academics only, since scholarly activity is assessed not only by publications in scholarly journals but also by reports written by scholars in their role as consultants. Indeed, much of the so-called applied work is published in outlets read more by practitioners, that is, in specialized journals of professional associations and in general serials such as *The Public Manager*.

As an area of study public administration has proliferated in the past 40–50 years. This is illustrated by an expanding range of topics (certainly in PAR), by a growing number of specialized journals, by a growing number of independent degree programs, and by a range of schools (e.g., public administration, public policy, public management). This proliferation is testimony to a

---

[1] Kelman (2007: 232) observes that PAR had to appeal to practitioners and academics both and that this inhibited advances in methods of public administration research. He claims that the study separated from organization studies and thus cut itself off from methodological advances in social psychology, sociology, and political science (specifically econometrics, lab experimentation, and computational analysis) (ibid.: 227). Kelman's chapter is a strong advocacy for a performance centered and scientific approach to public administration.

vibrant study, yet at the same time underlines the extent of its fragmentation. Various authors have tried to provide a framework for the study based on conceptual maps of topics.

4.2 Comprehensive Conceptualizations of the Study of Public Administration

After the Second World War, scholars began to organize the study's content through analytical models and/or on the basis of distinct intellectual and/or disciplinary approaches. For instance, Simon et al. suggested that public administration had three major areas of interest: how the various levels of government should be (re)organized, the behavior of human beings, and the relation between politics and administration that were interconnected and could be presented "...through a realistic, behavioral description of the processes of administration" (1967: v–vi). In their view the problem area of the study included the activities of the executive branches at all levels, as well as those of independent boards, and commissions, corporations. Excluded were the judicial and legislative branches as well as NGOs (ibid.: 7–9). In the fifth edition of his handbook, Pfiffner distinguished between three schools of thought: the legal–historical approach that focused on normative and philosophical views upon the formal relations between the branches of government, the structural–descriptive approach that worked with "scientific management" assumptions and paid attention to the relevance of business methods for public administration, and the behavioral approach which was occupied with the "...systematic study of human behavior in organizational context" (1967: 11–13). As noted above, the table of contents did not change. Pfiffner did observe that it was important to pay attention to the environment in which government operates, defined as the political framework, as the normative questions of administrative responsibility, and as the administrative structures and procedures that reflected the values of the larger social system (ibid.: 15). Seven out of thirty-one chapters were devoted to it.

From the 1960s onward, traditional public administration handbooks were complemented with handbooks that conceptualized public administration in terms of public policy, public management, or governance, often presenting government as a system model. For instance, Sharkansky presented the study as a policy process because he desired to make public administration "...relevant and interesting for the student of political science" (1978: 6). The administrative system, as he called it, consisted of five elements: the environment (that both stimulates administrators and receives the products of their work), the inputs, the outputs, the conversion of inputs to outputs, and the feedbacks that transmit immediate outcomes back to the administrative system as new inputs at a later time. Following a chapter on comparative administration, showing that his process-framework could be used in any setting (ibid.: 53), were four chapters on the conversion process (decision-making, administrative organization and control, personnel, and management) and three on the inputs (political culture, citizen demand, and executives, legislators, and administrators). The two chapters on outputs included attention for intergovernmental relations and for various types of outputs.

A few years later, Wamsley and Zald regarded public organizations as systems "... for producing 'output' of the organization [through] the combination of men, money, machines and facilities..." (1973: 19). They organized the topics of interest to the study in a political economy model (Table 4.5). In this model the external aspects of public organizations concerns the exchanges between public organization and external actors. What distinguishes public from private organizations is that in the former external actors are much more directly involved in determining goals, allocating resources, and

Table 4.5 The Political Economy Model of Public Organizations

	Environment: structure and process	Internal: structure and process
Political	• Superordinate and authoritative executive bodies and offices (and organized extensions: budget, personnel offices) • Superordinate and authoritative legislative bodies and committees (and organized extensions: ombudsman, inspectorates) • Independent review bodies: courts, judiciary • Competitors for jurisdiction and functions • Interest groups and political parties Media-communication entrepreneurs • Interested and potentially interested citizenry	• Institutionalized distribution of authority and power: dominant coalition or faction, opposition factions, etc. • Succession system for executive personnel • Recruitment and socialization system for executive cadre • Constitution: ethos, myths, norms, and values reflecting institutional purpose. • Patterns for aggregation and pressing demands for change by lower personnel
Economic	• Input characteristics: labor, material, technology, facilities, supply and cost factors • Output characteristics: demand characteristics and channels for registering demand • Industry structure (in and out of government) • Macro-economic effects on supply–demand characteristics	• Allocation rules: accounting and information systems • Task- and technology-related unit differentiation • Incentive system: pay, promotion, tenure, and fringes • Authority structure for task accomplishment. • Buffering technological or task core

Source: Wamsley and Zald (1973: 20) (reprinted with permission from Professors Wamsley and Zald).

so forth (ibid.: 21). What makes their model unique is that they treat specializations that were generally regarded as technical subfields (e.g., public budgeting and finance, personnel management) as, at least partially, behavioral topics, since they are critical to organizational behavior and have significant political and economic causes and consequences (ibid.: 22–3). Their model also explicitly connected public administration's traditional attention for organizations to policy analysis (ibid.: 11).

A system or process approach was also adopted by Starling in his handbook of public management (2008: 16). He labeled his model as "the process of public administration." He mentioned that the many skills public administrators are expected to have can be summarized in three categories: public or political management (the political–legal environment, intergovernmental relations, and administrative responsibility and ethics), program management (planning, decision-making, organizing, leading, implementation), and resources management (human resources, financial resources, and information management) (ibid.: 15). Thus, it appears that his model should really be labeled as concerning "the process of public management." Starling's 2008-edition included explicit attention for the nonprofit sector, something that has become normal in public administration textbooks in the past 10–15 years.

At the time that public policy and system approaches were very popular (since the 1960s) and that public management approaches were on the rise (since the early 1980s), Rosenbloom published a textbook (1983) that combined the traditional attention for law and politics with the more recent attention for management, thus explicitly focusing on the three branches of government. A legal approach to understanding government was necessary because of the importance of sovereignty, constitutions, and regulations. The political approach drew attention to " . . . legislative policy making concerns" (2005: 14). The managerial approach included two subtypes: traditional public management and New Public Management (NPM). Underscoring the complexity of contemporary government, Rosenbloom and Kravchuk write in the sixth edition of the 1983 handbook that

> Public administrators are called upon to be managers, policy makers, and consti-
> tutional lawyers. They are stuck between the proverbial rock and a hard place
> when called on to act in a fashion that will integrate administrative approaches
> that may defy successful integration. This is one reason why politicians and the
> society generally have become so critical of public administration. It is virtually
> impossible to satisfy frequently all the managerial, political, and legal/constitu-
> tional demands placed on public agencies and public administrators. (2005: 38)

Any conceptual map of the study should capture that complexity in the real world and not just at one point in time. Interestingly, the models of Wamsley and Zald, Sharkansky, Starling, and Rosenbloom present the study in a time-less, abstract fashion. The Sharkansky and Starling systems models do not say anything about what topics are considered central to the study. Their conceptualization of public administration is so abstract that it can be applied to different times and places. The Wamsley and Zald and the Rosenbloom tables provides a listing of topics and perspectives, with the latter including a sense of temporal development (from traditional management to NPM).

This notion that the study develops over time is visualized in McCurdy's diagram (Figure 4.1). It shows the multidisciplinary origins of the study (e.g., sociology, psychology, political science, law, economics, and business admin-istration; but leaving out, e.g., history, philosophy, and mathematics,

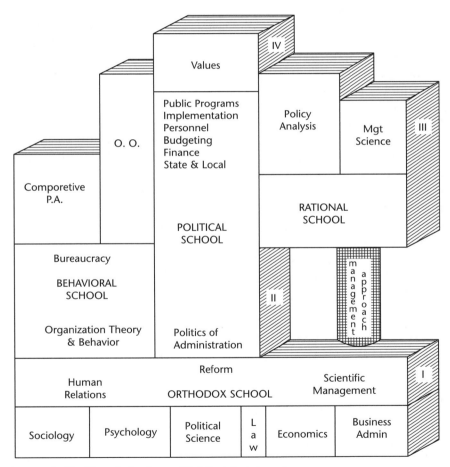

Figure 4.1 The Knowledge Base of Public Administration
Source: McCurdy (1986: 17).

mentioned on p. 72 of his book). McCurdy argues that during the orthodox period (I) (1880–1945), human relations continued with themes from sociology and psychology, reform-minded scholars grounded themselves predominantly in political science and law, while scientific management built upon economics and business administration. During the second phase (II), labeled as the period of description (1945–65), two of these broad groups of approaches fleshed out into the behavioral school and the political school. A third approach became the rational school during the third period (III), the era of applications (1965–80), that included attention for comparative studies, management science, policy analysis and organization development (OD). Finally, in the fourth phase (IV), that of reconsideration (1980s), values and ethics emerged on the agenda against the background of pluralist politics, cutback management, and declining trust in government. The political school situated at the center of the diagram suggests that it is the dominant school of thought, the central pillar of the study where less is borrowed from other fields than is the case in the extremities " . . . where the propensity to borrow is most pronounced" (McCurdy, 1986: 18).

McCurdy seems to regard the study of public administration as part of political science, but the imagery in his diagram is qualified in the subsequent discussion. Political science, he writes, surfaced at a time that hopes for unity of social science were high (i.e., the 1850s) (McCurdy, 1986: 19). In contrast, public administration emerged at a time that hands-on skills and instruments were desired to help local administrators deal with societal demand for better working and living conditions, and at a time that social sciences were confronted with the need to train professionals, to provide usable knowledge, and, consequentially, to reach beyond disciplinary boundaries (late nineteenth, early twentieth century) (ibid.: 21).

McCurdy starts his overview of the conceptual developments in the study in the 1880s, while Stillman starts his with the publication of the first handbook in public administration by Leonard White (1926). In Stillman's view, public administration seems to " . . . transform itself into new shapes and purposes every generation, or on twenty-year cycles, to respond to the particular needs of the times" (2010: 27). The McCurdy and Stillman conceptualizations of the development of the study provide a sense of what topics were considered relevant and important at a given point in time; that these have changed suggests that the study has responded to changing environmental circumstances. This adaptability is the study's strength as well as its weakness, since societal developments prohibit an authoritative definition of the study that travels over time. It is thus even more important that conceptual maps of the study are developed that incorporate the traditional as well as the more recent interests. This cannot be done through top-down and abstract analytical models (Sharkansky, Starling) or top-down analytical lenses (Rosenbloom) since they are heuristics for capturing the real world and do not show the range of topics that are addressed in the study. By contrast, a bottom-up approach calls for conceptual maps of topics in the study. The advantage of such an approach is that it is much more concrete then abstract approaches (Sharkansky, Starling) and does not use stage models that provide one way of sketching the topical development over time (McCurdy, Stillman).

4.3 A Wheel of Public Administration

Initially, the study of public administration was defined in terms of characteristics internal to organizations. After the Second World War it became more common to adopt a particular analytical approach. Simon et al. organized their textbook by starting with individuals, then moving to groups in organizations, then organizational structures at large, and then processes in organizations. Sharkansky and Starling both used a systems approach. Finally, Rosenbloom introduced the idea of using three disciplinary lenses.

In view of the fact that the topics considered part of the study of public administration have been increasing, especially since the 1960s, it has become more and more difficult to provide a conceptual map that captures that topical diversity. There are two conceptualizations available that have tried to do so and they start by addressing the nature of the study. The first of these is by Richard Stillman. He believes that determining the scope and purpose of public administration is " ... perhaps the most difficult, central intellectual problem in public administration today" (Richard Stillman, 2005: xxii–xxiii). Six chapters in his handbook constitute the inner ring of "The pattern of public administration in America." The second ring provides readings and cases on major activities, responsibilities, and roles of public administrators and, thus, concerns functions internal to the organization. The third ring focuses on enduring and unresolved relations between politics and administration, between public and private sectors, and between ethics and the public sector. The environment is represented in both the inner and the outer rings. Less clear is how the three rings are positioned vis-à-vis one another. Why would Chapter 7 (on key decision-makers) in the inner ring be aligned with Chapter 13 in the middle ring (implementation)? Why would Chapter 4 (political environment) and Chapter 10 (executive management) be aligned with Chapter 15 (on relations between public and private sectors) and not with Chapter 14 (on political–administrative relations)? The potential conundrum of Stillman's wheel can be resolved by imagining that the three rings can revolve, that is, that each of the chapters in each of the rings can be related to each other.

Stillman is careful to note that " ... no one has produced a simple definition of the study of public administration – at least one on which most practitioners and scholars agree," and that such a definition would be difficult to establish given the continued expansion of government in the twentieth century (Stillman, 2005: 1). What Waldo once called the "identity crisis" has become even more urgent because " ... a plethora of models, approaches, and theories now purport to define what public administration is all about" (ibid.: 4). Stillman suggests that it is pretty difficult, if not impossible, to define the content of the study for all time because government is not a static phenomenon, neither in terms of its activities in society nor in terms of how it is conceptualized. However, the methodological and intellectual pluralism so characteristic of the study of public administration, and so overwhelming to many of its scholars, need not be a factor in the effort to define its content. Is it possible to disregard and circumvent this theoretical and methodological pluralism, and proceed to define the topics of the study?

To do so requires rather plain and simple questions. What legitimizes government, the swiftness and adequacy of response to citizen demand and changing environmental circumstances, is expressed best in the ability to make binding decisions about matters of a public and collective nature. Government is empowered to make public decisions that have bearing upon (hence, are binding for) both public and private actors. The core function of public decision-making includes the entire process from preparation, via implementation to monitoring at the level (i.e., tier of government) and at the degree (i.e., intensity of government intervention) considered appropriate and morally acceptable at a given time. That said, four basic questions can be raised:

- About what are public decisions made?
- Who are involved in making these public decisions?
- Why are public decisions made?
- How are public decisions implemented?

These four questions will be briefly discussed in general terms. Any attempt to provide detail will fall short of the intention to focus on the study of public administration as a whole. The four questions represent four quadrants around the core of the study (Figure 4.2).

The inner circle represents pure theory, and in each quadrant three elements are analytically distinguished. These elements are not indivisible, because each would not make much sense without the others (hence the dotted line dividing them). The outer ring represents theory developed through empirical research (i.e., evidence-based theory: Meier and O'Toole, 2009). The three elements in the outer ring of each

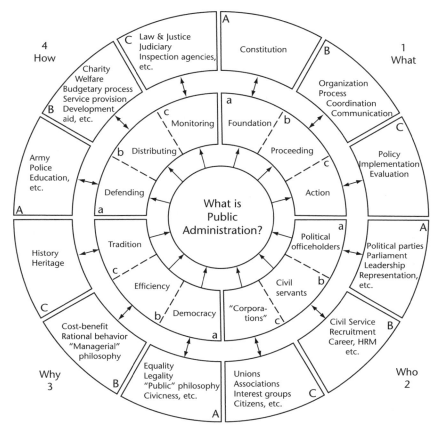

Figure 4.2 Conceptual Map 2, Public Administration as a Body of Knowledge
Source: Raadschelders (1999: 292) (with permission from Oxford University Press).

quadrant are divided because each has multiple theories of its own. In each of these, scholars have made a name.

The first quadrant is concerned with the question what public decisions are made about. Basically, decisions are made within the existing arrangements for the *foundations*, the *proceedings* or *processes*, and the *actions* of government. One core theory that can connect these three elements (sections 1a–c) is that of the levels of choice and levels of rules (Kiser and Ostrom, 1982). Focusing on the element of "foundation" only, empirical work with strong theoretical meaning in section 1A is concerned with *constitution* (e.g., Rohr, 1986; Lane, 1996). The proceedings or process section 1B in the outer ring contains research on the organizations within which these decisions are made (e.g., Gulick, 1937; Blau and Schoenherr, 1971; Meyer, 1979). Also important are the ways in which these decisions are communicated (e.g., Garnett and

Kouzmin, 1997) and coordinated. This would today also include studies in information technology and e-government. The third element in the outer ring concerns all research on policy implementation and evaluation (e.g., Pressman and Wildavsky, 1973).

Once we are down to the action level (1c), the question emerges of who are involved in making these decisions. The inner ring of the second quadrant represents pure theory about iron triangles, networks, and so forth (2a–c) (e.g., Heclo, 1978). It is in this type of theory that the three main actors in government are intricately linked: *political officeholders*, *civil servants*, and *corporations*, the last being a generic term to describe the amalgam of unions, citizens' associations, interest groups, the business community, and so forth. In the outer ring the three sections represent separate bodies of empirical work (2A–C). Section 2A comprises research on political parties, parliament, elections, leaders of government, issues of political representation, etc. Section 2B contains all research on bureaucracy as a personnel system, as a civil service: training, recruitment, career development (Bekke et al., 1996; Raadschelders et al., 2007), human resource management (e.g., Hays and Kearney, 1995), and the assumed tendency to aggrandize their own importance (e.g., Downs, 1967) or their influence/power over politics (e.g., Page, 1992). Sections 2A and 2B are connected in the topic of political–administrative relations (e.g., Aberbach et al., 1981). Section 2C concerns all research about the influence of individual citizens (through referenda, public hearings, participation on local boards, etc.) as well as of organized segments of society upon public decision-making such as nonprofit organizations, labor unions, and interest groups (e.g., Peters, 1989). Obviously, section 2C is linked with the other two: both political and administrative officeholders are heavily intertwined with citizen collectives.

From this we can move almost automatically to ask what propels these three groups of actors into making decisions. Why are public decisions made? Each public decision and action is motivated by and embedded in values that people hold about society and its governance. The inner section of the third quadrant is thus the pure type of theory that focuses on ideological motives (sections 3a–c). There are three basic and highly interrelated motives: *democracy*, *efficiency*, and *tradition*. These three are intricately related. Democracy and efficiency have been called the classical dilemma of public administration (Self, 1979: 277–8). Also, decisions do not come out of the blue but are almost always a consequence of *casu quo* rooted in past decisions. Hence, while democracy and efficiency represent two sides of the same contemporary coin, the presence of the administrative past (Fesler, 1982; Raadschelders, 2009a) provides the perimeters within which democracy and efficiency were and are defined. As there are pure theories of democracy (e.g., Dahl, 1970), there are pure theories of efficiency (e.g., Simon, 1957), theories about the impact of time (e.g., Bartolini, 1993), and theories about the sequential, hence, dynamic nature of decision and policymaking (e.g., Lindblom, 1959; Rose and Davies, 1994). In section 3A of the outer ring, research can be situated that includes such topics as equality, citizens, and civicness (e.g., Almond and Verba, 1963; Putnam et al., 1993), and public administrative philosophy (e.g., Hodgkinson, 1978). Section 3B comprises empirical work on cost and benefits, rational behavior, managerial philosophy, and so on. The last section in this quadrant is concerned with research in the area of administrative history (e.g., Finer, 1997; Raadschelders, 1998*b*) and the history of management (e.g., Wren, 1972; Barley and Kunda, 1992).

This quadrant calls for a little extra justification. While the topics of the other quadrants are considered part of mainstream public administration, perhaps with the exception of 2a and A), those of this quadrant may raise some eyebrows. Many will agree with the observation that a political theory of administration is essential to a balanced understanding of the contemporary structure, the functioning, and the challenges of government. Waldo pointed this out sixty years ago (1984) and yet it seems as if the relation between democracy, efficiency, and tradition is not a concern in mainstream public administration. Adams suggested that more attention for this relation is necessary:

> The tension between a meaningful, democratic politics and an expert, specialized administration, embedded in our nation's founding and intensified greatly by the flowering of technical rationality barely 100 years ago, remains at the forefront of any possible claim to legitimacy for public administration in the American state. An atemporal public administration has considerable difficulty even addressing this question, because in its very essence it is an historical question. [...] Remaining enthralled with modernity, we remain unable to locate ourselves in our present historical circumstances, and thus relegate ourselves to issuing "new" calls for science and rigor on into the future. (1992: 370)

Would public administration's identity crisis be less prominent and pressing if the rationalist-scientific approach, which is piecemeal by nature, is supplemented with more attention to configurations, interpretations, and cultural context that takes a more comprehensive approach to government?

The last quadrant concerns the matter of how these public decisions are maintained. In the inner ring (4a–c), three basic activities are situated: *defending/protecting*, *distributing*, and *legislating/monitoring*. Defending and legislating are based on the norms and values shared in society and generally upheld through social control. Where spontaneous social control fails, the military and the police are available to assure peace and prosperity (section 4A) (e.g., Reiner, 1992; Bailey, 1995). Distributing represents shared convictions about charity and welfare (welfare state) and civic culture (e.g., Heater, 1990). In the

119

outer ring we find such processes as budgeting and public finance (e.g., Peters, 1991; Mikesell, 2007), public service delivery, development aid, and so forth (section 4B). The inner ring of the final segment concerns law and justice (e.g., Rawls, 1971) upon which activities of the judiciary, of inspection agencies, etc. (the outer ring) (e.g., Cavadino and Dignan, 1996; Stojkovic et al., 1996; Hurst, 1977). With this twelfth element we are, literally, back to square one, since law and law enforcement emanate from the Constitution.

This wheel of public administration presents the study as an intellectually coherent body that has, at least, seven features. First, the bottom part of the framework, quadrants 2 and 3, represent the input side, while the two top quadrants represent the output side. Actors and motives upon which they act provide the input; the output consists of actions and the ways in which these actions are pursued and monitored. The nature of the input varies from country to country and is dependent upon who participates in decision-making given a particular arena of ideology, practical problems, and traditions.

Second, it is clear that the various elements are interrelated, since each output element can be analyzed in terms of each input element. Taking section 3cC as example, it will not take much convincing to argue that tradition (input) is highly influential upon output. Students of government can and have analyzed, for instance, budgeting in a historical perspective (e.g., Webber and Wildavsky, 1986), the development of organizations in terms of their dominant managerial ideology (e.g., Barley and Kunda, 1992), the origins of the legal system of the Western world (e.g., Berman, 1983), the development of state government in the United States (e.g., Garnett, 1980), the emergence and development of the welfare state as a function of interest group input (e.g., Flora and Heidenheimer, 1990), and the development of political–administrative relations since the Atlantic Revolutions of the late eighteenth century (e.g., Raadschelders and Van der Meer, 1998).

Third, in this presentation of the study the point of departure is the material object (see Chapter 1) of government and governance, not a particular theoretical, methodological, or conceptual approach (the formal object). Public administration scholars can draw upon a large body of disciplinary approaches. This framework does not require commitment to a particular methodology nor does it claim or provide commensurability. It is nothing more, nothing less, than a way of organizing the study as an integrated whole. The various topics mentioned in the quadrants can be analyzed from various approaches (interpretative, positivist, postmodernist, etc.) and at different levels of abstraction such as the macro-social, the organizational, and the micro (individual) levels.

Fourth, this wheel presents a mix of theory and practice. The practice of governing cannot be defined by looking solely at theory or practice. What constitutes government varies with time and place. For instance, the Roman distinction between *res publica* and *res privata* was not revived in Western Europe until the late eighteenth century (see Dyson, 1980: 115). Since the late nineteenth century government has grown not just in size (as measured in terms of personnel, revenue and expenditure, regulations, organizational differentiation) but also in its interactions with organizations in the market and with citizen associations. Sometimes practice influences theory and sometimes theory influences practice. That is, sometimes developments in practice become "codified" in law, or in accepted and explicit procedures, while at other times developments in theory (such as thinking about a welfare state in the eighteenth century) become possible in practice later (i.e., in the twentieth century).

Fifth, this framework does not indicate how important each topic is. There is no specific core to the study other than its material object. All topics are relevant to the practice of government and to the study of public administration. When an author claims that one particular feature or approach is more central to the study than another, we know more about the identity of the author (i.e., disciplinary background, outlook on science, ideological preferences) than about the identity of the study.

Sixth, this framework transcends the differences between the continental-European taxonomical approach and the Anglo-American pragmatic approach. What separates them is less important than what combines them: the interest in government and its impact upon society.

Finally, seventh, there is no topic in the recent past, the present, or the proximate future in the study of modern[2] public administration that does not fit in this framework, because the labeling of the various quadrants and their sections is sufficiently broad to allow for the placement of time-specific developments. For instance, efficiency was as relevant in the 1910s and 1920s (scientific management) as it is today (performance management and measurement). Also, processes of organization, coordination, and communication involved the telephone, the telegraph, marketing tools, etc. in the 1930s, while nowadays it would include attention for information technology and e-government. As a final example, quadrant 2bB easily accommodates the concern for representative bureaucracy and diversity that was pretty much irrelevant before the 1940s. One could argue about the positioning of these topics. For example, ethics, the core values of government, the notion of due process, and charity and justice as manifestations of moral authority could be

---

[2] The use of "modern" refers to the modern period, that is, the time since the late eighteenth century; hence the use of "recent past" and of "proximate future." To develop a conceptual framework for the study of government that transcends not just a few centuries but millennia would be a challenge, to say the least.

placed in various quadrants (e.g., 1aA or in 3aA or...?). This framework is, therefore, a means to show how topics in the study of public administration can be conceptualized as an integrated whole; it is not intended as finite.

4.4 A Meta-framework for Studying Government

In the previous two sections, several examples were provided of how topics in the study of public administration can be mapped. They only, though, concerned the study of public administration itself. The net could be cast wider by conceptualizing a study of government. Until the 1960s, many universities in the United States had Departments of Government. While it is possible that a study of government is best served by an umbrella discipline such as public administration (see Chapter 2), it is equally conceivable that a study of public administration concerns a more limited range of interests and topics than a study of government.

Given the variety of disciplinary approaches in the study of public administration, it would be useful to develop a meta-framework for the study of government that meets several criteria. First, a meta-framework has to be defined in such a manner that knowledge from various disciplines can be included. Such a framework is thus not one that is identified by a particular theory, method, discipline, or study, but by a material object.

It follows, second, that a meta-framework should be grounded in the widest possible conception of government in the modern era. Traditional public administration excludes a variety of topics that are relevant to understanding government itself and to the understanding of the interaction between society and government. This is perhaps best expressed in the distinction between the concepts of "government" and "governance." The latter includes attention for collective actors outside the public realm who influence to smaller or larger extend what happens in the public realm (such as NGOs, interest groups, lobbyists, private corporations, media representatives).

Third, a meta-framework should include attention for collective and individual levels of analysis. This criterion requires more detail since there are contrasting schools of thought that fundamentally disagree with each other. Rational choice theorists consider collective action in terms of the action of individuals who just choose to accomplish something collectively rather than individually (e.g., Buchanan and Tullock, 1962: 13). In this approach, institutions are not assumed to have an existence of their own. By contrast, neo-institutionalists argue that institutions have a life of their own. Could it be that both approaches are legitimate? A meta-framework should facilitate a linking of the micro and macro levels of analyses because what is observed at individual level may not apply at organizational level and vice versa (Mouzelis, 1967: 118–19). In the words of Mouzelis:

> ... as one passes from one system level to another, each higher level (e.g., referring to more inclusive systems) cannot be reduced to the properties of the lower one because, although there is relative interdependence and interpenetration between a system and its subsystems, there is also relative autonomy between them. (1967: 149)

While Mouzelis argues that a system perspective facilitates the study of individuals, groups, organizations, and society, in 1991 he suggests bridging the micro- and macro-groups through a *system perspective* upon social positions and institutions and a *social integration perspective* upon actors (Mouzelis, 1991: 106). He recognizes that most individuals will not have major impact upon the macro-institutional order, but the same cannot be said for the so-called macro-actors. He distinguishes between two types of macro-actors: collective actors who make decisions through interaction (e.g., political parties, legislators, governmental agencies, interest groups, etc.) and mega-actors who are single individuals that have such a large social power base that the consequences of their decisions can be widely felt (ibid.: 107) (i.e., of the stature of a Nero, Charlemagne, Frederick the Great of Prussia, Hitler, Mandela). He convincingly argues that micro–macro analysis, while not simple, will help avoid the downward reductionism (where subsystems are assumed to have little if any autonomy) and upward reductionism (where the subunits have so much autonomy that the system is only an aggregate of its constituent subsystems (ibid.: 137).

A fourth criterion follows from the third and that is that government ought to be regarded as a layered phenomenon. There are at least two dimensions to that. The first dimension is that of different levels of abstraction or meaning. Authors in public administration and in other disciplines increasingly recognize that what is visible to the observer is embedded in a deeper level. The constitutional level is the most abstract and provides the framework for collective action (i.e., of rules and choices), which in turn serves as the framework for the operational and most concrete level (Kiser and Ostrom, 1982). The second dimension is that of levels of time, recognizing that human activities are expressions of and embedded in longer term developments. A short-term, contemporary perspective on societal challenges and social problems should be complemented with an understanding of the middle range perspective (spanning two to five years) and the long-term perspective (twenty years or more).

A fifth criterion involves recognition of the fact that anything that concerns government and its interaction with society can be looked at through (formal) juridical and through (informal) sociological lenses. A juridical perspective upon public administration dominated in the first part of the twentieth century with attention for rules and law but also with attention for formal organizational structures and principles, and for separation of politics and administration. Comparative legislation and jurisprudence, international law and constitutional law, and all these in historical perspective, were at the heart of the study at the time (Hill, 1992: 30). During the second part of the twentieth century, a sociological perspective (i.e., a generic term encompassing all of the social sciences, including economics) came to dominate prompting scholars to map structures and search for law-like generalizations (i.e., structural-functionalists) or for regularities in the interactions and differences between actors (i.e., behavioralists). Yet others pointed to the futility of earlier research by pointing to the extent in which "interpretation" plays a role in everyday life (postmodernists). However, both structure (statics) and process (dynamics) of governing need to be understood. A juridical perspective draws attention to the degrees of standardization and formalization of rules and interactions in society and to the role of government in this. A sociological perspective draws attention to the many informal rules and interactions between various actors in and around the public arena. On the basis of those criteria, a meta-framework for the study of government can be developed (Figure 4.3).

In view of Mouzelis' advice to connect micro and macro levels of analyses, Figure 4.3 provides two main levels: an institutional and an actor level. At the institutional level, a distinction is made between the ideational level (the foundation of society) and the societal level. At the actor level, both organizations and individuals are regarded as agents. Each of these levels can be analyzed in terms of each of the dimensions outlined above. The individualism–collectivism continuum draws attention to the fact that people (whether as citizen or as a public functionary) are always challenged to balance the needs of a collection of individuals with those of communities of people through a government of citizens. It is a major political challenge. The juridical and sociological perspectives help to recognize that public officials are required to balance

	Individualism		Collectivism		
Juridical	**Institutions**				Historical
perspective	*Ideational level*: people need government; legal, moral, and ethical constitution of society				perspective
	Societal level: democracy; justice and social justice; traditional and welfare services				
Sociological	**Actors**				Contemporary
perspective	*Organization level*: efficiency: organizational structures and cultures; decision and policy making				perspective
	Individual level: political, bureaucratic and citizen actors and interest groups				
	Abstract level	More concrete level	Concrete level		

Figure 4.3 Conceptual Map 3, a Meta-framework for the Study of Government
Source: Raadschelders (2003*b*: 374) (reprinted with permission from M.E. Sharpe).

fairness from a legal point of view (i.e., due process and equality before the law) with fairness from a social point of view (i.e., discretion in determining extend of government support relative to individual need). Both these angles highlight that governing is not an activity that provides clear-cut solutions to equally clear-cut problems. An either-or mindset is not helpful in seeking guidance for the real world. These two angles also emphasize that analysis of the cultural context within which human thought and interaction acquire meaning is in its infancy. The third and fourth angles emphasize that government is a multi-layered phenomenon both in terms of abstraction as well as in terms of its embeddedness in the past. Examples of how a variety of variables can be perceived in each of these four angles had been provided in my 2003-study (376–90).

The framework presented in Figure 4.3 is nothing more, but also nothing less, than a bookcase where knowledge about and theoretical perspectives upon government from different disciplines is placed. The content of each bookshelf is determined by the fact that it has to do with government. What is placed on the bookshelves is subject to differences of opinion. It is up to an individual author to determine the content of the bookshelves. The four shelves (ideational, societal, organizational, and individual) not only include attention for mainstream public administration (i.e., at the organizational and individual levels) but also for the democratic superstructure of society (i.e., the institutional arrangement of representative democracy and of intergovernmental relations) and for the values that undergird society at large (the ideational level).

4.5 Government: A Public Administration Perspective

In discussions about the identity of the study of public administration, it is often said that a coherent and unifying theory is lacking. This claim, however, does not do justice to the study. Perhaps a coherent and unified body of theory does not exist, but that does not imply that the study lacks identity. That identity, however, is sooner rooted in the material object of the study than in a distinct theoretical and/or methodological approach. Bemoaning the lack of a coherent and unifying body debases the vast amount of theories available on specific topics and denies the multidisciplinary and interdisciplinary (see for these two concepts Chapter 7) nature that is essential to the study. Scholars who continue to strive for a coherent and unifying theory in an inductive manner are digging their own grave. Apart from the fact that this is not desirable from a personal and psychological point of view (will every citizen agree with one particular scholarly view upon and interpretation of government?), it is equally undesirable from a cognitive point of view (i.e., disavowing the fact that the material object can be viewed through multiple formal objects). The search for a coherent and unifying theory negates what is characteristic for public administration and, in fact, for all of the social sciences: they deal with and depart from the reflection and interpretation so basic to human nature.

In this chapter, several ways of framing, conceptualizing, and mapping topics in the study were discussed: features of internal organization (e.g., White, Walker), system approaches (e.g, Wamsley and Zald, Sharkansky, Starling), disciplinary approaches (Rosenbloom), and topical approaches (Stillman, Raadschelders). Each has its advantages and shortcomings. White and Walker provide solid introductions to the inner structure and workings of government organizations, but pay much less attention to relations with society. The Wamsley and Zald, Sharkansky, and Starling models provide a particular and coherent analytical frame but do not show how various theoretical approaches can be linked. Rosenbloom's disciplinary lenses upon government remind of the fact that it is studied in various social sciences, but the topical map is dispersed throughout his book. The wheels of Stillman and of Raadschelders show how the various topical areas in the study can be linked, but they leave it up to the reader to determine which theories are suitable for the various topics. Finally, Raadschelders' meta-framework shows how government can be understood as an embedded phenomenon. It is a highly abstract representation that invites a move away from a "disciplinary" approach to defining the study of public administration to one that departs from the material object of study. To understand government, a public administration perspective holds the best promise because of the earlier claim that it is the umbrella discipline (Chapter 2). The other social sciences are only interested in elements or aspects of government. But, government is not served by the partial understandings of the various social sciences. In its complexity, government is not captured by these other social sciences because they are limited by their own foci. Public administration as umbrella discipline draws upon these foci and thus has the potential to provide better understanding.

The academic community of public administration differs about the question how public administration can be defined respectively captured adequately. None of the examples presented in this chapter can claim superiority. The study of public administration is probably further away than ever from reaching a theoretical closure to its identity crisis. How far becomes clear when mapping the theories-in-use in the study of public administration (Chapter 5).

5

Bogey Man, Doctor's Bag, and/or Artist's Medium: The Dynamic Arena of PA-Theory

> A popular duality casts public [administration] as either "craft/art" (in an Aristotelian sense) or as "science" (in a Platonic sense). The fields' purpose is alternately viewed as providing either positive knowledge or normative guidance for practice. (paraphrased from Lynn, 2006)

We have seen that the study of public administration is a social science (Chapter 2) that taps into a variety of knowledge sources (Chapter 3), and is concerned with a wide range of substantive interests (Chapter 4). While this indicates both the complexity of the study itself and of what it studies, the nature of the study and its identity crises (Chapter 1) are mainly perceived as theoretical and methodological challenges in view of the multiple and conflicting theories-in-use. Scholars who perceive "science" in the narrow sense seek to develop the "scientificness" of the study by advocating the use of formal theories and models and by applying quantitative-statistical methods to research questions (Simon, 1947, 1952; Meier and O'Toole, 2009). Dubnick described opponents of a science of administration as being afraid of the "logical positivist bogeyman" (1999: 40). However, governing cannot not only be understood through science, it is also a craft where the practitioner grabs his "doctor's bag" (Waldo, 1968b: 10; Wamsley, 1996: 366) and searches for the right tool or instrument in a particular situation. Finally, there are scholars who regard public administration as a study that enlightens, that helps gauging and guessing appropriate action by intuition without solid guarantees of success. In that case the study is an "artist's medium," to use Berlin's phrase (2000: 113). Judgments about the state of public administration theory vary with perspective (science, or craft/profession, or art).

Some scholars say that the study's theory is in disarray (the positivist critique), while others believe it is in good shape (Frederickson and Smith, 2003). This confusion has been part of the study for almost 70 years, but the study thrives as never before (Wise, 1999). Assessing the nature and status of public administration theory is a challenge for it concerns both theory that is developed and tested in the study of public administration as well as theories used in the study but drawn from elsewhere. To understand the quandary in which PA-theory finds itself since Simon (1947, 1952) and Waldo (1948, 1952a/1952b) shredded the prewar optimism of having a "science of administration" soon, each suggesting a radically different direction, the following questions can be raised:

1. Why has a science of public administration not developed (with) a unifying theory?
2. Why has the craft of public administration not come up with timeless usable knowledge?
3. Why has public administration as art failed to convince that there are neither law-like generalizations about nor (quick-and-dirty) prescriptions for solving societal problems through government?

Whichever angle the PA-scholar identifies with (science, craft, art), apparently each has failed to deliver. But there are more positively phrased equivalents to these questions:

1. Why is the study of public administration an interdisciplinary endeavor?
2. Why can the study of public administration not be but time- and context-bound?
3. Why must the study of public administration be in part reflective?

In these two sets of questions we can see why PA-theory is hard to be found. Interdisciplinarity prevents the development of a unifying theory. Historical time and geographical context prohibit the development of timeless usable knowledge. Reflection upon complex social problems holds no promise that government might provide somewhat effective solutions. The study of government started in the fourth-century BCE as a king-philosopher's art. The practitioners' need for usable knowledge has, since the seventeenth century, turned them to a study of government that emphasizes administrative practices, skills, cases and examples. The unity of knowledge ideal has, since the eighteenth century, turned the study of government toward a science of administration. Two questions are addressed in this chapter:

1. Given the different origins (art, craft, science) of the study of public administration as it is today, what is the nature and status of PA-theory?
2. Given the fact that public administration's material object of study is government, can the study develop a theory of government?

In Section 5.1 the nature and challenge of PA-theory will be outlined. In Sections 5.2–5.4 an overview is given of the nature and challenges of PA-theory when defined as science, as craft, and as art. For each of these the major features, the critiques, the problems, and the central hopes are discussed. In Section 5.5 these three approaches will be positioned in a model of the PA-theory arena. To be clear, this chapter does not provide an inventory of PA-theory. This would be a useless exercise in view of the many theories developed and used by public administration scholars. The arena in Figure 5.2 provides an impression of the complexity of any effort to capture PA-theory.

5.1 The Nature and Challenge of PA-Theory

Determining the state of PA-theory depends upon various considerations. First, is the study of public administration a monodisciplinary or an interdisciplinary endeavor (see also Chapter 7)? When public administration is seen as a monodiscipline, it would suggest that there are theories and models that originated in it and circumscribe the entire study. There are many more theories and models when perceiving public administration as an interdisciplinary study that, because of its material object, has to draw from any body of knowledge that is relevant to understanding government. PA-theory is most certainly found in various specializations that also draw upon other disciplines. Scholars of public personnel management use behavioral psychology. Decision-making theory draws significantly upon rational choice theory from economics and cognitive psychology. Organization theory acknowledges the extensive work in organizational sociology and in business administration. Studying the distribution of power and the use of authority, one cannot but look at, i.a., political science and political theory. Public sector ethics considers moral philosophy, virtue ethics and theology. There are no theories or models at the level of the study as a whole.

Second, the state of PA-theory also depends on how we define "theory." In the logical positivist approach a good theory describes, explains, and predicts on the basis of an empirical analysis of objective facts and is universal, causal, and quantified (cf. J.S. Mill as quoted in Berlin, 2002: 43). Positivism assumes that all questions can be answered, that everything is knowable in principle, and that truths cannot conflict (Berlin, 1991: 21–2). To the "craftsman," a good theory is hands-on and case-based knowledge about a particular phenomenon, event, instrument, etc., that can be used time and again. Finally, to the reflective practitioner, a good theory is one that helps understand events and weighing these in intersubjective terms through shared understanding. Both the craftsman's experience and the artist's reflection accept that knowledge is culture-bound, relational, and partially tacit. There are multiple truths that complement and contradict each other, but this pluralism of truths is grounded in an intersubjectivity that rejects ultimate relativism (Berlin, 2000: 11–2).

The three approaches (science, craft, art) can be organized on a continuum from most objective (i.e., positivism) through less objective (craftsmanship), to somewhat subjective (art), to most subjective (skeptical postmodernism; see Chapter 6). In the study of public administration the majority of scholars appear to range from the "objective" side to the "somewhat subjective" side of the continuum. There is a sizeable number of scholars in public administration, though, who identify with affirmative postmodernism (see Chapter 6).

Third, the assessment of the state of PA-theory also depends on whether public administration is first and foremost considered as an academic pursuit of experimentally tested knowledge, as a practitioner's search for usable knowledge, or as a reflective practitioner's inherent need for wisdom. For some time, public administration has been struggling with this and, in view of its inherent interdisciplinarity, this should not come as a surprise nor should it be lamented. This struggle is both one of choice (i.e., consciously borrowing from others: the eclectic study without boundaries) and one of necessity (i.e., government is a material object of interest studied across the social sciences and the humanities).

Fourth, and expanding upon the third consideration, perhaps the state of PA-theory also depends on whether there is an identity crisis. Some scholars seem to think there is, while others appear to regard it as a non-issue. If there is an identity crisis, the assessment of the nature and status of PA-theory is that it is in critical need of being upgraded. If there is no identity crisis, PA-theory is in great shape.

Fifth, the state of PA-theory also varies with what the focus of PA-theory is and/or ought to be: theory about government in society?, theory about citizens in and with government?, theory about the internal structure and functioning of government?, theory about both structure and process? Until the 1970s the eclectic and boundary-less PA-theory mainly concerned structure (including analyses of the stages of the policy process). Attention for the process side is of much more recent origin (McSwite, 1997: 272–3).

Of the more than 5,000 theories listed in Bothamley (2002), 251 are categorized as "politics." While there are some glaring omissions (e.g., the life-cycle theories of Downs and of Greiner; Ayn Rand's theory of self-government), and where some are categorized as "economics" (e.g., Rawls' theory of justice), the listing is as good as any. Theories categorized as "politics" include epistemological theories (e.g., cybernetics, game theory, legal positivism), domination theories in the widest sense of the term (e.g., various types of rule), economics-inspired theories, mechanisms of social behavior, and theories about international relations. Only eight entries are labeled as "administration" or "management." Public administration must be poor in theory. For solace we can turn to Frederickson who embraces the theoretical richness of the study (1980: 16), to Wamsley et al. who celebrate the rich diversity of perspectives born from differentiation and specialization (1990: 46), and to Frederickson and Smith who categorized and assessed theories in public administration (2003: 231). They and most of their colleagues agree that "nothing is as practical as a good theory" and that theory helps to hone, otherwise chaotic, observations. What they question, though, is the possibility of a singular, unifying theory.

5.2 PA-Theory as Science in PA-Academe: The "Bogeyman"?

In the first postwar publication exploring the possibilities of a science of public administration, Dahl (1947) argued that the problem of public administration as a discipline and as a potential science is that it must deal with a much wider set of problems (including normative considerations) than those of mere administration (1947: 3). Science would not be achieved by creating a mechanized "administrative man" descending from the eighteenth-century "rational man" (ibid.: 7). In response to this, Simon replied that Dahl confused pure science (which discovers and verifies propositions) (cf. Stene, who wrote that pure science is based on clear premises that "permit objective scrutiny and verification," 1940: 1125) and applied science. As an applied science, public administration could not work within the boundaries of academic specializations and should define itself as "political economy" (Simon, 1966: 35–6) instead.

Simon's monodisciplinary science of administration is based on careful observation of facts. He started his study in the "academic backwater" of public administration that, at the time, did not attract many scholars interested in constructing a theoretical foundation for an applied field (Simon, 1991: 114) and worked in it for the first 15 years of his career (Simon, 1995: 404). His science of administration focused on decision-making in organizations conditioned by the bounded rationality of the decision-makers who had to be content with satisficing rather than maximizing results. The source of knowledge is facts that can be objectively observed and described, and which can subsequently provide a satisfactory explanation of real phenomena. Judged by the criteria of science (cumulative, unified theory, explanation, and objectivity), Simon made the effort to develop such an encompassing science of administration.

A science approach to public administration is sometimes regarded as superior to other types of knowledge. The influence of Simon upon the further development of the study and its theories is assessed differently. Simon suggested that the study had absorbed both the revolutions of Waldo and himself (1995: 404), but others have not been that convinced (Hood and Jackson,

1991). Frederickson and Smith wrote that Waldo's assertion about administration being fundamentally political, had sunk deeply into the study at large (2003: 47) and significantly influenced the study (2003: 164). To Dubnick, Simon's influence had limited the study because Waldo's emphasis on professionalism succeeded in (or was used to justify) linking the study to practice rather than to science (1999: 19). Waldo's spirit loomed so large in the Minnowbrook-I conference (1968; Marini, 1971) and in the Blacksburg Manifesto that Dubnick spoke of the mainstream's aversion to the "logical positivist bogeyman" that prevented any meaningful participation in discussions about the standards of social science research in general and how these applied to public administration in particular (Dubnick, 1999: 40).

As far as the scientific study of bureaucracy is concerned, one can say that Simon has had substantial influence. Studies such as those by Moe (1980, 1990), Bendor (1988), Bendor and Moe (1985), Hammond (1993), Krause (2001), Krause and Meier (2003) are representative of positivist perspectives. Theirs is a bureaucracy theory of a "first principles" variant and it is contrasted to the "institutional public choice literature" (e.g., March and Olsen, 1982, 1989; Olsen, 2001) that focuses on the societal level (the distinction from Dunleavy, 1991: 1). The "first principles" group is much more influenced by Simon than the "institutions" group, but only up to a point. After all, in the fourth edition of *Administrative Behavior*, Simon points out that his use of "rational" (in bounded rationality) is distinctly different from how game theorists, statistical decision theorists, and so forth, use it (Simon, 1997*a*: 121–2). More than the Dahl-Simon exchange in 1947, it was the Waldo-Simon debate in 1952 that shaped the controversy that later was referred to as the "identity crisis."

Since McCurdy and Cleary's article (1984), it seems that the number of publications probing the quality and scientificness of public administration has swelled, neither resolving the challenge nor alleviating the self-imposed yoke of objective, rational, and usable research. The critique of those who profess to a (natural-) science or positivist approach to public administration research is various:

1. It is hardly cumulative (Perry and Kraemer, 1986: 220; Houston and Delevan, 1990: 680). Earlier work is dutifully annotated but how earlier work contributed is seldom elaborated;
2. It is eclectic (Perry and Kraemer, 1990: 364; Rhodes et al., 1995: 11);
3. Dissertations are seldom published in the United States (unlike in Europe) and fail to satisfy criteria for mainstream social science research (McCurdy and Cleary, 1984; White, 1986*b*) although this situation was improving as Cleary later reported (1992);
4. Many articles are concerned with defining a research problem and conceptualizing it rather than developing theory (Perry and Kraemer,

1986: 219; Stallings and Ferris, 1988: 585; Houston and Delevan, 1990: 675–80);

5. Many articles are low in theory-testing (Perry and Kraemer, 1986: 219; Stallings and Ferris, 1988: 583; Rhodes et al., 1995: 11). Rhodes et al. also noted that only a small group of methods is used (mostly case studies), that articles are descriptive and that they contain simple forms of inductive statistics (1995: 11). But even case-studies need to be scientifically rigorous and consider generalizability, transferability, and replicability (Bailey, 1992: 51).

Indeed, that articles are increasingly written by academics and then especially by those of senior rank (Bowman and Hajjar, 1978: 208; Houston and Delevan, 1990: 19; 1994, 256; Raadschelders and Lee, 2011), has apparently not been sufficient to relieve the study's identity crisis. And even if scholars often work with case-studies it does not absolve them from trying to.

There are two major problems standing in the way of a more "scientific" public administration and thus of developing theories original to the study. The first is that students of government have found a home in either public administration or political science, each of which has moved in very different directions. Some advised that public administration should stay close to political science because the latter provides more rigorous scientific training and because both studies emphasize different yet compatible levels of analysis (Whicker et al., 1993: 532–5). In response, Keller and Spicer argued that the advice of Whicker et al. hinges upon an instrumental understanding of public administration and a strong belief in quantitative research (1997: 270). Whicker et al. politely disagreed (1997). The second major problem is that of specialization. Theory development mainly occurs in the specializations of the study. PA-theory at the level of the study as a whole attracts much less attention (but see Frederickson, 1980; Wamsley et al., 1990; Wamsley and Wolf, 1996).

Public administration is a study that trains both (future) specialists as well as generalists and the latter category of civil servants is not only served by pre-occupation with theory-development at the level of the study's specializations. Posner observed that specialization has resulted in the decline of a common intellectual culture. Intellectuals are now specialists who can make errors that their educated audience will not notice simply because the latter are not a specialist in the area of the speaker. But, the generalist is condemned as an amateur whose views carry little weight (Posner, 2001: 53–5). One can say that the study of public administration has many specialists and specializations but no common epistemological and methodological culture. Consequentially, there is a dearth of studies that probe ideas relevant to the study as a whole. Waldo's political theory of administration (1948) and Frederickson's study of citizenship and civicness (1997) come to mind as some of the scarce examples.

5.3 PA-Theory for the Craft of Management: The "Doctor's Bag"

Studying techniques, cases, and proper styles of communication in and for administration started in earnest in the seventeenth century. The growth of the state prompted a surge in the study of administration, and especially of the various skills in and practices of administration (Raadschelders and Rutgers, 1999: 21). Despite efforts in nineteenth-century Europe at developing grand theory and providing an encompassing framework for the study, attention for the craft of administration and management stayed very much alive. The desire of developing a science of administration was balanced with an equally strong desire to provide administrators with usable knowledge. In the professional circles on both sides of the Atlantic, higher level administrators at local, and later regional and national, levels took the initiative and developed and implemented reform programs and practice-oriented training programs (Raadschelders, 1998a; Stillman, 1998; Stivers, 2000). In Europe, the independent study of administration was more or less abandoned until the 1970s. During the first half of the twentieth-century "science" in the United States and in Europe was equal to deductively articulating universal principles of administration that would help managers (Stivers, 2000: 127) and then especially at the local level. That characterizes much of the prewar study as a craft that is studied at the university. In Europe the "craft" element of public administration is usually situated in institutions of higher vocational education (Rouban, 2008).

Public administration as craft contains various specializations particularly in the areas of organization and management, personnel management, budgeting and finance, policy analysis, and program evaluation. They draw from whichever body of knowledge relevant. The craft-element is emphasized in education as is illustrated by the various simulations and case studies (much less common in Europe) used to make students familiar with both practice and with the underlying theoretical considerations. In the 1960s, Waldo argued that the study ought to adopt a professional perspective (1968b: 9). He compared public administration to medicine where the doctor's bag contains identified and usable instruments and techniques. The charge of public administration was to identify the content of this managerial "doctor's bag" (Wamsley et al., 1996: 366).

In this approach the emphasis is on theory for practical use. Some "theory" is inductive by nature and continues along the lines of prewar public administration; some theory is more deductive by nature. However, theory in public administration as craft is not theory-for-theories' sake (which remains a necessary and important academic pursuit) and the question is whether it is fair to assess the quality of this type of work by the positivist criteria for good research. Box outlined three difficulties in applying "mainstream" social science research techniques to public administration. First, the assertion that positivist methods provide an appropriate standard is not investigated and cannot, therefore, be assumed accurate. Second, while research in public administration is compared to that of other disciplines, the comparison rests upon personal rather than empirical observations. Furthermore, the state of research in other studies or disciplines is not measured. Finally, the positivist critique upon public administration research does not include a comparison to " . . . other practice-oriented disciplines such as law, planning, architecture, business administration, education, etc." (Box, 1992: 63). Where Dahl expressed concern about narrowing a science of administration to administrative techniques and processes (1947, 1), Box added the concern that a science of administration would narrow acquisition, understanding, and communication of knowledge to scientific methods, thus excluding other sources of knowledge (1992: 68).

Box's challenge was picked up two years later. Comparing public administration research to that of social work administration and business administration, Houston and Delevan concluded that public administration did not come out favorably. While they argued that practitioner-oriented studies have a wider variation in purpose and in methodological rigor than academic disciplines (1994: 265), they found that public administration scholars needed to improve the methodological competency of scholars doing quantitative work, that more rigorous use of quantitative methods might be fruitful, and that the demand for rigor and science would only increase. At the same time, though, they advised that the study should be willing to accept a multi-method approach characteristic for practice-oriented research (1994: 268).

The main challenge for theory development in public administration as a craft is to successfully "marry" usable and scientific knowledge. Discussing the nature of applied science, Simon presented the example of an engineer who works with scientific knowledge about characteristics of speed, maneuverability, cruising range, etc., of airplanes, but still has to figure out how this knowledge helps him in the design of a plane (1966: 34; 1981). As an analogy to the applied nature of public administration, though, it is of limited value, mainly because public administration concerns more than mere technical knowledge as Dahl already observed.

Practitioner-oriented as public administration may be, there continue to be concerns about the relation between practitioners and academics not unlike what is experienced in other practice-oriented studies. Bolton and Stolcis discuss five areas of tension between the needs of scholars and practitioners (based on Buckley, 1998) and a few years later discussed the relevance of public administration research for practice (Bolton and Stolcis, 2003:

627–8). Of the five tensions, three are relevant to the state of PA-theory (development):

1. Theoretical versus pragmatic knowledge: scholars emphasize development of theory, while practitioners are more focused on improving their managing skills;
2. Data-supported versus logical generalizations: practitioners will use logic to generalize about what they observe, while scholars will only generalize on the basis of data;
3. Scientific method versus cases and common sense.

The other two areas of tension (academic vs. professional journals, and tenure vs. organizational considerations) concern the organizational environment to which the scholar respectively practitioner belong. The relationship between academic and practitioner will always be problematic in the study of public administration. To argue, though, that the study has not produced usable knowledge of the kind desired by practitioners, obscures the fact that the latter do not acknowledge the degree to which public administration is not just an application of mere techniques but also must consider and weigh normative judgments. Waldo may have embraced a professional approach but continued to express concerns about too much emphasis on technical matters: "It is possible that historians of the future will puzzle over our fascination with our "technology" while alarm bells were ringing in all directions" (Waldo, 1987/1968: 368). Rainey stated that the idea as that theory and conceptualizations were not relevant to practitioners seriously underestimated the intellectual qualities of leaders and managers (1997: xvi–i).

5.4 PA-Theory for the Art of Governing: The "Artist's Medium"

Is PA-theory still possible and/or useful when public administration is regarded as an art? In Berlin's words "...successful statesmen behave like artists who understand their medium. They undertake courses of action or avoid others on grounds which they find it difficult if not impossible to explain in clear theoretical terms" (2000: 139; also Berlin, 1996: 45). On the same page (2000), he writes that:

> Judgment, skills, sense of timing, grasp of the relation of means to results depend upon empirical factors, such as experience, observation, above all on that "sense of reality" which largely consists in semi-conscious integration of a large number of apparently trivial or unnoticeable elements in the situation that between them form some kind of pattern which of itself "suggests" – "invites" – the appropriate action.

Assuming for the moment this to be a reasonable observation, it means that social reality cannot be captured completely in a "science." But, what is the alternative?

When the study of public administration started in the United States in the 1880s it had clearly a multi- if not interdisciplinary orientation as is illustrated by the program offered at Johns Hopkins (Hoffman, 2002). From the early 1900s on, though, the study increasingly narrowed to a more monodisciplinary focus around the concept of efficiency (McSwite, 1997; Stivers, 2000). Public administration concentrated both on its scientific and on its craft-side and left its liberal arts aspect behind. After the Second World War the central question became whether it was a science or an art. The need for professional education and for research in support of further developing professional skills was no longer contested. The "science" or "art" question is at the core of the identity crisis but is actually relevant to the social sciences at large: Can there be social science theory?

This question was raised by Flyvbjerg who offered four considerations with regard to the (im)possibility of social science theory (2001: 47). First, it had not been demonstrated that it was impossible for social science to become a normal science (the pre-paradigmatic argument). Second, the social sciences can only be as stable as people's situational self-interpretations of reality (the hermeneutic-phenomenological argument, which, i.a., resembles that of affirmative postmodernists – see next chapter). Third, any study concerned with human activity cannot generate cumulative knowledge since humans both constitute these studies and are its object. Finally, a cumulative social science presupposes a necessary yet impossible theory of human background skills. This last issue is the most difficult to tackle, yet has been frequently acknowledged as highly relevant by practitioners and academics both: To what degree does tacit knowledge plays a role in action and how can we capture (some of this) tacit knowledge?

In the introduction to his attempt at a more systematic and rational analysis of organizations and managers, Barnard observed that company executives were " . . . able to understand each other with very few words when discussing essential problems of organization" (1968: xxvii). He hoped to articulate better the tacit knowledge that formed and informed the actions and interactions of executives. Simon approvingly quoted Barnard's thesis that executives generally rely upon intuitive or judgmental responses rather than rational analysis (1997: 130). Is it possible to identify all the "rules" a swimmer (or: executive) observes when performing his skill, even when the performer himself cannot identify them (Polanyi, 1962: 49)? Tacit knowledge is displayed by the scientific or artistic genius (think of Crick and Watson's double helix of DNA, Ritter, 2003; or Weinberg's discovery of electroweak theory, Weinberg, 2001: 184–6) or by the expert medical diagnostician (Polanyi,

1966: 14–17). Reminiscent of Simon's bounded rationality argument are the three ways Nelson and Winter explain why conscious knowledge articulation is impossible and why, thus, tacit knowledge will always play a role. There is a limit upon the time that information can be processed (e.g., a tennis player can only adequately respond to a ball coming at him at 100 miles an hour if drawing upon tacit knowledge); a limit to the causal depth of our knowledge (e.g., a performer does not need to be aware of all variables relevant to the performance); and a limit to the degree that we can understand the coherence between the whole and the parts (e.g., exhaustive attention to detail will only produce an incoherent message) (1982: 80–1).

A philosopher of science himself, Polanyi argues that tacit knowledge is relevant to and operative in both the natural sciences and the humanities (1966: 17; I assume that the social sciences are included). Especially in the third essay of his 1966-study, he considers tacit knowledge necessary for the exercise of responsible judgment by administrators (cf. Aristotle's prudence or practical wisdom; see next chapter). Tacit knowing achieves comprehension by "indwelling" (1966: 55–6) which is echoed in Self's "intellectual appraisal" (1979: 192) and in Schön's "reflective practitioner" (1983). It " . . . dwells in our awareness of particulars while bearing on an entity which the particulars jointly constitute" (Polanyi, 1966: 61). A theory of background or tacit human skills is not possible, but can we teach in such a manner that an individual decision-maker is able to tap into the widest possible sources of knowledge?

Berlin wrote that statesmen are unique in the ability to understand an individual, a particular state of affairs, some combination of economic, social and personal forces, while " . . . we do not readily suppose that this capacity can be taught . . . " (1996: 45). However, the response of teachers in public administration to the practitioners' demand for "specialists in generalization" (Tead, 1935), for a "new Democratic Ruling Class" (Durham, 1940) (both Tead and Durham, practitioners, are quoted in Waldo, 1984: 95, 119–20), for "synthesizers of social wisdom" (Brownlow in 1934 as quoted in Stillman, 1991: 111), and for "administrators as philosophers" (Dimock, 1936: 129) was to advocate a return to the interdisciplinary study of the 1880s and 1890s. Dahl's observation as that the study must rest upon knowledge of both administrative techniques and processes as well as of history, sociology, and economics, and Waldo as that public administration should cast its net across the branches of knowledge (1984, 203) are illustrative of this and garnered massive support (Wald, 1973). However, the "craft" and "science" approaches to the study are so strong that this support for "art" has not translated into significant curricular revisions.

5.5 The Dynamic Arena of PA-Theory

That PA-theory can be mapped according to whether it is a science, craft, or art is clear. To do so is, in fact, the easy way out of a phenomenal conundrum. If PA-theory is mapped according to criteria of "science" then a variety of theories will not make the cut, but is it possible to disregard public administration theories that can be labeled as craft or art? So far the only example of a conceptual map of PA-theory that seeks to be inclusive of science, craft, and art approaches is that by Stever (Figure 5.1).

In his view, public administration theories can be positioned on axes that range from positive to negative positions and share four characteristics:

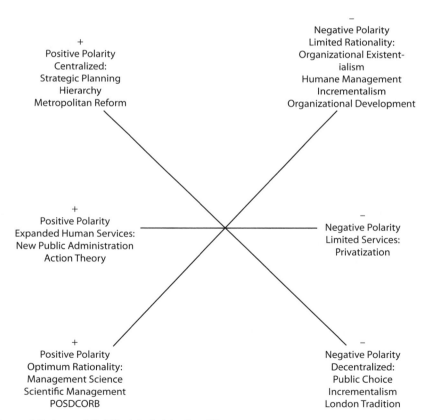

Figure 5.1 Axes of Public Administration Theory

Source: Stever (1988: 81) (N.B.: What Stever calls the London Tradition in Economics refers to the ideas of Von Mises and Von Hayek who condemned central planning, p.75) (reprinted with permission from Koninklijke Brill NV).

1. Theories of public administration are relative to others in that they express concern for a central problem or issue;
2. Theories of similar concern interact with each other along a common axis;
3. Within a given axis, there are theories taking positive or negative positions regarding the common, unifying issue of the axis; and
4. Numerous theoretical axes may occur within a given time period. Theoretical debates tend to occur among similar theories within a single axis, though they occasionally spill over and involve other axes (ibid.: 74).

He writes that public administration theory can be grouped along three axes: the structural, the rational, and the service axes and observes that, for instance, rational theorists cannot communicate with service theorists. In his view, developing public administration as a discipline requires that inter-action between theoretical perspectives is restored (ibid.: 83). This should not only be done just to meet the academic's desire for discipline but also to provide the public sector professional with an education that helps them to understand the meaning of their actions (ibid.: 98; Gawthrop, 1998: 19). Stever's conceptual map provides rather broad theoretical perspectives and few specific theories (e.g., public choice, incrementalism, scientific manage-ment). Problematic is that he does not clarify on what basis he determines that one concept or set of theories belongs to the positive respectively negative polarity. Can a conceptual map be made that categorizes various different types of approaches without mentioning specific theories, that is, without falling for the temptation to list public administration theories?

Public administration's identity crisis is mainly one between visions of "science" and of "art" but we must not forget that the study also has distinct elements of being a craft. What started in Antiquity as a study of the art of governing was complemented with a study of the craft of administration in the seventeenth century, and was finally completed with a science of admin-istration from the 1940s on, left the identity of the contemporary study of public administration unclear. The contemporary study of public administra-tion is the heir of these three very different, yet complementary, traditions in academe and practice (see for more Chapter 6).

Academics develop theories. All studies and disciplines that have found a home at the university are somehow involved in theorizing. Pondering the nature and status of PA-theory, two statements are relevant:

1. All academic endeavors manifest themselves as *science*, and/or *craft*, and/or *art*;
2. All academic endeavors can be categorized within a specific branch of knowledge: *natural sciences*, *social sciences*, or *humanities*.

With these statements, a 3×3 matrix can be plotted and one can attempt to fill the resulting cells with examples of authors. Such an exercise will quickly show how difficult it is to pigeon-hole authors in a study such as public administration.

In contrast to academe, practice looks for experience as well as for generalizable and usable knowledge. All knowledge studied and taught in a university setting has some practical application. Again, musing about the status and nature of PA-theory, two more statements must be considered:

1. Practical knowledge can be categorized as *theoretical*, and/or *applied*, and/or *reflective and interpretative*;
2. Practice works with *knowledge, experience*, and/or *intuition*.

This begets another 3×3 matrix and, again, it will be difficult to place public administration scholars in a single cell. To assess the nature and status of PA-theory these two matrices are combined.

The arena of PA-theory is influenced by four forces situated at the four corners in Figure 5.2: *scientific knowledge, historical and evolutionary knowledge, reasoned knowledge*, and *tacit knowledge*. Some comments are necessary on how to read this figure. It is not a traditional matrix. Instead, it is an arena (the nine cells in the middle of the matrix) where theories to lesser or greater extent "feel" the influence of each of the corners. Scientific knowledge in the upper-left corner is focused on pure science and based on rational knowledge that pictures the universe as operating according to universal laws and structures that can be discovered by pure reason (cf. Descartes) and/or through empirical science. This is the realm of the natural sciences. Reasoning involves processes of the mind such as imagining, experimenting, thinking, and reflecting (the

Scientific knowledge		Basic approach			**Reasoned knowledge**	
		Science	*Craft*	*Art*		
Branches of Learning	*Natural sciences*	Natural sciences	Principles of organization and management	Public administration as political theory	*Theory*	
	Social sciences	Positivism	Case study	Critical theory	*Application*	Type of knowledge
	Humanities	Administrative history, hermeneutics	Organizational memory	Berlin's "artist's medium"	*Wisdom*	
Historical and evolutionary knowledge		*Explicit knowledge*	*Explicit experience*	*Intuition*	**Tacit knowledge**	
			Object of study			

Figure 5.2 Conceptual Map 4, the Dynamic Arena of PA-Theory
Source: Adapted from Raadschelders (2004: 64) (with permission from M.E. Sharpe).

distinction between rationality and reasoning based on Vanelli, 2001: 1). Reasoned knowledge in the top-right corner straddles the art of governing and theorizing about government and governing. Historical and evolutionary knowledge in the lower left corner has the features of a humanities' study that tries to make sense of trends over time through understanding (e.g., *Verstehen*). Tacit knowledge, finally, draws upon intuition and wisdom. The more a particular theory can be situated toward a "corner," the less it will feel the "pull" of the other "corners." The identity crisis debate takes place most in the upper half of this arena, but it is clear that the practice of government and the study of public administration are more than just theory (the right side of this arena) and also include application and wisdom.

Each cell can be filled with theories, approaches, concepts, and examples of representative authors and one can only begin to imagine the objections to such an exercise. By way of example, positivism is placed in the left middle cell. Gulick's principles of organization and of management (cf. PODSCORB) fit very well in the craft category in the upper row, since he was convinced that such principles were universal. Scholars after the Second World War may be inclined to place Gulick's principles in the middle row, arguing that he was misguided in his belief that there are universal principles of organization.

Keep in mind that this arena is merely an attempt to conceptualize the complexity of public administration theory. There are various objections conceivable. A first objection is that some concepts in the model are not very well demarcated. For instance, is "explicit experience" not the same as "explicit knowledge" (consider the distinction made in Chapter 2 between pre-rational, experiential knowledge, and rational knowledge)? A second objection is that authors cannot really be placed in one cell. Some publications of an author may fit in one cell, other publications in another. A third objection concerns the structure of the figure. With two *X*- and two *Y*-axes the presentation is perhaps unnecessarily complicated. A fourth objection could be that the boundaries between the cells are fluid; perhaps a dotted line illustrates better the osmosis between the cells. However, the figure does illustrate why it is difficult to assess the nature and status of PA-theory. There is PA-theory in all cells except in the top-left corner and in this style of presentation none is superior.

5.6 What we Dare not Say...

The model in the previous section provides a map of the riches of theories and perspectives to which Frederickson and Wamsley pointed. It also shows that the study of public administration is "torn" apart by centrifugal forces. Any effort at strengthening the centripetal forces is quickly identified as coming from one "corner" and thus disregarded by others. Needless to say, the quality of communication between various approaches to the study leaves much to be desired (Section 5.6.1). In Figure 5.2 the interests of practitioners can be situated in the middle cell, because, as generalists, they are assumed to be cognizant of the degree to which the questions and nature of the study are influenced by all "corners." That being so, the interaction between academics and practitioners does not seem to rise beyond the usual stereotyping of the "too theoretical" versus the "too practical" variety (Section 5.6.2). This model also includes explicitly the importance of tacit knowledge. While we cannot teach it, we must assure that (future) practitioners are exposed to wide-ranging vistas across (at least) the social sciences and the humanities (Section 5.6.3).

5.6.1 ... about Academic Communication Concerning PA-Theory...,

In his speech accepting ASPA's Waldo Award, Simon suggested that "There was no real conflict between Dwight's vision and mine..." but that in 1952 they had "...managed to exchange some rather purple prose" (Simon, 1995: 404). However, anyone reading Simon's response to Dahl's article or his review of Waldo's book (1948) recognizes that, at the time, Simon perceived a vast difference between him and others and used strong language in advocating his approach. Nowadays, it sometimes appears as if "purple prose" is reserved for the anonymous review of submitted articles. There is some debate in public administration, but that mostly concerns exchanges about theoretical issues in the specializations. Debate about the nature of the study appears to be more a series of statements rather than a true back-and-forth between scholars of different persuasion.

The "mainstream" academics in ASPA talk with each other, but, do they mostly confer within their specializations or do they actually have substantive discussions about the nature of the study across specializations (see Stever, 1988)? It is also not clear what exactly constitutes "mainstream." The mainstream includes possibly those who embrace a science, and/or craft, and/or art approach to administration. In the "periphery," meanwhile, members of the Public Administration Theory Network (PatNet) and its journal *Administrative Theory & Praxis* happily converse with one another, with some publishing in "mainstream" journals (see Miller and Islam, 2003) while others do not.

The dialogue between mainstream and periphery is more limited than it ought to be. More precisely, the dialogue between representatives of the science, the craft, and the art approaches to public administration is much too limited. It is one thing to say that different viewpoints did not inhibit friendly and informal meetings (as illustrated by the lunches that Simon and Waldo continued to have together), but it is quite another to simply ignore the substantive issues and merits of approaches other than one's own. Simon did, and the heirs of both Simon and Waldo have. Is that mistake still made? That Frederickson and Smith (2003) and Denhardt (2004) consider, for example, feminist and postmodern approaches may be a sign that some scholars are considering approaches that used to be identified as periphery. At the same time, though, Dubnick's attack upon "mainstream" and anti-positivist public administration (1999) was never graced with a response in print even though it sought to revive that debate. This is especially important because in the closing remark of his paper, Dubnick writes that PA-theorists have been so much focused on the potential threat of valueless positivism that they failed to notice the degree to which the sharp distinctions between objectivism and relativism or between modernism and postmodernism have become blurred, and that the social sciences at large have moved toward more open and diverse positions on standards for research and theory (1999: 41).

The quality of communication between various approaches might improve when scholars manage to develop meta-frameworks that pull knowledge from various specializations together in combination with knowledge from other disciplines. Instead of stereotyping, scholars of the various approaches should look for strengths in each other and not only point to weaknesses in others. It is one thing to point out weaknesses in public administration research and theory of the past 20–30 years or so; it is quite another, and possibly more challenging, effort to outline its strengths.

5.6.2 ... about the Communication between Academics and Practitioners ... ,

ASPA was created in 1939 to provide an institutional home for pracademics (practitioners who adjunct in academe) and acapracs (academics who participate in, e.g., governmental think-tanks and commissions) (both constructs from Waldo). The Brownlow Committee had a membership drawn from both academe and praxis. The academic–practitioner balance was consciously built into ASPA. They talk with each other but represent two very different worlds with very different organizational needs. Academics are quite active in practice, especially when considering that many are employed part-time as consultants, are involved in citizen committees at various levels of government (especially at local level), or occupy political office. Practitioners still adjunct in various public administration programs, and certainly so in the United States.

Despite such interaction there is still a good bit of stereotyping going on between academics and practitioners. This is somewhat surprising since the practitioners who attend ASPA conferences are generally highly educated and hold advanced degrees. Practitioners hold that academics work too much in an ivory tower, that their research does not really meet the demand for usable knowledge, that their research runs behind current events, and that the standard answer to practical questions is that more research is needed. Academics believe that practitioners want simple and assured solutions to complex problems, that practitioners have no clue of how difficult it is to capture a complex reality in a theoretical framework or model without too much simplification, that practitioners only look at value for money, that practitioners are too much focused on immediate gratification of citizen demand, and that they lack the ability to reflect.

There are academics supporting the practitioners' concerns about the relevance of scholarly research. A few years ago " . . . a noteworthy disconnection between the published research [in PAR] and the knowledge needs identified by ICMA-members . . . " was reported (Streib et al., 2001: 522). Others made a case that different students may well need a different mix of theory and practice and that the market ought to be explored for an advanced practitioner degree (Denhardt, 2001: 532) or even a professional doctorate in governance (Dror, 2001: 124). A professional doctorate was, for instance, offered through the DPA – program of the Washington Public Affairs Institute, a branch of the University of Southern California, between 1973 and 2001 (Sherwood, 2008; Radin, 2010). The question whether the gap between academics and practitioners is growing has not been empirically investigated, but there probably is a gap and its consequences for public administration theory need to be addressed. In the Waldonian approach, theory and practice stay connected; it is the material object of study that determines what theories are used in a particular research project. Hence, Waldonians advocate interdisciplinarity. In the Simonian approach, theory is pursued and advanced for its own sake; to them it is the formal object of the study that determines how reality is studied. Thus, Simonians embrace monodisciplinarity.

Here we see another explanation for the identity crisis emerging. Practitioners may well find the Waldonian approach more palatable, more wide-ranging, and more practical. There are quite a few academics who identify with Waldo's heritage. Several academics, though, find Simon's pure science more attractive and are not as much interested in the degree to which their knowledge contributes to the solution of social problems. ASPA has members of all varieties (practitioners and academics in either the Waldo or Simon heritage).

Is it not about time, though, to emphasize that practitioners can and have been reflective (such as, e.g., Brownlow, 1937; Barnard, 1938; Hartmann and Khademian, 2010); that practitioners can and have pursue(d) theoretically informed interests; that practitioners acknowledge the importance of theory (Englehart, 2001; Denhardt, 2004: 187); and that mid-career practitioners in advanced programs are delighted to see how theory explains and enlightens the experiences in their own organization (as I heard from many middle and

145

higher level civil servants from the United States and a variety of other countries)? Is it also not time to emphasize that sometimes academics must withdraw into science; that academics do not cater to short-term needs only; that academics in their research simplify the complexity of the real world already more than they are comfortable with? One can even wonder whether the existence of a gap between academics and practitioners is so deplorable. After all, both work in very different arenas and developing a one-size-fits-all approach to the study of public administration may well dissatisfy both academics and practitioners.

5.6.3 ... and about what the Study Cannot and Can/Ought to Do

For much of the twentieth century the study of public administration focused on efficiency. Waldo pointed out that "efficiency" is not as value-neutral as initially had been assumed. Simon, on the other hand, pointed out that administrators must have a thorough appreciation of the theory of efficiency (1997: 327) as a basis for any broader understanding of an organization's work. Up to a point the study of public administration can teach about "efficiency" using various different methods of assessing it (e.g., cost–benefit analysis, SWOT-analysis, performance measurement, etc.). At the same time, it cannot teach a one-best theory of efficiency. What is efficient depends very much upon the task or service at hand, the organization, the officeholder, the time-context, etc.

From the early 1900s onward, the American study of public administration emphasized specialization and the development of technically oriented skills. Since the 1930s, several practitioners in and scholars of public administration advocated the need for generalists. Waldo warned against over-emphasizing technocratic approaches. Since the 1970s the study has become more interdisciplinary and its interests branched out into a variety of directions. In a way an interdisciplinary study provides the foundation of wide-ranging knowledge that the future practitioner can tap into when developing policy and making decisions about complex social issues. At the same time, though, the study cannot teach wisdom and there are no theories about how tacit knowledge can be put to better use.

A study that reflects and interprets, connects depth (specialized knowledge and theories) with breadth in such a manner that public servants can draw upon various bodies of and approaches to knowledge so that the tradition of public intellectualism – so strong in America until the 1980s (Melzer et al., 2003) – is revived. The study of public administration should not only teach theories and applications, it should also teach about the nature of history and society in any given country. After all, government serves society and the study cannot afford to be disconnected from the major questions about and challenges in the society in which it is embedded. Therefore, public administration curricula should include social commentaries of both left-of-center (in the United States, e.g., Croly, Lippmann, Bellah, Nisbet, Bok, etc.) and right-of-center (in the United States, e.g., Bell, Fukuyama, Lasch, Schumpeter, etc.) authors for it informs the student and future practitioner not only about the society in which they live and to which they will contribute but also helps them to recognize the ideological issues that underlie theories about government.

5.7 PA-Theory must Satisfy Generalists as well as Specialists

The first question in the opening section was: Given the different origins (art, craft, science) of the study of public administration as it is today, what is the nature and status of PA-theory? Science and craft can be found in the various specializations. At the generalist level, art and craft can be found. Where public administration is a study defined by its material object, its theoretical make-up is a mosaic with a rich variety of theories and conceptualizations about government that are successfully used in public administration scholarship. However,

> ...certain fields of human endeavor display an orderliness that lends itself to scientific precision and measurement, and to the development of rules, laws and principles [...] Other fields of human endeavor, while not random, are much less orderly and, therefore, less amenable to scientific precision and to management. There is simply no question that building more freeways is much easier than figuring out how to improve inner-city public education. (Frederickson, 2003: 1)

Hence, applying academic insights in practice will always be a challenge, to say the least. Middle-range PA-theory, as used in the specializations, is in good shape but we must remember time-and-again the limitations of that knowledge when not considered in its consequences for knowledge in other specializations and for application in the real world.

The second question was: Given the fact that public administration's material object of study is government, can the study of public administration develop a theory of government? Obviously, there is no theory of government. Such a theory is so far inhibited by strong convictions about public administration as science, as craft, or as art. A theory of government, though, might be possible when considering how knowledge generated by the science of administration, the craft of administration, and the art of governing can complement each other. Conceiving of public administration as a study working with different levels of abstraction and application is a start. The next step would be to bring scholars together of different persuasion (scientists, craftsmen, artists) to muse about a theory of government in an atmosphere of mutual respect. The challenges confronting government are not served by turf-battles between scientists, craftsmen and artists. They are served by cooperation and open-mindedness and are facilitated by dropping the shackles of any single approach.

Is this easier said than done given that there are so many theories and models used in public administration? When listing theories and models in an effort to be complete, it must seem an almost endless exercise, but it is possible to place these into an arena or "force-field" and thus acquire some level of clarity about the nature of our study. It is also possible to categorize the bewildering variety of theories and models into a few intellectual traditions as we shall see in Chapter 6.

6

Four Intellectual Traditions in the Study of Public Administration

> It is to be presumed and desired that students of government will play a larger role in the future than in the past in shaping of the types of civic education; but this will not be possible unless *a broader view is taken of the relation of government to the other social sciences, and the function of the political in the social setting.* (Merriam, 1934; emphasis CM)

The status of the study of public administration in academe is not as unproblematic as European handbooks tend to show, and, at the same time, much more coherent than comes across in American handbooks. In Europe the study is generally rooted in two, quite distinct, organizational settings. At the university level, on the one hand, curricula focus on teaching theory, while research concerns both theoretical and practical, applied challenges. At institutions of higher vocational education, on the other hand, teaching is much more hands-on, focused on particular skills in, for instance, personnel management, budgeting and finance, etc.

In the United States, public administration curricula and research are situated at the university where attention for theory and for practical skills are combined in an intellectual atmosphere that favors "science" and facts over *Wissenschaft*. Scholarship in Europe is generally more understood in terms of *Wissenschaft*. Another distinction between European and American scholarship is that handbooks in the former tend to develop an organic and systematic perspective upon the study as a whole, while US handbooks display the study more as a string of specializations. On both continents, though, scholars distinguish a scientific approach from other approaches. This highlights the specific problem of public administration's status in academe: Is it and ought it be a science in the restricted sense or has it, is it, and ought it be *Wissenschaft* which includes science, skills, wisdom, and a variety of relativist perspectives?

To answer this question the American crisis of identity crisis literature is used as point of departure (Section 6.1) since it clearly demonstrates the fundamental challenge of the study. In Section 6.2, four general traditions to the study of government in public administration are outlined, relevant to and salient for PA-scholarship anywhere in the world. Each tradition is host to a variety of theories, models, and approaches. Illustrative examples of European and American scholarship will be provided in the more detailed discussion of the four traditions (Sections 6.3–6.6). That the work of many more scholars is not referenced should not be regarded as dismissive, but is simply a function of the enormous number of publications available. Perhaps the four intellectual traditions can be regarded as ideal types, useful to characterize existing scholarship. To that end, similarities and differences between these traditions are outlined and summarized in Section 6.7. In the concluding section (Section 6.8), an argument is presented that advocates public administration as an interdisciplinary pursuit.

6.1 Once More: The American Identity Crisis in the Study of Public Administration

It is intriguing that public administration's "crisis of identity," as Waldo called it (1968a: 443), has been mainly debated between "scientists" and "holists," also referred to as positivists and "traditionalists" (White and McSwain, 1990: 5), or as rationalists' and "normativists" (Harmon, 2006: 31) (i.e., between "science" and "art"). Scientists like Simon then and Meier and O'Toole now advocate more rigorous research methods with an eye on developing public administration as a science and a true academic discipline in relation to specific problems and/or topics. Holists such as Waldo, Stillman, and Wamsley are more concerned with the understanding of government as a whole and emphasize its service to the community and the public sector at large. To them public administration trains professionals as well as scholars and is by nature an interdisciplinary study that moves between and draws upon the social sciences at large.

When Simon accepted the Dwight Waldo Award in 1995, he graciously observed that the study of public administration had absorbed two revolutions: his own call for a scientific approach (Simon, 1957) and Waldo's advocacy for an interdisciplinary approach (1984; Simon, 1995: 404). Simon criticized the lack of true scientific methods, and Waldo pointed to the fundamentally value-laden nature of the study. Simon stressed the need for science in his exchanges with Dahl (1947; Simon, 1966), with Waldo (1952a/1952b; Simon, 1952), with Banfield (1957; Simon, 1958), and with Argyris (1973a, 1973b; Simon, 1973a, 1973b), while Waldo increasingly came to regard public administration as a professional study. This was not novel. Already in the late 1930s William Mosher, Dean of the Maxwell School, argued that administrators could be trained "...in much the same way as physicians and engineers are equipped for the practice of their profession" (as quoted in McCurdy and Cleary, 1984: 49), but it was Waldo who gave this approach wide currency.

It took a while for this debate between scientists and holists to spread but by the end of the 1960s it was widely acknowledged that public administration suffered from an identity crisis (Waldo, 1968a and b; V. Ostrom, 1974). Was it a science, a profession, or...what? The debate was joined by a variety of scholars in the 1980s and 1990s, some siding with "Simonian" calls for more scientific rigor (McCurdy and Cleary, 1984; Perry and Kraemer, 1986, 1990; White, 1986a, 1968b; Stallings and Ferris, 1988; Houston and Delevan, 1990, 1994; Mainzer 1994; White et al., 1996; Dubnick, 1999) and others with "Waldonian" calls for an interdisciplinary public administration more rele-vant to society and operating with a variety of theoretical perspectives (Mar-ini, 1971; Waldo, 1971; Frederickson, 1980; Wamsley et al., 1990; Wamsley and Wolf, 1996). This contrast between "scientists" and "holists" has lost nothing of its intensity as is illustrated by De Zwart (2002) in his confronta-tion of Farmer (1999) and by the recent exchange between Luton (2007) and Meier and O'Toole (2007). The two groups of contestants have been so vocal that they overshadow the degree to which prewar, inductive public adminis-tration survives while at the same time it prevents a proper assessment of the most recent tradition in public administration, that is, the relativist perspec-tives generally associated with postmodernism.[1]

The search for identity in public administration may never be complete as long as it is cast in terms of knowledge rankings. American scholars of public administration are both guided and blinded by the contrast between scientists and holists and do not fully acknowledge that

1. the study of public administration may have one identity crisis engaging two groups of contestants, but that there are – at least – four intellectual traditions in the Western world at large;
2. specialization for epistemological purposes results in compartmentaliza-tion of knowledge, prohibiting the development of a comprehensive and multifaceted understanding of government.

This is both a practical and a pedagogical concern. It is interesting that Simon and Waldo could not be further apart when discussing the epistemological

---

[1] One can argue that there never really has been a debate. Advocates of one approach tend to talk past rather than with protagonists of other approaches. Harmon (2006: 34) observes that rationalists only engage in more philosophical debate when they are provoked.

objective of the study, but explicitly agreed with Merriam on the pedagogical need: that is, understanding government from a wide range of disciplinary insights:

> ...the proper training of "administrators" lies not in the narrow field of administrative theory, but *in the broader field of the social sciences generally*. (Simon, 1957: 247; emphasis added)

> ...administrative thought must establish a working relationship with *every major province in the realm of human learning*. (Waldo, 1984: 501; emphasis added)

6.2 A Conceptual Map of Intellectual Traditions for Studying Government

Scholarly attention to government dates back to Antiquity, but its concentration in two increasingly separated studies (public administration and political science) is only about seventy years old. Currently, the major challenge is to make sense of the vast range of approaches that proliferated against the background of an unprecedented expansion of government since the late nineteenth century. The desire to understand and explain this government growth has spawned dramatic specialization and compartmentalization of knowledge within public administration and across the social sciences. Indeed, looking at American handbooks, the study often comes across as a series of specializations each with its own theories, models, and interpretations. It is tempting to conceptualize the study as a large variety of theories, as for instance Frederickson and Smith have done (2003), but that only reinforces the long-standing impression that public administration lacks a core and consists only of a series of specializations and disjointed theories. The conclusion that the study lacks a core can only be reached, though, if one evaluates public administration's current status in terms of a scientific discipline, that is, with a logic, rigor, and epistemology that is distinct from other disciplines. An entirely different conclusion can be reached when public administration is regarded as an interdisciplinary study whose core is defined by the object of study (government) rather than by theories and methods. Public administration can and should be defined on its own ground, and not on inappropriate comparisons to other studies which claim to have (political science) or do have an epistemological and methodological core (the natural sciences). In other words, it is possible to develop a meaningful conceptual map of intellectual traditions in public administration.

Four intellectual traditions to the study of and the discourse about government can be distinguished. Each has a unique objective for the study of government. In order of their emergence over time, they are:

1. a study *for* the development of practical wisdom (e.g., Waldo, Frederick-son, Rhodes, Rutgers, Hood, König). The focus is on political (and since the late eighteenth century also: administrative) theory and includes attention for, among other things, world view, public morality, the ruler's (since the late eighteenth century both political officeholders and civil servants) disposition toward and his relation with citizens, and the development of "grand theory" (Section 6.3);
2. a study *for* the development of practical experience (e.g., Taylor, Gulick, Fayol, Hood, Mayntz). This work is more technocratic in orientation and focuses on instruments and techniques useful in day-to-day administration and for on-the-job experiential learning (Section 6.4);
3. a study *for* the development of scientific knowledge (e.g., Simon, Meier (in terms of "science"); Auby et al., Luhmann, Rhodes, Van Braam and Bemelmans-Videc (in terms of *Wissenschaft*). This work searches for a "scientific" or *Wissenschatftliche* and/or unifying theory (Section 6.5);
4. a study *of* relativist perspectives, more often referred to as postmodern-ism, a term that includes a variety of different approaches (e.g., Farmer, Fox, Miller, Box, Bogason, Frissen). This work emphasizes interpretation and subjectivity (Section 6.6).

These four traditions can be placed on a continuum from objective to subjective approaches (see Figure 6.1), but note that the continuum extends on both sides beyond the four approaches where complete objectivity respectively complete subjectivity reside.

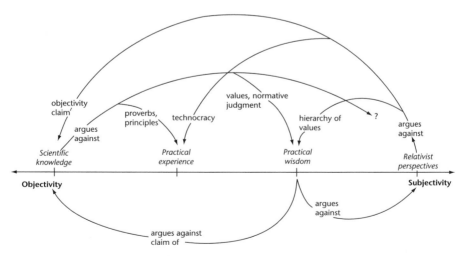

Figure 6.1 A Continuum of Four Approaches to the Study of Public Administration
Source: Raadschelders (2005: 607) (reprinted with permission from M.E. Sharpe).

The scientific knowledge approach, especially in the United States, is critical of the other traditions. It criticizes practical experience for working on the basis of proverbs, intuition, and induction. Positivists also consider the interpretivism, normative underpinnings, and eclectic interdisciplinarity of the practical wisdom tradition as flawed, especially for not distinguishing facts from values. Positivists basically ignore postmodernism (hence the question mark in Figure 6.1). In turn, postmodernists disagree with the hierarchy of values implicit in practical wisdom (that is the pluralism of truths grounded in an inter-subjectivity that rejects relativism; see Berlin, 2000: 11–12), criticize the "technocratic" focus of practical experience, and challenge the positivist's claim of objective reality. In this continuum, scholars focusing on the skills of practical experience or on the historical, philosophical outlook of practical wisdom do not criticize but augment one another. The four approaches can also be visualized as a force field (Figure 6.2).

The horizontal axis represents a continuum from theory to practice; the vertical axis represents a continuum of timeless theories versus time and context bound theories. The upper half of the model is the realm of laws and principles. Both scientific knowledge and practical experience look for these. Practical wisdom and relativist perspectives deal much more with interpretations. Scientific knowledge, practical experience, and practical wisdom seek to generalize and are in that sense comparable to each other. Relativist

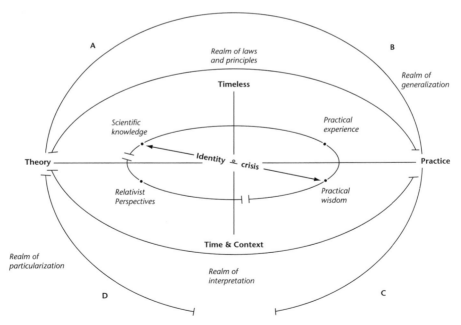

Figure 6.2 A Force Field of Four Approaches to Studying Government

perspectives focus on what is unique and they are somewhat disconnected from the other three perspectives or approaches as is visualized in a "break" in the outer and in the inner "ovals."

As mentioned earlier, the identity of public administration in the United States is mainly debated between representatives of scientific knowledge and of practical wisdom. European scholars debate the same issues but generally with much less purple prose than their American colleagues (e.g., Rhodes, 1991; Rutgers, 1993). More importantly, European scholars appear to have embraced public administration as an interdisciplinary study rather than as one that ought to strive for "science" or for professionalism (e.g., Chevallier and Loschak, 1974; Hesse, 1982; Bouckaert and Van den Donk, 2010). In other words, in Europe there have not really been two clear camps of contestants.

The positivist critique in public administration is that research is not cumulative enough, not rigorous enough, too eclectic, and too little focused on testing theory. Mainstream public administration has not taken its responsibility as a social science as, for instance, Dubnick (1999) and Gill and Meier (2000) argued, and this suggests that a pure science of administration is much less rooted in the study than an interdisciplinary and professional orientation. Simon's influence is larger among political scientists (including that group of more than half of public administration scholars who identify with political science; Ellwood, 1996: 56), business administration scholars, and organizational sociologists. Waldo's influence is believed to be greater in the study of public administration (Dubnick, 1999: 11–20; De Zwart, 2002: 485) and has inspired the search for an identity specific to public administration. In the United States, the Minnowbrook-I conference (that spawned the New Public Administration (NPA); see Marini, 1971; Waldo, 1971; Frederickson, 1980), the Minnowbrook-II conference (Frederickson and Mayer, 1989), and the Blacksburg Manifesto (BM) (Wamsley et al., 1990: 31–51) were all major attempts to flesh out a theoretical and/ or normatively grounded identity for public administration in the postwar era. The NPA, though, has not generated a major theoretical reform of public administration (O'Toole, 1977; Bozeman, 1979: 45; Stillman, 1999a: 2–3), but raised awareness for social equity, non-governmental organizations, social movements (Candler, 2008: 301), and participative values (Dyson, 1980: 214). The same can be said for the BM. Both continue, however, to inspire (White and McSwain, 1990; Wamsley and Wolf, 1996; Frederickson, 1997; Stillman, 1999a; Raadschelders, 1999, 2003a, 2003b). European handbooks so far clearly show a holistic public administration. Its scholars are much less confrontational than their American brethren, perhaps because of the more explicit acceptance of the study's interdisciplinarity.

6.3 Practical Wisdom

The earliest discussion of practical wisdom is found in Kautilya's *Arthaśāstra* and in Aristotle's *The Nicomachean Ethics* and includes attention for both intuition and "science" in the restricted sense (Aristotle, 1976: 209–16; Björkman, 2003). Ample attention is given to prudent leadership in a time when politics was central to government. Also part of the practical wisdom tradition is the so-called "mirrors of princes" (*Fürstenspiegel*) literature which dates back to the (West) European Middle Ages and Renaissance of which Machiavelli's *The Prince* is the best known example. In the practical wisdom tradition, three fundamental questions are raised: Where are we going? Is it desirable to go there? What can we do to get there? (Flyvbjerg, 2001: 63). To answer these questions, a ruler must understand the social context in which action is taken, understand the nature of the actual and desired relation between ruler and ruled, and have some command over knowledge about government.

Practical wisdom in Antiquity provided several crucial elements to the Western approach to understanding government, including the selection of moral reasoning and logical arguments as a knowledge base to be used by the guardians (or trustees, stewards) of society, a knowledge ideal of moral truth and grand theory (but see the challenge to this particular legacy from the late eighteenth century on in Berlin, 1999), a methodology of reflection and comparison, and a focus on drawing upon various bodies of knowledge commonly referred to as interdisciplinarity. Interdisciplinarity is often defined in terms of a unity of knowledge based on an integration of concepts and theories from various disciplines. For instance, Dogan appears to define interdisciplinarity in terms of relations between whole disciplines. In his view political science maintains only relations between sectors of different disciplines and is therefore not interdisciplinary (1996: 97). However, whenever there are active relations between disciplines, in terms of an exchange of knowledge regarding a particular material object, there is interdisciplinarity. Successful mapping of this interdisciplinarity, though, requires a meta-framework.

Representatives of the effort to develop such meta-frameworks in the nineteenth century include German scholars such as Von Mohl, Von Stein, and Wagner (cf. grand theory) (Rutgers, 1994: 400–1). Among the twentieth century authors, there is the monumental Weber who was deeply concerned with substantive issues and problems that he believed to be larger than any single approach could handle (Lindenfeld, 1997: 296; see also Waldo, 1965, 1978, 1984: 203). Post-war representatives of this approach include various American and European scholars. In the United States, Waldo's comprehensive approach to public administration fits well in the practical wisdom approach and perhaps represents "soft-core rationalism" (in contrast to Simon's "hard-core rationalism") (Harmon, 1995: 4). Frederickson fits in this approach given his interests in citizenship and public sector ethics (1997). Stillman's search for sources and themes of public administration represents an historical approach befitting practical wisdom (1999b). The habit of looking at public administration through different lenses (legal, political, managerial), as Rosenbloom did (1983), is equally characteristic for practical wisdom. Morgan's carefully developed argument for administrative phronesis, that is, the discretion and autonomy civil servants must have in order to develop workable, acceptable, and fitting solutions to social problems, is yet another example (1990: 73–4). Lindblom fits in this tradition since his partisan mutual adjustment is as much grounded in specialist knowledge as it is in lay probing (1990). Finally, Wamsley and Wolf may label themselves as high-modern (1996: 22–4), but their object (a normative grounding) and style of reasoning puts them squarely in the practical wisdom group. Representatives of this tradition in Europe include Hood whose study of the rhetoric of public management challenges the possibility of singular perspectives (1998). Another example is Rutgers and his attention for the development of public administration from its philosophical and historical origins (2004). European handbook authors fit equally well in this tradition.

This tradition is generalist by nature and eludes the modeling necessary for the development of a "natural science"-style public administration. Some scholars consider practical wisdom's interdisciplinarity its greatest weakness. For instance, Mainzer wondered whether "... hostility to disciplines reflects deep distrust of *discipline*?" (1994: 364; italics in original). He suggested that interdisciplinarity may mask a fuzzy eclecticism that lacks a sense of what is most significant because the study has failed to develop a theory at the core (1994: 383). He advised public administration to stay close to a "... philosophically sensitive, historical alert political science..." (1994: 384). In his view, mere interdisciplinarity may very well lead to pseudo-learning and superficiality (1994: 383).

However, there are several considerations supporting the notion of public administration as an interdisciplinary venture. First, a social phenomenon as complex as government, internally complex with its multiple organizations and policies, as well as externally in its multiple relations with society, cannot be understood within one discipline or approach. Public administration is a study that does not fit the disciplinary mold (Wamsley, 1996: 354) and is fed (in part) by theories and concepts of various traditional disciplines. At the same time, public administration must always balance the theoretical interests of its scholars with those of its practitioners since, in the end the latter must be synthesizers of social wisdom. Interdisciplinarity breaks through the linguistic

157

and conceptual isolation that may come from being too focused on unified theory and methodology (Nelson and Winter, 1982: 405).

Second, it provides an excellent context for a generalist outlook on government that goes beyond the applied skills knowledge of the specialists and considers a more expansive outlook on what is usable (Lindblom and Cohen, 1979). Third, practical wisdom draws upon common sense, and therefore allows for incremental learning through experience (Lindblom 1990). Related to this, fourth, it works with the existence of human background skills, that is with the tacit knowledge (see Polanyi, 1962, 1966; Nelson and Winter, 1982: 80–1) that supports the intuition and judgment (Simon, 1997a: 130) with which businessmen (Barnard, 1968: xxvii), statesmen (Berlin, 1996: 45), and civil servants (Self, 1979: 192; Schön, 1983) operate. Fifth, in its explicit philosophical, political theory, historical and comparative content, it acknowledges (not resigns itself to) different national traditions in public administration. Finally, in its embrace of moral reasoning, judgment, and interpretation, practical wisdom conditions "respect" for different viewpoints and approaches.

6.4 Practical Experience

The systematic pursuit of practical experience, a tradition with an eye for description and prescription, starts with Von Seckendorf's study (1656). Practical experience develops further in the eighteenth century *Kameralistiek* in the German principalities and in the French *science de la police* (also: policey science). Cameralism in the limited sense concerns the administration of the king's income and domains. In the broader sense it encompasses economics, politics, and social studies. While seventeenth century studies in the German principalities focus on the internal structure and functioning of government through examples/cases (Dyson, 1980: 86; Rutgers, 1994: 281), eighteenth century scholarship branches out into the study of public welfare services (Rutgers, 1994: 284; 2001: 33–41). Until the late eighteenth century, Germanic scholarship mainly concerns practical implementation techniques based in Aristotle's ethically directed practical wisdom (Lindenfeld, 1997: 2). From then on the state sciences split into politics as a natural law science that studies the nature of the state, types of government, and constitutions on the one hand and the study of laws and administrations of particular states on the other (Lindenfeld, 1997: 19). Likewise, the French policey science focuses on practical experience, non-juridical training for civil servants, and on the need for public welfare services (Rutgers, 1994: 281–2). In the nineteenth century, the German *Staatswissenschaften* and the French *sciences administratives* turn toward the development of a unified (i.e., in grand theory style) administrative science (as *Wissenschaft*).

By the end of the nineteenth century, the university-based study of government in Germany is supplemented with privately and municipally funded commercial academies because businessmen and industrialists find that academic theories no longer meet their need for practical skills (Lindenfeld, 1997: 286). In France (Fayol) and elsewhere in Europe, the enthusiastic adoption of Scientific Management (Fry and Raadschelders, 2008: 75) is an excellent example of practical experience. Other developments indicating a need for applied knowledge include the emergence of training programs at local and state levels in the United States and elsewhere from the 1880s onward (e.g., Raadschelders, 1998*a*: 17; Stillman, 1998), the emergence of (local) research institutes (e.g., Stivers, 2000), and the international exchange of information and experience between local administrators (e.g., US civil servants and scholars visiting local governments in Europe, see Saunier, 2003; Japanese civil servants visiting Europe, see Westney, 1987).

Characteristic for the "practical experience" approach is the search for applied knowledge in a narrow, technicist sense. Both Taylor's time and motion studies and Gulick's management functions and organization principles are excellent examples. In their 1937 Papers on the Science of Administration, Gulick and Urwick write that science "... can be arrived at inductively from the study of human experience of organization, which should govern arrangements of human association of any kind" (quoted in Martin, 1952: 667). Postwar practical experience continues along these lines and is in the United States and in Europe interested in prescription (Mayntz, 1978: 2).

The critique that scientific management is not scientific enough and too mechanistic is phrased in strong terms. Nonetheless, it continues to be of great relevance to the development of public administration in two very different ways. The first legacy of scientific management in the United States is the return of the case study approach characteristic of eighteenth century Cameralism. One of its premier advocates is Waldo. Several curricula in mainstream public administration work with the case study approach. Case studies serve as illustrations of a more general theoretical principle (Page, 2003: 159–60), requiring that the micro levels of concrete experience are linked to the macro level of social experience at large (Merton, 1967; Luhman, 1985; Simon, 1985: 303; Mouzelis, 1991: 106–7). The case study approach is as important as ever in American public administration. In Europe, case studies went by the wayside until the late twentieth century when network theory was built on the bases of case studies (e.g., Koppenjan and Klijn, 2004).

The second legacy is that of public administration as a design science based on experience. This is considered desirable because of "... the natural desire of practicing administrators to escape the harassment of human vagaries, [and move] towards a science of public administration specializing in the design of models for the machinery of government" (Davidson, 1961: 852). A good example of public administration as a practical design science is the development of a range of design principles to help practitioners with the construction and maintenance of self-governing organizations or common pool resource management institutions (E. Ostrom, 1992: vii). Design science as "science" will be further discussed in the next section.

What does practical experience have to offer? First, contemporary government must provide many services using instruments and techniques considered appropriate. As early as the sixteenth century, growing government activity creates a demand for learning by case and by example. This is even more important today. Public administration needs case studies to illustrate the challenges of contemporary government, providing practitioners with real-world applications of theory, and to develop theory. Second, a strong interest for the practice of public management (e.g., personnel, budgeting, organizational design, and leadership) developed especially in Anglo-American countries. Third, this approach is multidisciplinary by nature since the eclectic borrowing of techniques or even theories is informed by the needs of the day and not by pure academic desires. It is here that the practitioner can exercise influence over the extent of academic input in problem-solving. Related to this, fourth, is that a focus on practical experience helps to ground advice about the "what" and "how to" in specific settings. Efforts to generalize practical experience from one country in other settings have been difficult, if not disastrous (E. Ostrom, 1990; De Zwart, 2002: 490).

6.5 Scientific Knowledge

The scientific tradition of knowledge originates in the seventeenth century and gains momentum during the Age of the Enlightenment. Scientific, technical, and factual information is quickly perceived as superior to any other type of knowledge as noted by Hamann in 1765 (Berlin, 1993: 126) and Burke in 1790 (Dishman, 1971: 111; Yankelovich, 1991: 197). It is here that the divergence between the European and American approach to public administration in the twentieth century is most striking. In Europe, public administration is much less perceived as a study in competition with traditional disciplines, and generally not as one that ought to spend its energies toward the creation of an administrative science (narrowly understood) but rather as one that ought to attempt unifying the study around core concepts (e.g., Auby, 1966; König, 1970; Van Braam and Bemelmans-Videc, 1986).

In the United States, Simon is the most strident advocate of a narrow scientific approach in public administration. He focuses on organizational behavior and on the decision-making and thinking processes of, what Dreyfus and Dreyfus (1986) call, the "competent performer" (who focuses on the processing of logical information and analytical problem-solving), the "proficient performer" (who intuitively chooses on the basis of analytical evaluation prior to action), and the "expert" (who also operates upon intuition, tacit knowledge, and a holistic approach to the subject matter) (Barnard, 1968: 302; Simon, 1997a: 130–5; Flyvbjerg, 2001: 13, 20–1). The science of administration is a design science since the social world must start with the notion of bounded rationality and work through disconnecting the design or means from the final goals so that the design assures optimal future flexibility (Simon, 1981: 188–90; Jones, 2003: 407).

Simon operates upon a logic of discovery which holds that research starts with an idea (Simon, 1991: 107), such as bounded rationality, which is first explored through theoretical understanding and then through developing and testing hypotheses. However, when the major difference between substantive, objective rationality and procedural, bounded rationality is that the former implicitly operates with untested auxiliary assumptions about utility and expectations (Simon, 1985: 297), then the latter logically has inductive elements for starting with testing auxiliary assumptions through observations and recording of human thought processes in specific situations (such as diagnosis by a medical professional, the moves made by grand master chess player in simultaneous games, solving physics and math problems in high school and college) rather than in a generalized setting (Simon, 1985: 295) in order to arrive at a uniform theory of information processing in the human brain (compare this to Riker's discussion of substantive rationality versus procedural as operating on *ex ante* respectively *ex post* assumptions: 1990: 172). Hence, it is too simple to say that Simon's work is deductive or inductive by nature. Indeed, the natural and social sciences work with both (Daneke, 1990: 384; Babbie, 1998: 36, 60).

Simon's design science of public administration is descriptive and explicitly concerned with the activity of information processing and with the best division of labor for information processing which involves "... human and mechanized components of man-machine systems" (1973a: 270). Simon's design science catches on in public administration, but in a manner different from what he envisaged (finding "widely varying applications"; Daneke, 1990: 385). Moving away from Simon's intent, Miller argues that public management as a design science would be much more useful than public management as a natural science (Miller, 1984: 251–68). The same applied focus is found in Shangraw and Crow who argue that public administration as a design science "... can be separated from the behavioral sciences such as political science, psychology, or economics..." and "... that it has not accepted its role of designer and evaluator out of fear that it will not be accepted in the academic community" (1989: 156–7). Their understanding of design science, though, is very different from Simon's. They explicitly include description *and* prescription (ibid.: 155), and ground the design and evaluation of institutions, mechanisms, and processes in previous experience (ibid.: 156). Also, they present an inter-disciplinary curriculum for a design science (ibid.: 157). In contrast, Simon's curriculum example is clearly disciplinary (1981: 190). In a commentary upon Shangraw and Crow, Overman writes that design science is making headway in public administration, public management and public policy programs. At the same time he criticizes it for not providing a viable alternative to systems theory and for coming close to "discredited" notions such as comprehensive rationality, social engineering, and technocratic rule (Overman, 1989: 159–60). Like the case study approach, the design science approach – whether in Simon's pure sense or in Shangraw and Crow's applied and interdisciplinary sense – appears to keep the attention of scholars in public administration (especially in public management).

To be sure, Simon's design science is a pure science based on facts and tested propositions which " ... does not, or should not, have any illusions that it is prescribing for public policy" (Simon, 1966: 36; Lalman et al., 1993: 98). Instead, it designs decision processes in such a manner that three vital criteria are met: comprehensiveness, technical sophistication, and pluralism (Simon, 1973*a*: 276). If public administration includes a focus on applied knowledge, it cannot work within the boundaries of academic specialization and should be labeled "political economy" (Simon, 1966: 35). Simon's influence has been especially strong among scholars who study political and/or bureaucratic institutions (e.g., Moe, 1980, 1990; Bendor and Moe, 1985; Bendor, 1988; Alt and Shepsle, 1990; Hammond, 1993; Bendor and Shotts, 2001; Krause, 2001; Krause and Meier, 2003) and/or public management (e.g., Kettl, 1993: 411; Kettl and Milward, 1996; Brudney et al., 2000; Heinrich and Lynn, 2000; Bertelli, 2004; Meier and O'Toole, 2006). The big challenge that scholars in this tradition face is the charge that they have failed to produce predictive and law-like generalizations, and that generalizations are probabilistic at best (Harmon, 2006: 50, 54). Simon recognized this better than many of his followers as is clear from an observation by Landau: "The history of science and technology indicates that as we gain more knowledge we open new areas of uncertainty. Which is why, I suspect, that Simon says that " ... many, perhaps most of the problems that have to be handled at middle and high levels of management ... will probably never be amenable to mathematical treatment" (Landau, 1969: 358, footnote 51; quoting Simon, 1960: 21).

A less apparent and indirect influence of Simon is evident in E. Ostrom's extensive work that combines case study and design science and has both scientific and applied components, and that won her the Nobel prize in Economics in 2009. Two features make this project stand out. The first is the enormous number of cases that include data on thousands of common pool resource organizations (CPRs) all over the world, thus contributing to the validity of conclusions. The second is the implicit design science approach. Systematic analysis of successful CPRs has resulted in identifying features contributing to the longevity of institutions. Ostrom calls these features "design principles" (1990: 88–102) and uses these as elements of a theory of self-organization or self-government and as prescription for reality. Simon is much less influential among those who adhere to a pure public choice approach that only emphasizes rational and maximizing behavior (as observed by Bendor, 1988: 383, 390; and by Heckelman and Whaples, 2003). He states that scholars who work with game theory or rational expectations theory do not take the severe limits of the decision-maker's actual knowledge and computational powers into account (Simon, 1991: 122).

The assessment of Simon's influence in public administration is mixed. Recall that Simon suggested how the study had absorbed both his and Waldo's revolutions. Dubnick wrote that mainstream public administration was so influenced by Waldo's emphasis on professionalism that an aversion developed against the "logical positivist bogeyman." If Dubnick is right, a proper assessment of Simon's potential meaning for the study of public administration is prohibited by bias. For instance, Hood and Jackson wrote that Simon's influence must be limited because few proverbs have been laid to rest, administrative argument has not really changed let alone improved, and positivism commands less universal respect today than when Simon wrote about public administration (1991: 20–1). However, each of these observations can be countered. First, keeping the differentiation between pure and applied science in mind, Simon merely points out that "proverbs" have no place in a science of administration (1969). He never says anything about the role of proverbs in day-to-day government. Consequentially, and second, Simon studies the logic of administrative argument but never expresses a desire to change administrative argument in practice. From early on he regards himself as a scientist, not an applied scholar. Third, whether an approach (or theory) commands, "less universal respect" is not relevant as a measure of its theoretical quality. However, the impact of Simon's thought has been doubted. For instance, fellow Nobel Prize winner Kenneth Arrow wondered "Why [. . .] has the work of Herbert Simon, which meant so much to all of us, [. . .] had so little direct consequence?" (quoted in Williamson, 1996: 40). Simon argued (though not in response to Arrow) that economics operates upon a "preposterously omniscient rationality" having reached a stage of "Thomistic" refinement in game theory and rational expectations theory that have great intellectual and aesthetic appeal but little relation to actual or possible behavior (1997a: 87; 1997b: 26, 63). He was convinced, though, that bounded rationality and satisficing will become mainstream in economics (1991: 364) and he may well be right (Sarin, 1999: 82).

The strongest and most biased critique has come from scholars who find Simon's scientific approach dehumanizing (e.g., Storing, 1962), prompting others to support Simon's quest even though they did not identify with his approach (Schaar and Wolin, 1963: 133–7; Landau, 1972: 193–202). Some scholars argue that public administration should develop a methodology of its own with a rigor worthy of the positivist challenge (Gill and Meier, 2000: 9, 13). However, such rigor does not require unified theory but methodological pluralism, since what theories and concepts are relevant depends upon a particular research object and thus may vary from one research project to another.

The research tradition with which Simon and so many others are identified is that of logical positivism. Simon wants to adapt this approach to the needs of the social sciences since the fundamental difference between it and the natural sciences is that the former deals with far more complex social and organizational phenomena upon which experiments cannot be conducted (D'Andrade, 1986: 39; Simon, 1997a: 358; Meier, 2005: 655). Reflecting upon his "proverbs" article, Simon wrote in Humean fashion that "It is true that I am still accused of 'positivism' as though that were some kind of felony, or at least a venial sin; and there still seems to be widespread lack of understanding of why one cannot logically deduce an 'ought.' without including at least one 'ought' among the premises" (1991: 270). He revisited the issue of positivism in the commentary to Chapter 3 in the fourth edition of *Administrative Behavior*, saying that his initial use of "logical positivism" is meant to provide a philosophical foundation to the "is" and "ought" distinction. Recognizing logical positivism as widely discredited, he dryly remarks that replacing that term with "empiricism" makes the entire argument go forward just as well (Simon, 1997a: 68).[2]

Simon is obviously correct when observing that an "ought" cannot be derived from two "is'es" (1948: 844; 1973b: 348), but this observation draws attention to a major problem with the logical positivist approach to the study of government: the separation of facts from values. The notion that facts can be established rests upon the claim that an objective reality exists. Whether we are able to perceive this reality is a matter of disagreement and confusion (Meier and O'Toole, 2007: 786 versus Luton, 2007: 527). There are several other problems. The first is of methodological nature and concerns the level of analysis. For instance, in 1990 the economist Coleman argues that the social sciences should explain social rather than individual behavior and thus take

---

[2] Keep in mind, though, that logical positivism is a type of empiricism. Not all types of empiricism (e.g., taxonomy, typology) can be labeled as logical positivist. See Phillips (1987: 41).

the social system, not the individual, as the primary level of analysis (mentioned in E.O. Wilson, 1998: 187). However, why should we have to choose between studying social or individual behavior? E. Ostrom's work shows that one can profitably combine these.

A second problem is epistemological and concerns clarity of the philosophical justification(s) for how and why theory produces knowledge and clarity about the concepts (or proverbs) with which an attempt is made to capture reality. As mentioned earlier, the complex phenomenon of government attracted attention of scholars from various disciplines and this generated a wide variety of theories, while, as MacDonald argued, scholars seldom probe the epistemological inconsistencies of their reasoning. He illustrated this assertion with a discussion of instrumental-empiricist and scientific-realist approaches to rational choice theory (MacDonald, 2003). But, is a dichotomous presentation of theories useful? Overman argued that as long as reality is portrayed as dichotomous (e.g., democracy vs. bureaucracy, artificial vs. natural approaches), the study is doomed to eternal debate (1989: 160). In the same spirit McSwite wrote that public administration's legitimacy crisis is rooted in concept-pairs such as democracy – efficiency and politics – administration that are regarded as dichotomous rather than as complementary (1997: 148). Along comparable lines, Harmon argued that the study of public administration operates upon the so-called schismogenic paradoxes where each of two opposing principles is neglected in favor of the other. Instead, he suggested that public administration should work with antinomial paradoxes where two ideas or principles are presented in necessary and creative tension with one another (1995: 7; Wamsley, 1996: 354). Harmon presented fascinating examples of such antinomies (1995: 93, 112, 119, 150, 186–7) and later expanded on these (2006).

A third problem can be drawn from Polanyi's concern that objectivity and formalization of knowledge cause the destruction of other knowledge and this is reiterated in Yankelovich's reference to the philosopher Bernstein who believes objectivism to be a destructive force that distorts reality and undermines wisdom and common sense (Polanyi, 1966: 20; Yankelovich, 1991: 197). Too much emphasis on empirical public administration may jeopardize "the use of imagination" where "small matters" studied by the scholar carries him into the "larger questions" (Dahl, 1961: 772; Davidson, 1961: 854; Redford, 1961: 759). Also, in the pursuit of scientific knowledge there is a danger of too much focus on method. Some argue that a focus on method need not inhibit attention for real-world problems and puzzles, yet others raise concerns: "Method becomes ritual when the analyst concentrates on an elaborate or rigid 'conceptual framework' and limits his interpretive role to the internal structure of the data, as if he believed that only so far as he is able to neutralize his own judgment will his study be scientific and thus, by definition, meaningful" (Davidson, 1961: 851; see also Lindblom, 1997: 233). Findings may also be more specific to method than methodologically sophisticated scholars care to admit (Fiske, 1986: 68).

A fourth problem is normative by nature and questions a positivist study of public administration that lacks attention for the moral challenges administrators face and the value-laden choices they must make every day (Redford, 1961: 759; Waldo, 1984). Simon is dismissive of any other than the positivist approach (Crowther-Heyck, 2005) but this has met with objections. In public administration, the NPA approach, for instance, is very explicit in arguing that the study must be committed to the values of both good management and social equity. The post-positivist NPA is not against positivism but hopes for a public administration that is less generic and more public, less descriptive and more prescriptive, less organization-oriented and more client-oriented, less neutral and more normative than logical positivism. But, it is no less scientific so argues Frederickson (1980: xii, 11–12) who thus embraces a European sense of *Wissenschaft*. Indeed, the NPA, the BM, and the mushrooming public sector ethics literature are indicators of how much the study of public administration has started to deal with normative concerns in the past 40 years.

A fifth and final problem of logical positivism concerns that it seemingly fails to take the "human side of enterprise" into consideration. For instance, management information and performance systems may support managers, but at the same time cause anxiety "... because the use of the system reduces the role of their intuition, reduces their space of free movement, increases their experience of psychological failure" (Argyris, 1973a: 263). Hence, too rational an approach to organizations is tyrannical and may have unintended consequences for the interaction between supervisor and subordinate as well as for the amount of creativity needed to achieve the organizational objective of productivity and profit.

The issue of what constitutes "science" with respect to government may not be resolved, but it seems there is room for both a broader Waldonian and a narrower Simonian definition, especially when the former is helpful in identifying the contents of the administrative "black boxes" through qualitative research and when the latter can help identify, through quantitative research, which of these factors, elements, configurations, and so forth are the most influential (Lynn et al., 2000: 13). However, a parsimonious model cannot include every potentially explanatory variable and must indicate to which management or policy domains and jurisdictions it pertains (Ellwood, 2000: 329).

Critique leveled against Simon specifically and against positivism in general should not overshadow its merits. First, it generated valuable new insights and theories and channeled an explicit methodological disciplinarity with an eye on ultimately arriving at epistemological unity. It is generally agreed that public administration profits from quantitative studies in organizational sociology and from an economics-based rational choice theory and principal agent theory. Second, positivism forced a rigor of conceptualization, research design, and proof that is focused on providing a solid description of the phenomenon of interest. This description can be empirically grounded, that is, inductively developed on the basis of observations of reality, or can be theoretically inspired, that is, deductively, on the basis of logic and/or common sense. Equally valuable, third, is that its scholars did not give up pursuing objectivity while acknowledging that interpretation is a fact of life. It is too simplistic to consider positivism and holism as opposites with the former relying upon hard quantitative methods and the latter upon "softer" qualitative analysis. Such a dichotomous presentation obscures the fact that both types of analysis involve extensive interpretation (Goodin and Klingemann, 1996: 12; Kritzer, 1996: 13–15). Fourth, Simon's type of organizational theory and rational man is not devoid of attention for emotion and humanity (cf. Simon, 1973*b*: 347) but focuses on the power of reason: "In Argyris' Dionysian world, [...] the rational man is cold, constrained, incapable of self-actualization [...] In my Appolonian world, reason is the handmaiden of freedom and creativity" (Simon, 1973*b*: 352). Perhaps Simon was confused. The Nobel prize winner for medicine in 1937, Szent Gyorgyi, distinguished between two lines of thinking (following Nietzsche). The Appolonian tends to develop established lines of thinking to perfection while the Dionysian is more open to new lines of research (see Hall, 1989, 24). In this light, Simon was a Dionysian when developing a new line of research, and very much an Appolonian when refining it.[3]

Fifth, more than any other approach, positivism takes up the challenge of explanation (cf. *Erklären*), and thus complements the understanding (cf. *Verstehen*) provided by the other traditions. If there is a problem associated with positivism, it is that some of its advocates do not consider the merits of other approaches and that its critics may not always understand or are even unwilling to understand the "language" of logical positivism which even the initiated do not always find accessible.[4] But then we must also ask: Are logical positivists or scientists willing to consider and work with and in other

---

[3] In Greek mythology, Apollo is the god of sun, lightness, poetry, and music. Dionysis is the god of wine, ecstasy, and intoxication. In modern literary usage, Apollo represents light, individualism, and civilization, while Dionysis stands for wholeness, darkness, and primal nature. To Nietzsche, the Appolonian state is a dream state or the wish to create order, while the Dionysian state celebrates nature. See F. Nietzsche (2009 [1872]). *The Birth of Tragedy. Out of the Spirit of Music.* (translated by Ian Johnston). Vancouver: Richer Resources Publications (text available in full at: http://records.viu.ca/~jonstoi/Neitzsche/tragedy_all).

[4] Lalman et al. observed about political science that "Today, even for the mathematician, a great deal of technical skill may be needed to comprehend papers in the field [...] and even with the mathematician's technical advantages, a great deal of reflection is required to comprehend the 'political' content of the formulations and their solutions" (1993: 77).

traditions? Indeed, where Simon invites scholars to acquire "sufficient techni-cal skill" before considering logical positivism, logical positivists ought to consider the merits of other approaches and not only from their own ground. When Simon debated others, he generally emphasized the strengths of his and the weaknesses of other approaches.

6.6 Relativist Perspectives

This tradition includes, as an example, hermeneutics (Gadamer, 1975), phe-nomenology (Hummel, 1977), critical theory (Box, 2005), postmodernism (Miller and Fox, 2007), and various other approaches that can be lumped together under the label of relativist perspectives.[5] Focusing on postmodern-ism in the social sciences, Rosenau distinguishes, as she calls them, affirmative from skeptical postmodernists. Skeptical or radical postmodernists are pessi-mistic about the future and regard this age as one of fragmentation, meaning-lessness, vagueness, and one of lacking moral anchors (1992: 15). Their primary method is deconstruction of modernity's organization of reality in increments of linear, purposive, homogenous, and evolutionary time. As a consequence, past, present, and future are collapsed and only confusion remains (1992: 22). Skeptical postmodernism has no supporters in public administration while affirmative postmodernists have made inroads in public administration (Frederickson and Smith, 2003: 145–7; Denhardt, 2004: 165–71; *Administrative Theory & Praxis*).

Affirmative postmodernists wish to augment positivist epistemology and methodology with intuition, selective judgment, feelings, imagination, and various forms of creativity and play (Rosenau, 1992: 117, 172; Miller, 2003: 16–17), favor interpretation over deconstruction (Rosenau, 1992: 118), and believe that postmodern social science should be descriptive rather than predictive and policy-oriented (ibid.: 169). "Affirmatives" emphasize the importance of rejecting the grand narrative over time in favor of the local and regional narrative with which individuals can identify.

The "affirmatives" may very well trace their origins to Antiquity's skepti-cism and to nineteenth century Romanticism which held that there is no right answer to questions, that truth varies from individual to individual, and that human values are contradictory (Berlin, 1999). A more elaborate study of the intellectual origins of postmodernism is not necessary here, but would be rewarding and perhaps even remove it from the realm of the "suspect" approaches where "anything goes" (Bevir, 1999: 79). At the time that

[5] The term "relativist perspectives" is preferred here over "postmodernism" since the former concept refers to a variety of approaches that are implicit when using the latter concept.

Rosenau's study was published, postmodernism was emerging in public administration. Her only source of information was an article by Caldwell who wrote that public administration in a postmodern society has to transform information into validated, usable knowledge (1975: 570–1). As it turned out, postmodernism became quite a different animal.

Postmodernism gained momentum in public administration from the early 1990s onward, especially in the United States (Adams, 1992; Farmer, 1995, 2005; Spicer, 2001; Miller, 2002; Miller and Fox, 2007). In Europe, postmodernism was not nearly as important although some scholars have identified with this approach (e.g., Frissen, 1999; Bogason, 2000). Farmer's 1995 study provides the best introduction to postmodern thought in the study. He extensively compares characteristics of modernity (i.e., particularism, scientism, technologism) with features of postmodernity (imagination, deconstruction, deterritorialization, and alterity) and argues that the latter perspective accommodates the cultural diversity of today's society much better. Farmer claims that his study is one of deconstruction (1995: 148), but his writings do not come across as those of a skeptical postmodernist. Indeed, in the epilogue he writes that neither modernity nor postmodernity need to be rejected, but that the value of their contributions must be properly understood (Farmer, 1995: 248). Miller and Fox underline this by observing that a perspectivist epistemic community need not abandon "the old positivism" (2000: 682).

One of the critiques postmodernism faces is that it is an approach where "anything goes." This critique has merit since postmodernists deny any claim of objectivity. However, once such a critique becomes stereotypical, that is, condemning all that is published under that label, we may fail to see that it produces good and bad scholarship just as in any other tradition. One of the problems of the postmodernist approach is that its "value" cannot be assessed in the familiar disciplinary terms. It is fair to raise three fundamental questions. First, what can postmodernism offer once it has deconstructed the knowledge acquired on a mono-, multi- or interdisciplinary basis? Second, in what sense do the philosophical, historical, comparative, and interpretative contributions of postmodernism differentiate it from practical wisdom? And, third, the most serious of challenges, how can scholars who embrace a (skeptical) relativist perspective hold to a claim of describing social reality when they deny the possibility of an objective and even intersubjective reality? Indeed, when truth and facts are considered subjective, cognitive relativism cannot lay any claim upon the quality of its own analysis and "Cognitive relativism backfires" (De Zwart, 2002: 490). Affirmative postmodernists do not, however, reject the process of empirical verification, but support the use of multiple approaches and methods (Mouzelis, 2008: 189).

Postmodernism has several features important to the study of government. First, affirmative postmodernists advocate the inclusion of philosophical, historical, and comparative approaches (Spicer, 2001: 125, 133; Miller, 2002: 57) but they are not unique in this (see practical wisdom). Second, postmodernists warn against reification when they point out that organizations have neither material substance nor a purpose of their own beyond what individuals pursue (Miller, 2002: 53). Intriguingly, they have this in common with methodological individualists (scientific knowledge). Third, they object to Simon's advice that administrators must "...take as their ethical premises the objectives that have been set for the organization" (quoted in Spicer, 2001: 98). Surely, ethical premises rooted in societal and individual demands and preferences must be considered (Waldo, 1996). *In extremis*, the emphasis on organizational objectives can and has resulted in agentic shifts with disastrous consequences (Adams and Balfour, 1998). Fourth, postmodernists operate upon a holistic view of society and human beings and sometimes hold to a strong conviction that its scholarship must help to emancipate those who have been marginalized in the past, such as women and minorities (e.g., in critical theory, see Jun, 2006: 2). Postmodernists regard public and business organizations as fundamentally intertwined social constructions (Farmer, 1995: 60). Also, they remind us that the free market is not as free as some think (Miller, 2002: 46; cf. Polanyi, 1944: 71, 141). Fifth, and in line with practical wisdom, postmodern authors emphasize diversity of values, cultures, traditions, and styles of life (Berlin, 1999; Spicer, 2001: 90) which must be disseminated in a discursive community of people so that different solutions to social problems can be considered and a choice made for consensual solution (Miller, 2002: 97; quite like Lindblom, 1990). They are inclined to take the human being as the starting point of analysis (McSwite, 2002). Sixth, like the "Waldonians," high-modern and postmodern authors regard too much focus on techniques and instruments of personnel management, budgeting, organizational structuring, and the like, as severely impoverished when disconnected from the values which give these instruments meaning (McSwite, 1997: 15; 2002). Finally, and this is perhaps their unique contribution to the understanding of government, is that they have called attention to what is left out and unsaid (Goodin and Klingemann, 1996: 21). Catlaw's study of "the people" as an abstract and fabricated notion is a good example (2007).

6.7 Similarities, Differences, and How the Different Traditions Provide Understanding

At this point it is helpful to highlight similarities and differences between these four traditions, thus augmenting the brief outline in Section 6.2. Both practical wisdom and relativist perspectives emphasize interpretation, value, moral reasoning, judgment, emotion, reflection and discourse, and comparison. A fundamental difference between the two used to be that practical wisdom implicitly (in Antiquity) or explicitly (in the nineteenth century) pursued grand theory. Currently, the difference between practical wisdom and postmodernism is that the former holds to some hierarchy of values (i.e., intersubjective value-pluralism) and interpretations where the latter does not. Twentieth-century scholars in the practical wisdom tradition seek interdisciplinarity through the integration of substantive knowledge from different disciplinary traditions around an identifiable core. Thus, they will not exclude the potential of any theoretical approach. Postmodernists emphasize a methodology that challenges positivist knowledge. Like positivists, they take the individual as point of departure for analysis. But, where the former emphasizes rent-seeking and preference-ranking actors, the latter stresses the human being as a whole (*Gestalt*). Scholars in the traditions of practical wisdom and practical experience generally believe in an intersubjective reality, while those working in the tradition of scientific knowledge agree that there is an objective reality (the correspondence theory) that we can know. Scholars embracing a relativist perspective hold that reality is socially constructed and interpreted (see Table 6.1 for a comparison of the four approaches).

The first part of this table concerns the internal characteristics of the discourse about government, while the second part explores the link between these internal features and the social–political environment. The four approaches can be summarized best by showing how they define and/or provide understanding:

1. *Practical wisdom*: defines understanding as a satisfying description of some aspect of reality, that is, government, through moral reasoning and logical arguments applicable to the widest possible range of phenomena, and through reflection, interpretation, and comparison of time and context in an interdisciplinary manner;

2. *Practical experience*: defines understanding as a satisfying description and prescription of some type of administrative action, by means of cases or examples applicable to the widest possible variety of comparable phenomena through experimental testing of the best way to conduct activities in a multidisciplinary manner;

3. *Scientific knowledge*: provides understanding through a satisfying explanation of some aspect of administration with probabilistic statements and perhaps law-like generalizations or principles through experimental testing of laws or principles in a monodisciplinary manner;

4. *Relativist perspectives*: understanding is regarded as a potentially unlimited range of interpretations about some aspect of "reality" through

Table 6.1 Conceptual Map 5, Characteristics of the Four Intellectual Traditions in and Social Objectives of the Study of Public Administration

	Scientific knowledge	Practical experience	Practical wisdom	Relativist perspectives
Characteristics of the four approaches				
Origin	Seventeenth–eighteenth century; post-1940s in public administration and political science	Kautilya, Plato, seventeenth century; 1900 in public administration, 1950 in political science	Aristotle; Mirrors of Princes; 1950s in public administration and political science	Romanticism; 1990s in public administration and since late 1990s in political science
Knowledge ideal	Unity of knowledge and middle range theory: explanation, objectivity, epistemological integration	Standardized activity and grand theory: description, usable knowledge, professional integration	Moral truth and grand theory: description, understanding, inter-subjectivity, differentiated integration	No grand narratives or "formal" theory: interpretation subjectivity, no integrative ideal
Sources of knowledge	Facts, propositions, data	Precedent, experience, inventory of principles and techniques	Arguments, moral reasoning, judgment, interpretation, tacit knowledge	Interpretations, values, judgment, feelings, emotions
Methodology	Positivist; "natural-science" style; focus on rationality and episteme (science)	Case collection; comparison; focus on mechanism and techne (skill)	Hermeneutic; discourse; reflection; comparison; focus on rationality, substance and phronesis (prudence)	Discourse; reflection; comparison; deconstruction; focus on irrationality and uncertainty
Disciplinary desire/ status	Monodisciplinary	Multidisciplinary	Interdisciplinary	Nondisciplinary
Substantive interest	Bureaucracy, efficiency, decision, and organization theory	Universal principles of organization and management	Evolution of governing, authority	Language, culture
Representative authors	Simon, Meier, E. Ostrom, Auby, Luhmann, Van Braam	Taylor, Gulick, Kettl, E. Ostrom, case study authors, Fayol, Hood, Mayntz	W. Wilson, Weber, Waldo, V. Ostrom, Rutgers, König, Hood	Farmer, Fox, Miller, Spicer, McSwite, Frissen, Bogason (affirmatives)
Social objectives of the study of government				
Political objective = legitimation	No particular political objective other than legitimizing public administration as a science	Public versus private spheres, bureaucracy for a strong state, social stratification	Ruler–ruled relation	Politics and administration, complexity, relativity of existence
Policy objective	Policymaking upon objective facts	Policy implementation with the proper instruments	Support policymaking of king-philosopher	To question rationales of policies
Task of administration	Achieve satisficing outcomes	Organizational support of ruler	Improving ruler behavior	Linking individual and collective desires
Role of mid- to higher level administrator	Neutral advisor, specialist at middle level, generalist at higher level	Administrative advisor, generalist	Political advisor, generalist, intellectual appraisal, reflective practitioner	Interpreter or deconstructionist
Representative authors	Laswell		Kautilya, Aristotle, public intellectuals twentieth century	Foucault

Source: Raadschelders (2008: 942) (reprinted with permission from Wiley/Blackwell Publishers).

intuition, selective judgment, feelings, imagination, creativity, and play and through uncovering and/or deconstructing diversity of values, cultures, traditions, and styles of life in a non-disciplinary manner.

To whom are these approaches useful? Practical wisdom is of pedagogical value since it provides a broad and interdisciplinary basis of knowledge upon which the contemporary role and position of government in society can be assessed. Hence, it is useful to (under)graduate students, public servants in elected and appointed positions, as well as citizens. However, it is also useful to the pure scientist who should not avoid thinking about the potential social consequences of theory. Practical experience is attractive to policy and decision-makers from the lower up to the higher levels given the need for applicable skills. Some are specialists and some are generalists, but all are managers who must match means to ends and costs to benefits. This approach is equally useful in the classroom since it brings the real world of government closer to the student through cases and examples. Scientific knowledge is most attractive to researchers pursuing science. It is thus also an important approach in the classroom, but perhaps less at the undergraduate level and more so at the graduate (especially doctoral) level. The practitioner may find some use for scientific knowledge, but it is up to her/him, and not the scientist, to see how it can be applied to the real world. Finally, relativist perspectives are important if only because academics and practitioners must be willing to question the value and challenge the strength of convictions and orthodoxies. As far as studying government, this approach is perhaps most fruitful in an educational environment with advanced graduate students or mid-career professionals, because it requires a solid knowledge basis in the study of public administration. More specifically, the relativist perspectives are by some considered the avenue through which line managers' interests are best served. After all, the study of public administration caters mostly to specialists given its emphasis on professional skills (Cunningham and Weschler, 2002: 105–6, 109; Imperial et al. 2007).

6.8 The Argument for Epistemological and Methodological Pluralism

In this chapter, four intellectual traditions in public administration have been presented. Both in the United States and in Europe, scholars focused their epistemological concerns on the question whether public administration ought to be a "science" or a *Wissenschaft*. Especially in the United States, this contrast resulted in strong confrontations. These may have overshadowed the degree to which public administration hosts a wide variety of theories, approaches, models, and so forth. In that sense the American identity crisis literature has not been very helpful by suggesting irreconcilable differences between scientific knowledge and practical wisdom. While in the natural sciences scholars enjoy a methodology distinctive for their field, their colleagues in public administration advocate methodological pluralism, but one of a specific kind. For instance, when Simon refers to pluralism he explicitly means "... not a single analysis but several, prepared by protagonists that have different interests and different viewpoints" (1973a: 276). In 1995, O'Toole argued along similar lines: "... let many research designs bloom..." and it would even be better when individual scholars would "... apply differing research perspectives on a common subject and to compare and assess the perspectives, their relative values, and the ways that they can or cannot be used in coordinated fashion" (1995: 294, 296). This approach is difficult. O'Toole observed that "... executing such a project would require high levels of commitment from participating scholars, a shared willingness to grapple in good faith and in the context of an actual research agenda, and resources for research at a level rarely experienced in this relatively unsupported field" (1995: 296). The big question is: "How can mature yet diverse scholars actually collaborate with one another, embracing interdependence and difference..." (Harmon, 2006: 149).

The methodological pluralism advocated in this book is one that is not limited to various methods within scientific knowledge only, but one that makes use of methods, theories, and approaches in the other intellectual traditions as well whenever appropriate to the specific research topic. Indeed, the four intellectual traditions are in and of themselves not able to provide the kind of understanding that contemporary government requires. The unprecedented degree of organizational complexity of contemporary government and of government's penetration in society has made government an object of study in all of the social sciences. The epistemological and methodological diversity that results from this disciplinary variety of concepts and theories-in-use makes that, ontologically, the study of public administration cannot but be interdisciplinary. Public administration is the only study of which its scholars can claim to study government as a whole. Public administration's diversity is captured in this chapter in four traditions rather than in an eclectic listing of various concepts, theories, models, and schools. This diversity cannot and should not be sacrificed for the kind of specialization that results from narrower epistemological and methodological approaches in public administration. Again, any narrowing of perspective will lead to limited understanding. This means that arguments in favor of one approach and critical of other approaches are unacceptable. Together, the four approaches contribute to this more encompassing understanding of government. None can stand by itself.

Public administration ought not to be limited to "science" but, should, instead be *Wissenschaft*, an approach that works with scientific knowledge, practical experience, practical wisdom, and relativist perspectives. It requires, though, that scholars not only say what needs to be done – that is, work together across traditions – but actually do it.

7

Public Administration's Canon(s) of Integration[1]

> The backwardness of social knowledge is marked in its division into independent and insulated branches of learning. Anthropology, history, sociology, morals, economics, political science, go their own ways without constant and systematized fruitful interaction. (Dewey, 1927)

> Social Science has accumulated many diverse bodies of knowledge. Each specific parcel is separate, almost insulated from the others. (Fiske, 1986)

Some believe that public administration scholars are " . . . always squabbling over the precise (and priceless) boundary lines that define our identity" (Rodgers and Rodgers, 2000: 436). The word "squabbling" conjures up an image of scholars disagreeing on rather petty issues. But, there is nothing petty about the questions that surround the identity of the study and practice of public administration. The often-heard criticism that the study is not scientific because it lacks boundaries only makes sense when public administration is viewed as a traditional academic discipline that strives for a positivist unity of knowledge. However, public administration also offers "terminal" professional degrees and is obliged to serve practicing professionals in a fashion similar to applied fields such as law, medicine, business administration, and social work. That fundamental reality cannot be erased by the fact that many universities also offer Ph.D. programs in public administration. Public administration spans so much intellectual ground and has so many persons of different perspectives and orientations approaching the subject from so many different angles that it is difficult, if not impossible, to bring them under one or even several conceptual and theoretical perspectives. Dwight

---

[1] Waldo's article "Canons of Integration" (1952a: 88) focuses on integrating efficiency and democracy as well as doctrines of centralization, hierarchy, unity, and simplicity. I liberally use his phrase but then in reference to exploring and mapping possibilities of integrating knowledge about government in the study of public administration.

Waldo's description of organization theory as an "elephantine problem" fits public administration at large. In a book review in PAR, he described how a crowd of "wise men," all blindfolded, were told to feel and subsequently describe an elephant (Waldo, 1961). One feels the trunk and says it feels like a snake, another feels a leg and declares that it is a tree, and so on. When the breadth, multi-dimensionality, and multi-faceted nature of public administration are taken into account, traditional positivists' criticisms about the field's lack of boundaries are meaningless.

The dominant approach to establishing a traditional discipline's identity is to achieve knowledge integration through developing epistemologically and methodologically consistent models of a particular slice of reality that is distinct from comparable efforts in other disciplines of other slices of reality. Commentaries critical of public administration's lack of boundaries and identity are therefore implicitly biased toward, and misled by, the achievements made by disciplines that enjoy some degree of epistemological and methodological unity of knowledge. But such critiques, which maintain that public administration's epistemological and methodological problems are clear manifestations of its lack of boundaries, are based on a fundamental misunderstanding of the nature of the study.

The study of public administration is characterized by methodological pluralism and lack of boundaries, but achieving unity of knowledge is more likely for studies that claim a subject matter not claimed by other disciplines, do not have to be involved in the complicating demands of serving practitioners, and are either purely logical systems (e.g., mathematics) or more readily grounded empirically (e.g., physics, chemistry). If viewed as something quite different from natural science, public administration must have, and indeed should have, empirical *and* design components that not only aim at describing what *is*, but also what ought to be (Wamsley, 1996: 358; Meier, 2005: 655). This is not as simple as it may seem, because knowledge about government is compartmentalized in specializations within public administration and scattered across the social sciences. Hence, knowledge about government cannot and should not be claimed by public administration alone, but the study serves as the umbrella for knowledge about government. Consequently, it not only works with theories and models developed by its own scholars but also borrows and works with theories and models from other studies. More often than not this diversity and richness is challenged from the perspective of a positivist definition of science as objective, replicable, and non-contextual knowledge. If, however, knowledge is more broadly defined as a branch then various methods and approaches can be included (Mazlish, 1998: 234). Under what circumstances, and how, can these theories and methods be connected without losing the inter-disciplinary nature of the study?

To answer this question a distinction can be made between two ways that knowledge integration can be mapped. The first is a map of general types of knowledge integration across the three branches of learning (Section 7.3). The second is a conceptual map of approaches to knowledge integration in the study and is an effort to make clear that the study of public administration integrates knowledge not by establishing boundaries but by building bridges in various ways (i.e., differentiated integration, see Table 7.1 and Figure 7.1). Before we broach the subject of a conceptual map of public administration's types of knowledge integration (Section 7.4), it is useful, first, to explore phases of knowledge integration (Section 7.1) and, second, why efforts at knowledge integration (at the level of the study as a whole) based on a positivist conception of science cannot but fail (Section 7.2). Instead, meaningful and useful knowledge integration is possible in public administration when it is regarded as an interdisciplinary study that differentiates, or selectively integrates, knowledge specific to the subject matter that is studied. The nature of this differentiated integration will be explored (Section 7.4) and several types discussed (Section 7.5). Differentiated integration is the fundamental nature of the study of public administration. Setting boundaries is not only artificial but also denies public administration's most important function: knowledge integration to inform government decisions and actions with regard to specific social and/or theoretical problems.

7.1 Phases of Knowledge Integration

As a study marked by a widely differentiated scholarly community and by an equally diverse clientele and practice, public administration is a problem-driven field of study concerned with discovering inter-subjective truths, and featuring a wide range of theories and methods that are selected for their usefulness and applicability to a particular research problem. In other words, the study of public administration encompasses many second order formal objects. Some of these originate within the study, while others originate in traditional disciplines; some of these are general, while others are quite specific in nature. Many originate in practice. No other social science claims as its primary interest government and governance, yet aspects of government and governance are studied in other social sciences, and scholars, public office-holders, interested parties, and citizens can and do have opinions about the usefulness of the study of the administrative dimension of government (the static or structural dimension) and governance (the dynamic or process dimension). Therefore, there is every reason for public administration scholars to define the nature of their study in a manner that is inclusive of any knowledge and insights about government and governance.

The study of public administration should also be based on the assumption that government is an essential part of governance, the process by which hopes, symbols, demands, claims, and promises are translated into authoritative actions, programs, rewards, or deprivations. Whether public administration is thought of as the core of governance, it influences, and in turn is influenced by, social and economic forces. This means that it faces demands for useable knowledge or knowledge-in-action from many sources. By contrast, mathematics and theoretical physics are not only defined by their first order formal object of study (i.e., they work with concepts and theories relevant to their discipline as a whole as well as to the specializations in their discipline) but also by their specific ideal of knowledge (i.e., quantitative, descriptive, explanatory, predictive). They also have specific methods for pursuing "objective" truth. These methods are based upon replication of research at any place and time, and claim a preferred, dominant, and even a superior approach to knowledge (i.e., paradigm in the Kuhnian sense). Scholars of public administration who wish to establish boundaries for their study in the "natural science" style negate the study's fundamental identity as one that is:

1. concerned with the organized complexity of government in modern society (Kline, 1995: 65) that cannot be captured in any simplification of reality;
2. defined by a variety of scholars (cf. Kuhn) (e.g., scientists, postmodernists, critical theorists, hermeneuticists, etc.); and
3. faced with demands to solve wicked (cf. Rittel and Webber, 1973: 160) or complex problems (Fernandes and Simon, 1999).[2]

For these three reasons the study of public administration is much more permeable to other social scientists and to other actors than is the case in the natural sciences. Since public administration largely studies man-made or artificial phenomena, it would be nonsensical to declare boundaries on the basis of specific formal objects and knowledge ideals since the artificial is a product of negotiation rather than of "natural law."

---

[2] Contrasting the natural and the social sciences, Rittel and Webber wrote that the latter deal with "wicked problems": "As distinguished from problems in the natural sciences, which are definable and separable and have many solutions that are findable, the problems of governmental planning – and especially those of social or policy planning – are ill-defined: and they rely upon elusive political judgment for resolution [. . .]" (1973: 160). A few pages later they ask: "In a setting in which a plurality of publics is politically pursuing a diversity of goals, how is the large society to deal with its wicked problems in a planful way? How are goals to be set, when the valuative bases are so diverse . . . ." (168). Fernandes and Simon (1999: 225–6) outline four features of complex problems: intransparency (only knowledge about symptoms is available, only some variables can be directly observed, observer needs to select from among large number of variables), polytely (multiple, interfering goals), situational complexity (complex connection patterns between variables), and time-delayed effects (consequences of actions not always immediate).

So, the nature of public administration's identity is defined by its first order formal object of study (i.e., government and governance in general as knowable through the lenses of various concepts and theories) which it shares with political science, and its second order of formal objects of study, for example, the specializations like budgeting and finance, personnel, planning, performance management, implementation, etc. Public administration is neither defined by one specific ideal of knowledge nor by a homogeneous scholarly community. This means that the traditional use of the term discipline, defined as a distinct body of knowledge clearly demarcated from other studies in terms of both formal object and knowledge ideal, as well as by existence of a homogeneous scholarly community, does not apply to public administration. Instead, we must consider whether public administration is multi- or even interdisciplinary in nature.

Multidisciplinarity is a situation of proto-integration where various studies are juxtaposed and share an interest in a particular formal object of study but do not necessarily, nor actively, exchange knowledge (Klein, 1990: 56, 1996; for an example, see Infeld, 2002). In such a situation there is a potential for, but no serious effort at, substantively linking bodies of knowledge from different studies. The content of public administration as a "first order formal object" is shared and contested with political science; the content of its "second order formal objects" is contested with research interests in other studies, and by a wide range of actors and interests as well.

In the second half of the twentieth century, the study of public administration (like the social sciences in general: Kaplan, 1964: 408–9) has been moving toward interdisciplinarity. Mansilla distinguishes three approaches (2006: 2–3, 25):

1. *Conceptual bridging interdisciplinarity* examines single concepts, principles, laws (e.g., network behavior) that can account for phenomena studied in a broad variety of disciplines. This type of interdisciplinarity is modeled after the formal disciplines (mathematics, theoretical physics). Research outcomes are measured against standards of elegance, predictive power, and generalizability.

2. *Comprehensive interdisciplinarity* produces multicausal explanations of a phenomenon whose interrelated components are typically studied by different disciplines. This interdisciplinarity is modeled after synoptic disciplines such as history, geography, and anthropology. Disciplinary perspectives are interwoven so that complexity becomes apparent. The focus is on complementarity among disciplines.

3. *Pragmatic interdisciplinarity* offers viable solutions to problems in the social, political, medical, technological, and so forth, realms and is used, for instance, in engineering, architecture, and journalism. The

outcome is judged in terms of relevance, effectiveness, and immediate problem-solving.

The study of public administration has features of comprehensive and pragmatic interdisciplinarity, and is defined by a process through which theories, methodologies, and research questions are selected in a rather eclectic manner from any discipline or specialized focus of study and practice considered relevant to a second order formal object of research. It represents a conscious, yet eclectic, effort to substantively connect (elements of) different bodies of knowledge that is motivated by problem-driven concerns (Klein, 1990: 83).[3] In Figure 7.1 this development from multi- to interdisciplinarity is graphically depicted. Note that in stage 4, and at the level of second order formal objects (d in I = subdiscipline or specialization), active interaction (indicated by dashed lines) is maintained between the various specializations within the interdiscipline of public administration (I) as well as with relevant specializations in various social science disciplines (d in D).

It is important to emphasize that interdisciplinarity refers to a process as well as to a particular substantive interest or problem. There is a substantial literature highlighting the pedagogical advantages of interdisciplinary teaching as well as outlining steps of interdisciplinary research (Newell, 2006: 248). The ultimate test of the quality of interdisciplinary studies, though, is when they result in an understanding of a particular phenomenon that is more comprehensive than what is possible through a disciplinary approach. Some even argue that interdisciplinarity has proven its worth if it actually brings solutions to real-world problems closer and leads to more effective action (Etzioni, 1988: 124–5) or leads to better probing of social problems (Lindblom, 1990).

At the level of individual scholarship, interdisciplinarity is visible in efforts to become acquainted with another field of study to enhance the understanding of the subject matter of research. Thus, public administration scholars study, have drawn upon, or migrated from behavioral psychology (Simon), theology (Gawthrop), constitutional and administrative law (Rohr, Rosenbloom, C. Wise), organizational sociology (Mayntz, O. White, Wamsley), economics (Simon, Lindblom), political science (Meier, O'Toole), political theory (Frederickson, Waldo), history (Stillman, Stivers), philosophy (Cooper, Farmer, Rutgers), and so forth. Interdisciplinarity is also visible in the application of economic theories (see Alt et al., 1999) of rational choice, game theory, principal–agent theory and, to a lesser extent, of bounded rationality to the study of bureaucracy and public management. Efforts to develop systematic

---

[3] Klein's distinction (1985, 1990: 41) between synoptic and instrumental interdisciplinarity does not make sense. She describes the former as concerned with methodological unification and internal coherence, but that seems to fit disciplinarity.

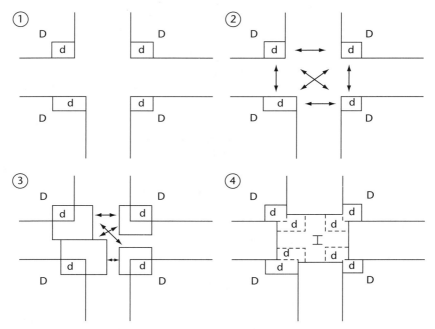

Figure 7.1 From Multidisciplinarity to Interdisciplinarity

Legend: D = (mother) discipline; d = subdiscipline, specialization; I = interdiscipline; 1 = multidisciplinarity; 2 and 3 = transitional phases; 4 = interdisciplinarity (adapted from: Rutgers 1987: 305).

Source: Raadschelders (2010*b*: 134) (reprinted with permission from Sage Publications).

inventories of the influence of disciplinary theories and methods upon public administration are few and far between. The closest example would be Kettl and Milward's description of the various disciplinary sources of public management (1996: 47–142). Interdisciplinarity can also emerge from cooperation between researchers in different disciplines, but can degenerate into a borrowing of concepts and theories that distort and change initial emphases and resemble piracy more than cooperation in theory development. It has been suggested that this has been fairly common in the social sciences (Gortner et al., 2007: 8).

By way of conclusion, it is not possible for public administration to claim meaningful boundaries. At the level of the "first order formal object," it shares occupancy with political science. Although it would be stretching a point, it could be argued that public administration comes closer to studying government as a whole than political science does. Public administration not only focuses on the internal structure and functioning of politics and governance (the so-called black box of Easton's system diagram) but also pays attention to relations between governmental actors and the stakeholders outside government (citizens, non-profits, and corporate actors). The study certainly cannot claim boundaries at the level of its "second order formal objects" since at that level research is being done both in public administration and in other social sciences. It thus cannot but strive to be interdisciplinary. Does that mean that the pursuit of knowledge integration, desirable in any academic endeavor, is doomed in public administration from the start? As indicated by the definition of interdisciplinarity, it is not but to answer that question we must see what efforts have been made to solve this boundary and identity crisis so far (Section 7.2) and what type of efforts have, or could and should be, made (Sections 7.3 and 7.4).

7.2 Disciplinary Solutions to the Identity Crisis and their Problems

At the level of first order formal object solutions, some public administration scholars identify the nature of the identity crisis as paradigmatic and seek to enhance the epistemological unity of knowledge for the study as a whole around concepts or theories considered relevant. This is an internalist approach to discipline formation, that is, treating the discipline as a product of a set of coherent scientific theories, research programs, and schools (Lenoir, 1993: 76). The best-known representative of this approach in public administration is Herbert Simon, who strived for a "pure" science of administration. In his view, applied work assisting the decision-maker was not considered scientific (Simon, 1966).

Desires for epistemological unity of knowledge have been expressed especially since the late eighteenth and early nineteenth century and have not lost any of their appeal. Efforts across the social sciences toward that objective range from efforts to encompass all branches of knowledge to efforts focusing on a small body of knowledge. As an example of the former, E.O. Wilson claims that a theory of gene-culture co-evolution has the potential to explain the development of human societies, and thus might unite the natural, social, and humanist branches of knowledge (1998: 126–7). Slightly different, but also aimed at uniting all branches of knowledge, is the idea that theories about the origins of preferences and behaviors can unite the social and natural sciences (Alford and Hibbing, 2004: 707, 718). A somewhat less ambitious effort was that of Sober and Wilson who developed a theory about altruism through combining evolutionary and psychological insights (1998: 331). In the same spirit, but for an even more limited universe, Coleman suggested (in 1989) that rational choice theory offers the promise of greater theoretical unity across the social sciences (as referenced in MacDonald, 2003: 561; but

183

see MacDonald's critique of this: 560). Shepsle (in Monroe et al., 1990: 42) expressed the hope that rational choice theory would center the effort to develop a core to political science and Moe (2001) argued that rational choice theory would unify political science in the twenty-first century.[4] Has rational or public choice theory left a mark in the study of public administration, and if so, to what extent, if not, why not?

In public administration, rational choice theory is mainly expressed in terms of principal–agent theory (on schools of rational/public choice theory, see Mitchell, 1988, 1999; Orchard and Stretton, 1997). The pure principal–agent model assumes a one-on-one relationship between a principal (supervisor or a political institution such as legislature, executive) and an agent (employee or bureaucracy). The agent needs to be supervised, that is, controlled, in order to constrain shirking and information-withholding behavior. In light of reality's complexities, this simple model has been abandoned in the 1990s for one that acknowledges the existence of multiple principals. Public administration studies that discuss and/or reference public choice and/or principal–agent theory seem to focus on dynamic processes of decision-making in bureaucracy (Meier and Krause, 2003a: 7–10). However, a unifying theory that truly enters the "black box" of bureaucracy is still sorely missing (Meier and Krause, 2003b: 296).

There is one feature of rational/public choice and principal–agent models that confronts the researcher with steep problems, and that is the fact that they often depart from an unspecified "objective reality." It is seldom, if ever, made explicit that a distinction ought to be made between a broader and a limited definition of objective reality. In its broad understanding, objective reality refers to anything "out there," observable actions, nature, physical structures, as well as beliefs, meanings, and interpretations (i.e., the material object as defined in Chapter 1). In a more limited definition, "objective reality" merely refers to measurable facts and observable actions/responses perceived through concepts and theories, hence a formal object. Meier and O'Toole (2007: 793) claim the existence of an objective reality in terms of a formal object, in response to Luton (2007: 527–8) who claims not to know whether an objective reality exists or not. Meier and O'Toole on the one hand and Luton on the other are not communicating, for neither specifies how they define "objective reality." Meier and O'Toole approach objectivity in terms of the formal object (i.e., we can know social reality only through concepts and theories), while Luton hints at a material object that we cannot fully know (see

---

[4] Rational choice theory assumes that individuals display maximizing behavior. The economist and Nobel laureate Paul Samuelson expressed the belief that maximizing behavior will provide "... a unified approach to wide areas of current and historical economic thought" (as quoted in Mäki, 1999: 491).

Chapter 1, Section 1.1). Meier and O'Toole's definition is a bare necessity when we wish to map, model, or correlate actions of individuals and/or institutions on an empirical basis. That is, we must agree that at some level, some degree of value-free empirical description is possible. However, the meaning of these actions can only be assessed in terms of personal interpretations, the aggregate of which results in an intersubjective reality (created through consensus, or better, integration seeking behavior; cf. Follett and Lindblom; see Fry and Raadschelders, 2008: 119–20, 277) where opinions, actions, and beliefs are subject to moral appraisal and judgment (Harmon, 2006: 32). So far, a unifying theory for public administration on the basis of rational/public choice and principal–agent theory is not available, for the simple reason that available methods and conceptualizations operate at the level of second order formal objects.

A more modest level of aspiration for unity is implicitly proposed by Gill and Meier (2000).[5] An example of a public administration specific model is O'Toole and Meier's model (1999) of the link between program performance and public management in its organizational environment (in the terminology of Chapter 1: a second order formal object). They propose that this be developed in the hope of arriving at more rigorous conclusions about determinants of good public management. They and others tested this model through a quantitative analysis of several large data sets on Texas school districts spanning the past fifteen to twenty years. One cannot but have respect for the impressive number of publications in which they have explored the various components of this model, but that very same work also serves as an example of some of the problems that such a mathematical and quantitative approach to knowledge acquisition has.

First, when using quantitative-statistical analysis, the findings can only be about *past* events, situations, and/or perceptions, provide only correlations between variables, and, hopefully, insight into a particular phenomenon as it was manifested in the organization(s) that was/were the source of the data. But, while American school districts are public they are not necessarily representative of the public sector in the United States let alone the world.[6]

---

[5] The use of the word "implicitly" indicates that Gill and Meier do not explicitly advocate unity of knowledge. Their reasoning that sophistication of methods will establish a more rigorous science of public administration, however, implicitly suggests that this will be a step toward removing barriers to knowledge integration (cf. Redhead's "unity of method," 1984: 275). The desire to elevate public administration theory and knowledge to a higher level of quality by developing more rigorous methods, though, places the cart before the horse. One cannot develop a study-specific methodology unless the nature (i.e., ontology and epistemology) of a study has been explicitly outlined.

[6] As is implicitly recognized by Meier et al., when observing that "...school districts are the most common public organizations in the United States [yet] they have some distinct characteristics. [...] If the findings here can be generalized, they would be applicable to *similar types of organizations*" (2006: 29; emphasis added).

Their hierarchies are generally much flatter than that of large government agencies. They are specific purpose organizations, usually independent (but not isolated) from general purpose governments (such as municipalities, states). They are monitored by an elected body that is non-partisan, and their managers (principals and superintendents) supervise a workforce that is much more self-directed (i.e., teachers) than is common in most public organizations.

Second, unity of knowledge through modeling and quantitative-statistical testing raises the challenge that its theoretical quality may be fine but that its relevance for the real world is limited because of the assumption that little – if anything – changes over time. In other words, would a data set of management and performance indicators in Texas school districts for the 1987–92 and the 2007–12 periods yield the same conclusions as those based on data for the 1997–2002 period?[7]

Third, this approach cannot provide universal causal generalizations, because that would require a replication of findings through comparable data sets of similar and different public organizations in different historical and geographical contexts. Clearly, this would be very difficult, if not impossible. Furthermore, it would seem likely that the broad explanatory power of a model diminishes radically when data are collected from among programs and/or functional fields of significant specificity (e.g., different local government units such as a water plant or a police department, as well as different state and federal agencies). How valuable can findings for the broader science and practice of public management be that are based on a very limited group of public servants and organizations?

Fourth, O'Toole's and Meier's formal theory of public management only addresses a small subset of public administration interests.[8] There is every reason to pursue formal modeling and quantitative-statistical testing in public administration, but the value of such research is generally limited to one type of policy or one kind of organization. A formal model that encompasses public administration in its entirety is so far inconceivable. Hence, this type of research does not do much for defining the study of public administration as a whole. That being the case, it becomes more difficult to argue that the study of public administration ought to develop only as a "science." To be

---

[7] That is, any generalization that coincides with a closed range of application (in this example: 1997–2002) does not qualify as a universal statement. See Kaplan (1964: 92) and Corcoran (1993: 102–3) about research findings as expressions of timeless forces rather than as a representation of a specific moment in time.

[8] In his 2006 Gaus Lecture, Ken Meier argued that political science has much to learn from public administration and he illustrated that with the research that illustrates his and O'Toole's formal theory of public management, which he called only "…one small subset…" of public administration (Meier, 2007a: 8).

sure, public administration can be "science" in the positivist sense but at best[9] at the levels of its specializations.

There are three other limitations to quantitative methods in general. First, the notion of measurement as a basis for analysis negates the importance of qualitative information. Ideally, any research project should combine both quantitative and qualitative methods and draw inspiration from the four major intellectual traditions in public administration (e.g., practical wisdom, practical experience, scientific knowledge, and relativist perspectives, see Chapter 6) and to see whether different methods and perspectives lead to different conclusions (see O'Toole, 1995). In other words, the main challenge to public administration is not to make all research efforts either quantitative or qualitative, but rather to increase the simultaneous and complimentary use of both quantitative and qualitative methods in individual research projects. Max Weber is one of the first scholars to actually attempt this (McDonald, 1993: 300–12; Mazlish, 1998: 180; Fry and Raadschelders, 2008: 25; Radkau, 2009: 80–4).

Second, how much of reality can be captured with quantitative methods and in mathematical models? In Chapter 6, Simon was quoted about the limits to which problems and decisions made at middle to higher levels of management can be modeled.

Third, any model of reality can only be used as a guide for the collection of information. It cannot be tested for its own validity. This being so strengthens the argument to employ, whenever possible, a variety of methods in the pursuit of understanding a particular social phenomenon.

Scholars working with quantitative-statistical methods are inclined to claim that their analysis is more scientific and rigorous than what is possible through other types of analysis (e.g., critical theory, case study, hermeneutics, narrative study, historical study, postmodern study, phenomenology). A respectable study questions the explanatory power of formal models, by trying to expand the sample size across different organizations. This would facilitate a more holistic understanding of government as a large-scale social phenomenon in which development and change occurs. A scientific epistemology and methodology specific to public administration (cf., Gill and Meier, 2000) can and surely should be advanced but not without recognizing the usefulness and complementarity of other approaches (Landau, 1972: 203; Brower et al., 2000) and not without exploring the societal meaning and practical usability of scientific findings. After all, "the theoretical needs for an interdisciplinary

---

[9] "At best" is used advisedly. Perhaps it is possible to develop a formal model that captures a specialization. However, it is more likely that in each of the specializations a variety of formal models is used.

field that serves a sociopolitical practice are much different" from that of a traditional academic discipline (Wamsley, 1996: 354).

In the discussion above the word "disciplinary" is used in its limited meaning of a rigorous, study-specific set of methods that enable the development of "science" in the limited sense as defined in Chapter 2. As a consequence, the focus in this section is on quantitative-statistical methods. To be sure, pointing to the limitations of this set of methods is not the same as singling them out without attention for other methods. However, the only set of methods that some scholars consider as befitting a "science" of public administration are quantitative-statistical methods. When we expand the definition of "disciplinary" to include any systematic, thoughtful, and reasoned study of reality, then other methods and/or approaches come into play. These too have their limitations (see Chapter 6), but they are not discussed in this section since they do not fit what is characteristic for "discipline" in the narrow sense.

To date, the discourse in public administration provides few, if any, reasons to believe that theories and models independent of context and observer biases can be developed. The alternative is to examine whether other solutions to the identity crises are more promising. Such an examination must be primarily concerned with integrating compartmentalized or fragmented bodies of knowledge through differentiated integration (the distinction between multidisciplinarity, interdisciplinarity, and differentiated integration is based on Rutgers 1987: 305).

7.3 Types of Knowledge Integration across the Three Branches of Learning

Knowledge integration across the three branches of learning can be conceptualized at four different levels (Table 7.1).

The first is *professional integration* on the basis of eclecticism and pragmatism. What different bodies of knowledge do students have to master to be properly equipped for a career in the public, the nonprofit, or even the private sector? Integration of knowledge at this level is left to the recipient of education. This type of integration is provided in handbooks of public administration (Barth and Green, 1999). There are no shared concepts, let alone a central theory. From an academic point of view this type of integration is unsatisfactory.

The second type could be called *specialist integration* which is more inductive by nature, since what is integrated depends upon what an author claims as the major topics. The advantage is that students are not only presented with in-depth discussions of various specializations but also with some

Table 7.1 Conceptual Map 6, Four Levels of Knowledge Integration and the Branches of Learning

Study and branches of study	The study	Interdisciplinary	+ Humanities on and relevant to government	+ Natural sciences relevant to government	Extradisciplinary
	Study of public administration	+ Social sciences on government			+ All knowledge relevant to government
Integration type					
Professional	Most common				
Specialized	Common	Possible and desirable			
Differentiated	Desirable			Desirable (C.P. Snow)	Tacit knowledge (Polanyi)
Epistemological	Impossible			Impossible (but see E.O. Wilson)	Divine knowledge

Source: Adapted from Raadschelders (2000a: 209) (reprinted with permission from M.E. Sharpe).

overview. The handbooks in the various specializations are an example. With this type of integration, however, it is even more difficult to develop a holistic overview of the entire study since there are no shared concepts and theories. While specialized handbooks are testimony to the amount of knowledge already available about government, they are by the same token a triumph of compartmentalization.

The third type is that of *differentiated integration* which can be achieved in various ways (see below). Central to differentiated (i.e., "not one-sided") integration, also referred to as "integrative pluralism" (Mitchell and Dietrich 2006, S76) or as "analytic eclecticism" (Sil and Katzenstein, 2010), is that the nature of integration depends upon the researchers' objective: organizing the study around a core concept, mapping concepts along a continuum, shining different disciplinary "lights or lenses" upon a particular research topic, or developing meta-framework and/or theories. Differentiated integration is thus problem-driven research: "To state and solve any one of the significant problems of our period requires a selection of materials, conceptions, and methods from more than one [discipline]. A social scientist need not 'master a field' in order to be familiar enough with its materials and perspectives to use them in clarifying the problems that concern him" (Mills, 1959: 142). This set of options for knowledge integration indicates clearly that it goes beyond the "law of higgledy-piggledy," that is, that everything is subject to chance, a charge that philosopher and mathematician Herschel laid before Darwin's theory of natural selection (Lennox, 1999: 299; Vanelli, 2001: 60–3).

The final type is *epistemological integration* that operates upon belief in the unity of knowledge. It is the most ambitious and is achieved to some degree in each of the natural sciences. There is, though, so far no knowledge integration of the natural sciences, let alone of all the branches of knowledge. Whether this type of integration, based on a deductive-nomological framework, will ever be possible remains to be seen.

Given that knowledge about government is compartmentalized, each type of integration can be pursued at four different levels. At the level of integration within the study, the goal is to develop unity of knowledge across the specializations in the study. This is the level where the identity of the study is debated. The net is cast wider at the second level, that of *interdisciplinary integration* within the social sciences. At this level, understanding of government is dependent upon meaningful conceptual and theoretical linking of the various social sciences that (partly) study government. At this level we can apply again the four types of integration and the most ambitious goal is to establish a scientific identity for the social sciences at large. While most social scientists pay little attention to this, every now and then a voice can be heard that fundamental unity at this level is within reach. Thus, Braybrooke argued that the interdependence of causal regularities and the *naturalistic side* of the social sciences, on the one hand, and settled social rules on the *interpretative side*, on the other hand, is so intimate that the three major sides of the social sciences (i.e., the naturalistic and interpretative parts + critical theory) make an overwhelming case for unity (Braybrooke, 1987: 1, 112). Professional and specialist integration of knowledge are possible and desirable.

At the third and fourth levels, that of *interdisciplinary integration* across the great branches of learning, a Herculean attempt is made to cross the divide between them. Again, we can apply the four types of integration. This is a Herculean task given that, even at the least ambitious level of professional integration, mastery and basic understanding of a vast amount of knowledge is assumed. Professional and specialist integration of knowledge about government in the social sciences and the humanities is possible and desirable as various authors have argued. It is also desirable to include knowledge about government as generated in the natural sciences in view of the policy choices government officials have to make on the basis of technical and scientific knowledge. Public servants should be able to evaluate the political and societal consequences of technological and scientific developments and for that reason professional and specialist integration between the three branches of knowledge is desirable. Differentiated and epistemological integration of the social sciences, the humanities, and the natural sciences is impossible given the fundamental differences between them (Chapter 2). This utopian ideal of unity of knowledge is lost in Western scholarship (Van Baalen and Karsten, 2007: 5), and unity is only pursued at the level of individual disciplines. This endeavor has been more successful in the natural than in the social sciences, but the emergence of interdisciplines in the three branches of knowledge suggests strongly that disciplinary boundaries are incapable of addressing problems that cross several disciplines.

Table 7.1 includes one element that is not discussed. What Polanyi called tacit knowledge, and what is called extradisciplinary knowledge in the table, is acquired through experience rather than through instruction (Polanyi, 1958; see also Kuhn, 1973: 44). This knowledge is based on professional experience as well as experience in a relevant past that is not of a particular disciplinary nature (experience in writing, in presenting, in interaction in society at large). The prefix "extra" in extradisciplinary knowledge underlines that this is an added and valuable dimension to explicit, disciplinary, or interdisciplinary knowledge.

7.4 Differentiated Integration

Differentiated integration is the effort to connect different sources of knowledge about one particular topic (Rutgers, 1993: 299; 1994: 295; 1995: 81;

2004: 263).[10] Before defining it more precisely we can describe how this works in practice. Let us take the study of the oath of office by way of example (Rutgers, 2009). One could study the oath of office within one discipline and then proceed to collect literature on it from within that discipline. However, one could learn more about the oath of office when considering other disciplinary perspectives. For instance, the oath can be regarded as an expression of loyalty in general which calls for the inclusion of psychological and sociological concepts and theories. The oath can also be regarded as a legal act, binding an individual to uphold the Constitution and the law. Hence, a scholar should consult legal literature on it. The oath is also an expression of loyalty to politics and elected officeholders and this invites attention for political science. It can also be an expression of loyalty to the public at large, again requiring attention for what political science has said about the relations between politics and administrators on the one hand and citizens on the other. Any oath of office requires an individual to balance the loyalties to the public at large, to an executive, to a legislature, to the law, etc., with loyalty to self, to God, to family. Waldo rightly observed that a civil servant serves many masters and that their biggest challenge is to balance external demands with an internal moral compass (Waldo, 1996: 507–8). To properly understand this, philosophical and ethical perspectives are useful. It is also a highly symbolic act (an anthropological perspective) which, deep-down, commits an individual to something beyond her/his self-interest (philosophy, theology). Also, it can bring out how and why the use of oath of office varies with culture. Why do most civil servants in the Netherlands and the United States take an oath of office while in France only some judges do? (Rohr, 1995)

In the example above a public administration perspective is not mentioned because public administration is an interdiscipline where any topic studied by its scholars ideally includes knowledge sources from other disciplines. Public administration is a differentiated study that can study government from various perspectives. The effort to connect knowledge sources from the various specializations within public administration on the one hand with knowledge sources in other disciplines on the other hand presumes active exchange of ideas and sharing of knowledge, and such discourse is as useful for policy and decision-makers (cf. Berman, 1974: 116) and for the public at large (Dewey, 1927: 208) as it is for the advancement of comprehensive understanding of government.

---

[10] It might be useful to briefly reflect upon the concept of differentiated integration. It could be seen as an oxymoron, that is, a contradiction in terms. But, it is only a contradiction when one holds to a positivist idea about knowledge integration (i.e., unity of science). Positivist knowledge integration is impossible in the social sciences because no one can lay an exclusive claim upon a particular body of knowledge (for convenience I disregard this is also not really possible in the natural sciences, but they have more exclusive claims).

Interdisciplinarity or intellectual polymorphism is sometimes regarded as illustrative of amateurism and dilettantism (Mainzer, 1994; Dogan, 1996; Finkenthal, 2001: 13) and " . . . widely viewed as perverse" by the academic community (Knights and Willmott, 1997: 10). It is, however, much more challenging than disciplinarity, and it challenges " . . . the culture and career ladders of academia [that] endorse a defensive kind of disciplinary closure that inhibits critical self-reflection" (Knights and Willmott, 2007: 10). Indeed, interdisciplinarity and methodological pluralism are not indicative of identity crisis, inferiority, and dilettantism, but are rather testimony to the scholarly maturity that public administration has achieved (Fry and Raadschelders, 2008: 343, 363).

Based on the premise that knowledge about government is compartmentalized in the specializations within the study of public administration and fragmented across other disciplines, and based on the claim that this compartmentalization severely limits the development of comprehensive understanding of government, there are at least three obstacles in the way toward differentiated integration (Raadschelders, 2005).

First, this type of integration is impossible under a narrow definition of science that emphasizes the search for objective truth. Indeed, public administration scholarship narrowly conceived increasingly uses the "language" of statistics and mathematics, while knowledge in the more classic and broader sense also includes judgments, interpretations, and narratives. This difference in the conceptualization of "science" was believed strong enough that the Department of Economics of the University of Notre Dame decided to split in the Fall of 2003 into an orthodox (quantitative) graduate program (Department of Economics and Econometrics) and a heterodox (qualitative) program for undergraduates which focused on, for example, economic thought, social justice, and public policy (Department of Economics and Policy Studies) organized in a Faculty of Economics (see website of both departments at the University of Notre Dame's main website). Hopefully this will not happen in public administration.

Second, substantive coherence is difficult to achieve in research projects with scholars from different disciplines. It presupposes that all participants understand the disciplinary background of one another and are familiar with the empirical and normative work in the participating disciplines. Even the best can only collect and digest so much information. Individual efforts at differentiated integration deal with the same problem.

Finally, knowledge about government is relevant to practitioners in general, whether they are specialists or generalists. However, the degree of specialization in public administration is such that, increasingly, only the specialists are served. Presumably, someone who works in budgeting will keep up with the professional and academic literature on it, but, if ambitious, must also develop the generalist's habit of considering, for instance, the organizational objectives at large in relation to society's needs. The use of the concept of "old" generalist (one who has a background in classics and history and who, by the early 1960s, was called a myth: Presthus, 1964) presumes that there are now "new" generalists in government who have a specialist's background but develop in the course of a career a deep understanding of the structure and functioning of an organization at large, of its objectives, and of its relation to the needs of society. This new generalist, implicit in the conclusion of Mosher's study (1968: 219), is the one who profits most from interdisciplinarity and differentiated integration. This begs the question, though, whether the study of public administration caters to these new generalists (both in academe and in government) who throughout the twentieth century expressed a need for wisdom and comprehensive understanding of government (Redford, 1961: 758; Kaplan, 1964: 406; E.O. Wilson, 1998: 269; Bennis and O'Toole, 2005: 98; and – as far as applied public administration is concerned – Simon, 1966: 35; see also Chapter 5, Section 5.4).

7.5 A Conceptual Map of Knowledge Integration in the Study of Public Administration

In the previous section, differentiated integration was defined and discussed. In this section, several types of knowledge integration in and relevant to public administration will be presented along a continuum that ranges from multidisciplinarity, via approaches within the study, to interdisciplinarity and disciplinarity (Table 7.2).

Table 7.2 Conceptual Map of Knowledge Integration in Public Administration

Knowledge integration			
Multidisciplinarity	Approaches in the study of public administration	Interdisciplinarity	Disciplinarity
Government studied in various disciplines through multiple formal objects; ideas exist about what fits together, but lack theoretical coherence. Example: Wheels of public administration	One concept to unify the study; 1st example of differentiated integration From dichotomies to continuums; 2nd example of differentiated integration Miniparadigms Disciplinary matrix	Disciplinary lenses; 3rd example of differentiated integration Meta-framework; 4th example of differentiated integration Meta-theory; 5th example of differentiated integration	Epistemological and methodological integration

Source: Adapted from Raadschelders (2010*b*: 135) (with permission from Sage Publications).

In the case of multidisciplinarity, no explicit effort is made to develop a substantive connection between kernels of knowledge from different disciplines. Models about the coherence of public administration are available that implicitly allow for the inclusion of knowledge from other disciplines ("wheels" of public administration: Raadschelders, 1999; Stillman, 2010). These "wheels" provide a conceptual map of public administration, but do not provide unity of knowledge.

Characteristic of approaches within a discipline is that they focus on mapping the substantive content of a study itself. First, there is the notion that the study can be centered by selecting a core concept. The big problem, of course, is that of selecting an ultimate concept (Kaplan, 1964: 78) that a majority of scholars can agree on. Several concepts have been suggested over the years. For instance: Simon (1997: for whom a core concept was decisions and decision-making), Wamsley and Zald (1973: core concept = political economy), Ostrom (1974: core concept = association), Debbasch (1989: core concept = the state), Van Braam and Bemelmans-Videc (1986: core concept = decision-making), Lan and Anders (2000: 158–61: core concept = publicness), and Raadschelders (2003*b*: core concept = public realm) are examples of efforts toward such integration of knowledge within the study of public administration. As for subject-matter or formal object, the study of public administration has expanded far beyond its initial focus on organization, management, and leadership, which makes it even more difficult to determine what its boundaries are and what concept best captures the study as a whole.

Second, and much less recognized as a method of integration, is the notion that public administration should move away from a dichotomous presentation of reality and go toward using continuums. It has been said that dichotomous thinking is "...the curse of intellectual and scholarly action..." (Etzioni, 1988: 203; see also Finkenthal, 2001: 68) since it inhibits understanding of the context in which social problems unfold and can be solved. With regard to public administration, Harmon persuasively argued that dichotomies, which he calls schismogenic or evil paradoxes (where two principles oppose, ignore, or even reject each other; cf. Simon's proverbs) result in incomplete understanding of reality. In his view, antinomial paradoxes (where two opposing principles exist in creative tension with one another, for example, night and day, two concepts that cannot be understood separately) provide a more complete understanding of reality (Harmon, 1995: 7; 2006: 15–23). Consider the following examples: public–private sector, centralization–decentralization, politics–administration, facts–values, mechanistic–organic organizations, and academics–practitioners. When concept-pairs are perceived as a schismogenic paradox, they invite *either-or* thinking, expressed by the use of the word "versus" (e.g., public versus private sectors) that suggests a choice between alternatives. When such concept-pairs are regarded as antinomial paradoxes, they encourage *and-and* thinking and emphasize how both concepts are to be regarded as two sides of the same coin.

Third, Golembiewski argued that the study of public administration ought to develop as a family of miniparadigms (he mentioned three: traditional, social–psychological, and humanist–systemic miniparadigms) (1977) in the hope that at some time in the future these would blend. There are several problems with this. First, it confirms the compartmentalization of knowledge about government and, more importantly, does not specify a roadmap toward how such blending of miniparadigms could be pursued. Second, it is focused on the internal structure and functioning of public organizations. Third, public administration is full of (mini?)paradigms, although not in the Kuhnian sense of a discipline as a whole but in terms of a theoretical pluralism characteristic for the social sciences (Lakatos, 1970: 155).

Fourth, there is the effort at developing a disciplinary matrix. At first sight, this fits a positivist perspective given the use of the concept of discipline and given the basis in Kuhn's work. Kuhn initially developed the concept of "paradigm" to describe the nature of a scientific revolution (1973: 2nd ed.). Later he endorsed Masterman's concept of co-existing multiple or sociological paradigms (1970: 67–74) as better than his own, but preferred to speak of disciplinary matrix instead since "disciplinary" refers to that which is common in a particular disciplinary community and "matrix" to ordered elements that require individual specification (Kuhn, 1970b: 271; 1973: 183). Lan and Anders made an effort to develop a disciplinary matrix for public administration (2000: 158–61), but when looking at their paradigm matrix it is inconsistent. Their matrix includes political, managerial, judicial, ethical, historical, and integrated approaches (2000: 145). That is, a mix of "disciplinary angles" (political science, business administration, law, and history), one specific topical angle (ethics), and an odd duck (the integrated approach) defined as "not specifically [identified] with any of the above approaches but which regards public administration as an institution that does whatever necessary to keep the government functioning" (Lan and Anders, 2000: 158).

Perhaps public administration can only hope to be a disciplinary matrix at best (Raadschelders, 2003a: 342). However, considering that the concept of "discipline" is central to that of "disciplinary matrix," it offers neither a solution to the boundary challenge nor to the identity crisis in public administration since it assumes consensus about the identity of the study in an identifiable scholarly community.

With interdisciplinarity, we arrive at consciously incorporating knowledge sources from other disciplines under the umbrella of public administration and there are several ways in which this can be done (Table 7.2). The first example is the attention to disciplinary/theoretical lenses of which Rosenbloom's political, managerial and legal lenses upon government as a first order formal object are an excellent example (Rosenbloom and Kravchuck, 2005). White's distinction between three types of research (1986*a*: positive, interpretative, and critical research) also concern the study as a whole. Other examples include Martin (1992: three approaches to culture studies, i.e., a second order formal object for public administration), Radin (2002: policy and political lenses upon leadership, a second order formal object), and Gortner et al. (2007: 9, disciplinary perspectives upon organization theory, a second order formal object).

A second and more challenging example is the development of a meta-framework that substantively connects theories and concepts from different disciplines around a particular set of theories or a particular topic of study, pre-empting the compartmentalization of knowledge which is commonly a consequence of specialization. To be sure, it connects theories and concepts, but does not result in epistemological integration. In fact, a meta-framework considers different (theoretical) perspectives as alternative pictures of comparable processes without nullifying any perspective. This definition of meta-framework comes out of two excellent articles that meaningfully discuss and connect six perspectives and debates in organization theory (Astley and Van de Ven, 1983: 245–6) and four ideal–typical theories about organizational change and development (Van de Ven and Poole, 1995: 510–1).

Third, the most challenging of interdisciplinary efforts toward knowledge integration is the development of a meta-theory. A meta-theory is a theory about theories and examines groups of related theories, and may arrive at identifying classes of theories and perhaps even a taxonomy. It is the type of interdisciplinary knowledge integration closest to mono-disciplinary unity of knowledge. Whether meta-theories actually exist is debatable[11] and two examples in publications well-known in public administration will illustrate why. The first is Katz and Kahn's monumental work where they describe "Open-system theory [as] rather *a framework, a meta-theory*, a model in the broadest sense of that overused term." (1966: 452, emphasis added). A second example is Aldrich's and Ruef's evolutionary approach that overarches different theories about organizational development (institutional theory, interpretive approach, organization learning theory, population ecology, resource dependence theory, and transaction cost economics) (2006: 12). But, they write that their "...evolutionary approach may be described as *a metatheory, an overarching framework*

[11] The German mathematician David Hilbert formulated a program to give mathematics a consistent logical foundation. This program was "...concerned with formal deductions rather than with concepts of truth, satisfaction and validity." It launched the concept of "meta-theory" into academic parlance. Any hope that such proof would be found would be obliterated by Kurt Gödel who proved that this an impossible dream through his incompleteness theorem that holds that truth can never be captured entirely within a formal system. See Bothamly (2002: 233, 253–4). Applied to, for example, public administration it is thus impossible to verify or falsify statements about government since it is not possible to determine whether the verifying or falsifying test is true or false (see Miller and Fox, 2007: 18–19).

197

that permits comparison and integration of other social scientific theories" and one that hopes to achieve integrated understanding " . . . although perhaps not an integrated theory" (ibid.: 32, 34; first emphasis HA/MR; second emphasis added). In Europe, König is a clear advocate for a meta-theory on government (1980). To date there is little real meta-theory in the social sciences and there certainly is not in public administration.

7.6 Conceptual Maps of Public Administration's Interdisciplinarity

One of the earliest statements about the interdisciplinarity of public administration was by Waldo:

> During the past decade increasing attention has been given to the possible contributions of other disciplines to the special interests of administrative study, notable of the other social sciences. At the present time there is considerable – and important interaction. Writers professionally associated with such discipline as sociology and social psychology publish in the journals of public administration. Often they are addressing their attention directly to phenomena in, or related to, administration that have been the focus of study by students of administration; but they have a different perspective and bring to bear different conceptual tools. Increasingly too student of administration are turning their attention to these outside fields. . . . (1965: 49)

He observes that what is being used ranges from research findings, research methods, and symbolic logic to concepts and models. He then briefly discusses the interactions between public administration on the one hand and political science, history, cultural anthropology, sociology, social psychology, economics, and business administration on the other. At the end of that discussion, he observes that even the " . . . physical sciences and technologies supply grist for the mill of the administrative student. Indeed, no discipline is without its relevance for administration – and administrative study has relevance for every discipline" (1965, 57). Almost a quarter century later, Zorn wrote how

> . . . public administration has become a hodgepodge of individual (sic) with varied backgrounds and training. This has resulted in a discipline that has notable strengths and weaknesses. A major weakness and source of criticism from outsiders in (sic) the discipline's lack of a paradigm – there is no identifiable intellectual structure. Its strengths lies in the diverse theoretical conceptual, and methodological contributions borrowed from other disciplines. (1989: 213)

Focusing on the use of economic theory in public administration, Zorn observed that this required careful attention to the extent that " . . . economics is not appropriate to all questions" of administration and that positive and normative questions should be addressed in public administration (ibid.).

So, if public administration is relevant to every discipline and vice versa, and if it is a hodgepodge of disciplinary influences, how can this interdisciplinarity be mapped? Since meta-frameworks and meta-theories are non-existent, the public administration scholar is left with the challenge to develop a conceptual map of the study's interdisciplinarity. One straightforward example is provided by Shafritz et al. who place "core public administration" in the center of a circle surrounded by a variety of studies: management, political science, and law each occupy a sixth of the circle, the other ten (economics, anthropology, criminology, social work, medicine, engineering, psychology, logistics, sociology, and a miscellaneous category) occupy the other half (2007: 27). This figure, however, does not provide any information about the type of knowledge (concepts, theories, topics, etc.) that public administration draws from these other (social) sciences. Shafritz et al. (2007) also note that several of the study's constituent elements have moved to other fields (public policy to political science, public finance more to economics, management to public management; ibid., and we can add "organization studies" to sociology and psychology, see Kelman, 2007).

In an effort to capture the topical relations between five disciplines, Bovaird identifies a variety of concepts, theories, and topics that public administration draws from these (Table 7.3).

He is careful to observe that "... this is an artificial tool for illustrative purposes only. In most cells, far more areas of public administration could be included. Some areas of public administration should appear in several boxes (and some do), because they arise from the interrelationship between more than two core disciplines" (Bovaird, 2002: 353).

There are two shortcomings in the literature on public administration's interdisciplinarity. First, there is no systematic analysis of the interaction between disciplines in a manner comparable to what has been done for public administration and economics (Thompson, 2007) and for political science and economics (Alt et al., 1999). Second, there is no attention for the differential impact of disciplines upon specializations within public administration. For instance, it is reasonable to assume that economic theories and concepts have more impact in organization theory, policy analysis, budgeting and finance, civil service behavior, and decision-making theory, than in intergovernmental relations, human resource administration, and public sector ethics. In Table 7.4, a conceptual map of public administration's interdisciplinarity is presented with an eye for the impact of various social sciences in the study's specializations.

This table, admittedly, provides only an impressionistic overview of some concepts, theories, and topics important in the study of public administration. Several cells are empty and this illustrates the variation in influence of other

Table 7.3 Disciplinary Background to Public Administration

	Political science	Economics	Sociology	Psychology	Systems analysis
Political science	*Political behavior, political parties*	Budgeting systems, resource allocation	Organizational culture (ideology), elites (oppression), *self-organizing systems*	Leadership	*Policy analysis, network analysis, evidence-based learning*
Economics	Public choice theory (regime theory), *stakeholder analysis*	*Macro-economics, market behavior (exploitation), welfare economics, resource accounting*	Resource mobilization, social marketing	Motivation, consumer behavior, voter behavior	Evaluation, resource forecasting, *evidence-based action*
Sociology	*Stakeholder analysis*	Equalities (oppression)	*Socialization processes*	HRM, management of change	*Network analysis*
Psychology	Psephology (winning elections)	Service marketing	Organizational behavior (alienation)	*Individual self-actualization, group dynamics*	Games theory, network analysis
Systems analysis	Control systems, legal systems	Strategic management	*Self-organizing systems*	Ergonomics	Operations and project management

Source: Bovaird (2002: 352). Legend: Bovaird considers the italicized topics (i.e., stakeholder analysis, network analysis, self-organizing systems, and evidence-based action) as emerging in the study.

Table 7.4 Conceptual Map 8, Interdisciplinary Sources in Public Administration's Specializations

Social sciences and humanities	Sociology	Psychology	Economics	Law	Philosophy	Political science/political theory	Anthropology	Theology	History
Public administration specializations									
HRM	Leadership theory; social stratification	Mayo experiments; public service motivation	Standardization for efficiency	Diversity; representative government; AA, EEO; labor unions	Philosopher-king	Political appointees; citizen rights	Leadership theory	Equality; fraternity	History of HRM
Organization theory	Organizational sociology; bureaucracy as ideal type	Industrial psychology	Theory of the firm; organizational efficiency; systems analysis			Role and constituency of agencies	Organization culture	Participation	History of organization theory
Policy analysis	Social planning; social engineering		Preferences; welfare economics; planning			Public interest; interest groups; delegation	Cultural context	Common goods	of etc.
Budgeting and finance			Maximizing budget; program budgeting			Budget process; winnowing		Redistribution of surplus	of etc.
IGR	Social stratification; sociology of the state; institutional superstructure		(Neo-) institutional analysis	Constitutions	Democracy	Grants-in-aid; types of political system	State-making		of etc.
Civil service		Satisficing bureaucrats	Maximizing bureaucrats	Politics–administration relations; accountability	Hegel: civil servants as guardians	Administrative discretion; accountability; responsiveness		Brother's keeper	of etc.
Ethics				Ethical codes; whistle-blowing	Utilitarianism	Ombudsperson		Religious system values	of etc.
Decision-making theory		Cognitive psychology; group think; bounded rationality	Rational choice theory; methodological individualism	Positive law	Authority	Voting behavior		Authority	of etc.

disciplines, but also is testimony to the limitations of this author's knowledge. A more systematic investigation of the extent to which the study borrows from and "gives" to other disciplines would be useful, if only because that would actually provide substantive support for the claim that public administration is, indeed, interdisciplinary. There is some evidence, though, that public administration is somewhat disconnected from other disciplines and studies (Wright, 2011).

7.7 Concluding Remarks

It appears that Dewey's observation early in the last century has not lost any of its relevance (see mottos at beginning of article). Specialization reigns supreme. This is definitely the case in the study of public administration, which, some claim, suffers from a lack of unifying theory. This is, however, only "true" when assessing public administration in a positivist or empiricist perspective. In this chapter, public administration is defined as an interdisciplinary study that draws upon a great variety of theories, models, and concepts in order to capture the complexity of government in society. This means that positivist approaches are used side by side with other approaches, each providing a particular perspective upon government, and – when connected – providing more comprehensive understanding of government.

Integrating different approaches upon a positivist foundation is impossible since attempts at the level of the study as a whole (first order formal object) are lacking and attempts at the level of specializations (second order formal objects) are few and far between. Moving beyond a positivist approach to science, thus defining science in a more classic sense as "branch of knowledge," public administration's boundaries are defined by its first order formal object (i.e., government and its interaction with stakeholders: the "I" in model 4 of Figure 7.1). In Figure 7.1, four main stages of knowledge integration were presented, and it is through differentiated integration that public administration can serve as an umbrella in the effort to combine positivist, hermeneutic, etc., approaches to the study of government. Full disciplinary integration as presented in the right column of Table 7.2 is inconceivable at the level of the study as a whole, but could perhaps be pursued at the level of its specializations.

This chapter is more than simply a call for interdisciplinarity in public administration research. It outlines the challenges of and opportunities for knowledge integration in the study and, thus, provides an ontological and epistemological basis to the study that was lacking hitherto. This chapter will not "end" debates about what constitutes "real" science, but one can hope that fences are removed and attempts made to taking each other's approach(es) seriously and work with it. Whether this is naïve or visionary, only time will tell.

8

Intellectual Challenges in and to the Study of Public Administration

> ...it remains necessary to remember that no one investigator is to be trusted to give a survey of the whole field. (Bertrand Russell, as quoted in Hofstede and Hofstede, 2005)

> Knowledge is what we get when an observer, preferably a scientifically trained observer, provides us with a copy of reality that we can all recognize. (Christopher Lasch, as quoted in Sanderson, 2001)

> ...the degeneration of real curiosity and enthusiasm into a "planned economy", under which so much research time is stuffed into more or less standard skins and turned out in sausages of a size and shape approved by our own little printed cookery book. (Tolkien, 2006: 239)

The conceptualization maps of public administration in this book are wrapped around the question raised in the introduction of the first chapter: Is the lack of boundaries a threat or an opportunity when pondering the nature of the study of public administration? Quite a few public administration scholars conclude that the lack of boundaries signifies lack of rigor and, thus, of discipline. Implicitly or, though less, explicitly they refer to a "hard" science approach reminiscent of, although not necessarily the same as, the rigor and discipline achieved in the natural sciences.

There is, however, a sizeable group of scholars who beg to differ about what constitutes scholarship and they, more explicit than implicit, emphasize that there are various ways to understanding reality none being superior. Some of these scholars reject quantitative-statistical methods outright, but do so without reasonable justification and, sometimes, even upon prejudicial grounds. Many have no problems using quantitative-statistical methods as long as it is appropriate to the topic and not used exclusively at the price of rejecting other methods.

This book is about the epistemological identity of public administration, it is not a survey of the study. It is also not about method(s) for the study, since that can only be determined when ontology and epistemology are explored. Method should never come before ontology and epistemology. Could it be that scholars who develop ever more elegant models and methods, push the substantive issue, that of understanding government in society, to the background? This book wants to bring that back to the foreground. In reference to Bertrand Russell (see the first motto at beginning of this chapter), no single scholar is able to develop a satisfactory survey of an entire field of study and, as a function of specialization, this is even truer today than it was 100 years ago. The ambition with this book is more modest: to develop conceptual maps of the study in order to make the case it has a clear identity. In this concluding chapter, some of the arguments made throughout the book will be revisited.

First, public administration is not the only study with an identity crisis. In fact, the question of unity of knowledge has been on the agenda of most of the social sciences since the 1950s (Section 8.1) (Wylie, 1999: 295). Indeed, it has descended upon the natural sciences as well. Second, and unlike many other social sciences, the concept of public administration is problematic and needs to be revisited briefly (Section 8.2). Third, public administration's nature is not easy to establish because its scholars have different substantive, organizational, and pedagogical agendas (Section 8.3). Notwithstanding this conceptual and organizational ambiguity, it is possible to map the study's nature and identity. Thus, in Section 8.4 the conceptual maps presented in Chapters 3–7 are briefly reviewed, knowing full well that other ways to conceptualize public administration are conceivable. What makes this book unique is showing that the study's nature and identity is interdisciplinary with its characteristic theoretical and methodological pluralism. It is a study that builds bridges. It would be impossible to establish the study's nature and identity on the basis of study-specific methods, theories, and topics, which is what is needed when one wishes to determine boundaries. Fifth, whether the study of public administration has global features or is mainly local/national by nature also influences the answer about the study's nature and identity (Section 8.5). In the concluding section, the argument is made that the interdisciplinarity requires an unusual discipline and creativity that is not necessarily fostered in research programs built around the interests of senior scholars (see motto Tolkien at opening of this chapter).

8.1 Specialization, Field and Method Fixation, and the Unity of Knowledge

Unity of knowledge is an ancient Greek belief that at some point the one law will be discovered that explains everything in the universe. This unity is expressed as a parsimonious, elegant, generalizable, reproducible, and predictive theory that can withstand any Popperian falsification. Between the seventeenth century and the 1930s, especially natural scientists pursued such a theory, usually at the level of their field of study. Darwin's evolution theory is an example of a unifying theory for the field of biology. However, it appears that unity of knowledge is a "problem" or challenge in all of the social and the natural sciences, and in the humanities, as a function of continuing specialization and of increased efforts to capture the complexity of the natural and the social worlds by combining the strengths of different disciplines in interdisciplines.

In Chapter 1 the identity crisis in public administration was discussed and compared to that in political science. There is no difference between them, but they are not the only social sciences divided into specializations which, in turn, are further subdivided. For instance, where Henriques observes that psychology is divided, Good (2000: 398) shows how social psychology, one of psychology's specializations, is divided in itself as well. One can say the same about economics when looking at Small's topics of economic analysis at levels two, three, and four of his global map (see Chapter 2). Some scholars argue strongly in favor of unifying psychology (Staats, 1991), yet others question whether that is desirable (Kukla, 1992: 1055), whether diversity is not an indication of the study's vitality (McNally, 1992: 1054) and of its heterogeneous subject matter (Kunkel, 1992: 1058). Henriques may "suffer" from bio-envy but Mitchell and Dietrich (2006) do not, since they argue that biology not only is but ought to be divided. Discussing the state of the art in the study of international relations, Wight (2002) observes that it is character-ized by various approaches and methods. With respect to archeology, Wylie (1999) notes that historical archeologists (i.e., those who work, for instance, on medieval excavations) are perceived as inferior by pre-historical archeolo-gists. These are just a few examples from the social sciences. The natural sciences are as divided. The curriculum of any major research university will show this. Some of the divisions are the result of increased interdisciplinarity. The French physicist Gökalp suggested that many topics require an interdisci-plinary approach. For instance, environmental law requires knowledge of law combined with knowledge about, for example, the chemistry of pollutant emissions (2000: 39). For closely related fields or disciplines with a short cognitive distance, Gökalp believes that *weak integration* is sufficient, while *strong integration* is necessary for disciplines with a larger cognitive distance. How difficult this is becomes clear when considering the problems involved linking micro-, meso-, and macro-levels of research within one discipline or study (see Chapter 4).

Knowledge of natural and social phenomena has been recorded since Plato and Aristotle made the first attempts at identifying bodies of knowledge. The growth of knowledge, though, has accelerated in the past 150 years or so, as is illustrated by the proliferation of specializations in every branch of knowledge. With specialization theoretical and methodological disunity increases and this stimulates polarization between representatives of different approaches (Wylie, 1999: 299). This polarization is often expressed in field (specialization) and method fixation (Sternberg et al., 2001: 104). Scholars invest in particular approaches and are unwilling to peruse other approaches simply because this is perceived as possibly devaluing their own work. Gans and Shepherd showed how early work of living Nobel Prize and Clarke Medal winners in economics was often rejected to became classics later (1994). Field and method fixation potentially stifle innovation, but the idea and appeal of "unity of knowledge" is so strong that field and method fixation are the equilibrium in most of the sciences. Disturbing the status quo is more often than not looked upon with derision and irritation. Wylie suggests that scholars should not assume unity of knowledge as a normative ideal or even as a "working hypothesis" since the world is not orderly (1999: 294). This is certainly the case for social phenomena that are perceived in so many different ways.

The emergence of interdisciplinary studies is a clear indication that reality's complexity can less and less be understood in terms of one disciplinary approach only. There are two main categories of interdisciplinary fields. First, an interdisciplinary field can exist as the interplay between two or a few disciplines (e.g., law and chemistry for environmental law). Public administration is a somewhat different interdiscipline. It is an umbrella discipline that serves as the intellectual harbor for the many ships that probe aspects of the role and position of government in society. It is a true interdiscipline and not a specialization in another discipline such as in political science or law. When regarded as a specialization within political science, public administration is, more often than not, reduced to being a technocratic study that is expected to leave the attention for the democratic context to political scientists. Outside political science, public administration scholars have explored the public administration perspective upon democracy (Raadschelders, 2003b: 49–94; Hendriks, 2010).

Public administration has, though, become so much more than just a technocratic study. If, in fact, the study was just a toolbag of skills and methods, it might have been possible to develop it as a discipline, but what academics study and what practitioners do not only requires the technical skills of budgeting, program evaluation, and performance measurement, to name a few skills, but also the reflective skills (i.e., why do we do this?) that help to legitimize particular actions and choices. As Sayre insightfully wrote almost sixty years ago:

> The central concern about values in public administration in a democratic society turns around the arrangements for the responsibility and accountability of the

administrative agencies for their policies and their programs of action. [This suggests that] the basic search in the study of administration is more for a theory of government than for a science of administration. (1951: 9)

Such a theory of government can only be developed under the umbrella of the interdiscipline of public administration.

It seems that public administration's identity crisis is no different from what is reported in other studies. As a social science, it is not different from other social sciences that deal with the same complex environment. Having said that, we need to explore, briefly, why public administration's identity is traditionally perceived as problematic?

8.2 Public Administration's Conceptual Problems

Depicting the identity crisis as resulting from a lack of disciplinary rigor is too simple. If there is a crisis it has to do with how the study is conceptualized. First, the concept of "public administration" denotes both the study as well as the object of study. Other studies have the good fortune that study and object of study are clearly differentiated (e.g., psychology and psyche, economics and economy, sociology and society). This is the reason that in this book a distinction is made between the concept of "government," which refers to the object of study, and the concept of "public administration" which is the study itself.

Second, as any other social scientist, public administration scholars must confront the so-called challenge of "double hermeneutics," the situation that they are not independent from the social reality they study (Flyvbjerg, 2001: 32–3, following Giddens and Habermas). The ambiguous distinctions in day-to-day language between "government," "governance," "public administration," and "public sector" are replicated in the debate about the nature of the study and its object.

Third, given that we can and do study the study of public administration, there may even a "triple hermeneutics" (Raadschelders and Rutgers, 2001) that requires the creation of a meta-framework for analyzing the nature of the study (example: this book) which can ground, in turn, a meta-framework for the study of public administration (Raadschelders, 2003*b*), which, in turn, facilitates better understanding of government. Scholars who identify with traditional public administration may conceptualize the study differently than those who identify with public policy, public management, or the study of governance.

Fourth, Van Braam (1989: 11–12) argues that the study can be conceptualized in two ways. In the broad sense, public administration concerns government and governance and is then a topic relevant to and studied in various social sciences and the humanities (political science, law, economics, sociology, psychology, history, philosophy). These studies and disciplines are, in his view, *administrative sciences* insofar as they are concerned with understanding government and they are then auxiliary to the study of public administration. By contrast, he speaks of the *integrative or synoptic study of public administration* when referring to a more specific body of knowledge or study whose interests, theories, methods, discourses, and participants are connected by the material object of study that is exclusive to it. It is in this latter sense that public administration is called an interdiscipline and an umbrella discipline.

Fifth, the study of public administration is marketed in at least four different ways. Some speak of traditional *Public Administration* (PA) as a study of public organizations and policy processes with a strong emphasis on the legal aspects of public action. Others emphasize that government is about policymaking and policy implementation that involves power struggles and the label then used is that of *Public Policy* (PP) studies, a focus advocated by Harold Lasswell and found in public administration and in political science departments since the 1950s. A third group suggests that government is about management and thus advocate *Public Management* (PM) studies, especially since the 1980s. Finally, there are those who champion the *Study of Governance* (SG) in the desire to go beyond the traditional public sector orientation so that, for instance, the nonprofit sector and self-governing institutions are included as well. Reminiscent of a remark made by Simon (1991: 114), Kettl wrote that "... public administration sits in a disciplinary backwater..." (1999: 127) and believed that many sought to replace it with public policy, public management, or governance studies. Is it not a paradox, he asked, that public administration as academic label is outmoded while at the same time it is increasingly important as social phenomenon? Wise notes that categorizing publications and dissertations as PA, PP, PM, or SG may reflect a trend or fashion (1999: 150; see also Frederickson, 1997: 92–3) but does not constitute a substantial shift in theory, topic, or methodology. If this is so, then using labels such as PP, PM, or SG is merely a marketing tool, masking that old wine is sold in new bottles. Is what is offered as PP, PM, or SG so much different from what was offered as public policy and public management within the folds of "traditional" public administration? One could point to the many new topics and approaches that emerged when PP and PM developed their own programs, but one could also ask whether these would not have emerged when still within "traditional" public administration. In other words, is it the environment that drives changes in the study, or is it changes in the study that generate new topics of research?

These five problems in conceptualizing public administration are compounded by its varying organizational and professional identities.

8.3 Public Administration's Varied Organizational and Professional Identities

In Chapter 6 the emergence of public administration as an independent study was briefly described. Half a century after the publication of the first handbook by Ludwig Veit von Seckendorf (1656), independent chairs in and studies of public administration were established in France and in the Germanic principalities. It is not until the late nineteenth century that the study in Europe becomes embedded in the study of law in order to improve the implementation of law.

In the United States, public administration did not emerge until the late nineteenth century and when it did it was mainly in political science (Thompson, 1999: 119). In the study of law, some paid attention to (comparative) constitutional and administrative law, but scholars like Goodnow (1893) felt that jurists and political scientists distrusted each other's leanings (Chase, 1982: 49). Historians were especially interested in the constitutional and institutional origins of the American Republic and wrote administrative histories about local and state government at colonial times and the early years of independence. Some of that comparative-historical work was also pursued in political science (Raadschelders, 2000*b*, 2002). At the time the political science curriculum included courses in history, public administration, and law (Haddow, 1969). This was also reflected in what the American Political Science Association listed as its core interests in the year of its birth (1903): comparative legislation, comparative jurisprudence, international law and diplomacy, constitutional law, [public] administration, politics, and political theory (Hill, 1992: 30).

As discussed in Chapter 1, public administration became quickly a discreet body of knowledge in the United States based on a theoretical distinction between politics and administration on the one hand (that Goodnow labeled as necessarily imperfect as far as the real worlds was concerned, 1900), and a utilitarian orientation on "principles of administration" on the other hand. The first handbooks appeared in the 1920s, but the first journal not until 1940. In Europe, public administration became distinct first in the publication of journals (between 1912 and 1934) and only after the Second World War in the appointment of professorial chairs[1] and the publication of handbooks.

In the United States, practitioners and academics together formed local, state, and national reform leagues and established research bureaus for contract and consultancy work. In Europe, practitioners and academics cooperated especially at the local level in the desire to address municipal challenges. Thus,

---

[1] The first professorial chair in the Netherlands was established in 1928.

a municipal studies program emerged in Germany, while in the Netherlands an association was established in 1922 that focused specifically on the training of local civil servants (Rutgers, 2004: 73–4). In the United States, the increased intertwinement of public administration academics and practitioners resulted in the creation of an association reflective of the need to balance both interests and audiences (ASPA 1939; Chapter 1). From then on, public administration and political science went their own way. While political scientists dived headlong into behavioral research in the hope of achieving the coveted scientific status, public administrationists visibly split along two dimensions: academic versus practitioner orientations and research versus education orientation (the following from Raadschelders and Rutgers, 2001: 8–9).

Those oriented toward *academic research* pursued public administration along more formal and positivist lines of research. They heavily borrowed from economic, organization–sociological, and social–psychological theories and subjected these to formal empirical testing in order to ascertain their validity. Herbert Simon was their prime source of inspiration (1947). The objective of scholars in this group was value-free and objective research. Their main focus was decision-making and bureaucracy and organization studies. In Europe and in Asia, public administration continued to embrace a legalist and political science approach until the late 1970s (Raadschelders, 2009*b*). In France and Germany, separate institutions of public administration were established, such as the *École National d' Administration* (ENA) in Paris, France (1945; nowadays in Strassbourg) and the *Hochschule für Verwaltungswissenschaft* in Speyer, Germany (1947). Other countries followed with comparable actions in the 1970s and 1980s. Independent university departments emerged in a variety of European countries from 1955 onward (Toonen and Verheyen, 1999: 403–4). In Europe, much attention was paid to American developments in the study. At the same time, the study was firmly embedded in the state traditions (with its strong focus on law) as is demonstrated in a study of French public administration (Van der Eyden, 2003). Sixty years after Simon, positivist administrative science in Europe, and even in the United States, is less prominent (Hood and Jackson, 1991: 20–1).

Scholars with interest in *academic education* advanced a generalist's type of curriculum more or less along the lines of the liberal arts educators of the nineteenth century who believed that a mix of history, language, comparative studies, and political theory was the best preparation for aspiring public servants. Their twentieth century "offspring" acknowledged that, while public administration needed empirical research, its programs would provide little service if no attention was paid to the philosophical and normative underpinnings of governance and government. In contrast to the academic-research oriented group, their approach is not positivist but interpretative. The main advocate for an interpretative approach in the United States was Waldo who, in the course of his Ph.D. work, had come to the conclusion that public administration had profound roots in political theory (1984). This broader orientation upon public administration was much more common in Western Europe. England had long emphasized a liberal arts education for public servants (Rhodes, 1996) and the same was the case in continental Europe (e.g., Weber).

Those who were focused on *practitioner-oriented research* emphasized that public administration ought to focus on the problems of the real world and thus had to provide research that would enhance government's problem-solving capacity. Public administration scholars went into the study of policy-making processes, while the study of substantive policy by and large was left to the political scientists (Henry, 1999: 347). Among the early leaders of policy process study in public administration are Harold Lasswell (1948) and Charles Lindblom (1959). Other scholars in this group turned to the study of managerial practices, heavily borrowing from colleagues in business administration such as Henry Mintzberg (Matheson, 2009). Yet other scholars worked in think tanks and government-sponsored research institutes (e.g., in the United States, The Urban Institute, The Brookings Institution, the Cato Institute), striving to develop solutions to public policy problems. Both the policy and the management scholars built extensive consultancy practices, the work of which served as the basis for their research output. Widespread consultancy-based research also emerged in Europe, but not until the 1970s.

Finally, scholars who focused on *practitioner education* in the United States emphasized specialization in pre-entry education so as to prepare students for jobs in the public sector. This resulted in the proliferation of a large number of specializations, such as in public budgeting and finance, public management, public policy, human resource management, regulatory policy, intergovernmental relations, and so forth. To them the ideal curriculum provided simulations and case studies in which the students could exercise, and thus become familiar, with procedures and techniques as used in the field. In the 1960s, Waldo came to support this arguing that public administration ought to adopt a "professional perspective" (1968*b*: 9). In Europe, and especially at the continent, public administration was and is first and foremost considered as an academic discipline working on the basis of a deductive theory of state (e.g., Van Braam with Bemelmans-Videc, 1986; Debbasch, 1989). This reflected also a different focus on the nature of scientific study and the relation between academia and administrative practice that persists to this day. The learning of practical skills is still left to institutions of higher vocational education (Rouban, 2008: 139).

The end of the 1960s set the stage for an enormous proliferation of the study of public administration into a variety of different avenues. The market for handbooks of public administration must have been good, because their numbers increased steadily since then both in the United

States and in Europe. The generic handbooks in the United States defined mainstream public administration largely in terms of themes outlined by the practitioner-education oriented group with little attention for democratic theory. At the same time, general introductions to American government for freshman students were charged with lacking any substantial attention for bureaucracy (Cigler and Neiswender, 1991). Mainstream public administration in Europe commonly included attention for the democratic superstructure, for political–administrative relations, and for the political regime (e.g., Thieme, 1984; Van Braam with Bemelmans-Videc, 1986; Debbasch, 1989). The American focus was on administration, organization, techniques of financial and personnel management, and leadership. As is to be expected, the market for specialized handbooks (those that focus on, e.g., personnel, public finance, intergovernmental relations, management, policy, etc.) in the United States was equally booming. The same trend was visible in the journals. Initially, the generic journals (such as *Public Administration Review*, the British *Public Administration*, *Revue Française d'Administration Publique, Die Öffentliche Verwaltung*) dominated, but from the 1960s onward specialized journals appeared. In Europe there is perhaps less compartmentalization of public administration in specialized handbooks and journals. The main split is that between traditional public administration texts and journals on the one hand and policy and management-oriented texts and journals on the other.

The major consequence of this compartmentalization of knowledge in America was that various communities of scholars emerged that hardly communicated with one another. There was enough to do in each of the specializations (see on this, i.a., Oleson and Voss, 1979; see also Ross, 1991, especially Chapter 3). The upside of this was an enormous expansion of empirical research. The downside was that fewer and fewer scholars attempted to develop more encompassing perspectives of government and public administration.[2] Theoretical development was focused on micro- and sometimes the meso-levels; macro-theoretical developments were hardly given any attention. The generic handbooks did not provide such overview, but rather were testimony to the triumph of compartmentalization.

European handbooks, on the other hand, seemed to comprehensively capture knowledge, collected and systemized from the perspective of public

---

[2] An example of a scholar who did so was Dwight Waldo, but at what price? Quoting Waldo's remark (1952b: 503) that Simon may become a major political theorist "...if he can resist the temptation to make a career of defense of his first book." Bertelli and Lynn observe that "That, of course, is the fate that awaited Waldo, who never again produced a work of the originality of *The Administrative State*" (2006: 179, endnote 13). However, one can just as well argue that Waldo was concerned with the centrifugal consequences of specialization, and that the study benefitted from his efforts to see the forest instead of the trees. Furthermore, Waldo wrote a variety of creative essays over the years that should not be dismissed (Fry and Raadschelders, 2008: 302–42).

administration in the narrow sense of (national) state administration. In Europe, compartmentalization is less pronounced than in the United States, perhaps because the much smaller number of public administration scholars allows for more substantive interaction between them and, perhaps, because there is simply less opportunity to specialize. What is more, however, there are also splits in Europe between sociological and juridical approaches to the object of study on the one hand and between the national discourses on public administration on the other. This is caused by differences in language, culture, history, and academic traditions, making it even difficult to translate key terms such as "administration" and "policy" (Rutgers, 1996). Contrary to the United States, there is no shared vocabulary or, as yet, a study that encompasses the continent.

Considering the fact that the concept of public administration has at least two meanings, that it re-emerged as part of political science (the United States) or law (Europe), that it became autonomous from these studies and developed its own specializations, and that there are at least four groups of scholars with regard to orientation upon research or teaching for academe or for practice, it is no surprise that attempts to conceptualize the study on the basis of its theories and concepts have so far not been very successful. Avoiding the pitfall of trying to be complete in a survey of theories and concepts, the study can be conceptualized in various steps.

8.4 Conceptual Maps of the Study of Public Administration

In this section the steps taken in this book to describe the nature of the study of public administration are summarized. Two features are foundational to this book. First, in Chapter 1 the notion of conceptual maps was introduced as the way to capture the study in its ever changing environment, thus avoiding that a study's identity is based on a snapshot in time. Second, in the introduction of Chapter 2 a distinction was made between the Anglo-American and continental-European connotation of science. If the premise of that reasoning is considered acceptable, that is, that science in its pre-eighteenth century meaning (*Wissenschaft*) is scientific, then the conceptualizations developed in this book make sense. What are the various building blocks of the nature of the study?

First, in Chapter 2 the study of public administration was labeled as a social science mainly focused on studying proximate causes of events in the here and now. There is much less attention for ultimate causes, perhaps because these are more difficult to determine and there certainly are no datasets available that capture these ultimate causes. Also, public administration seems to be more focused on analyzing rational, goal-intended behavior, although in the past three to four decades attention for pre-rational behavior appears to be increasing somewhat (e.g., groupthink). The public administration research that uses quantitative-statistical methods often use data gathered at the individual level and conclusions are then generalized upward (i.e., fallacy of the wrong level). Qualitative research is more case-based and focused on the group and/or organizational level.

A second feature of public administration is that its sources of knowledge are dispersed within the study, fragmented across the branches of learning, fragmented across thousands of organizational units in the public sector, and dispersed among many, many societal associations. With such fragmentation of knowledge it is no wonder that a comprehensive overview of the study based on an inventory of its theories, concepts, and experiences is pretty much impossible.

A third building block is looking at how the study itself has been and can be mapped. Thus, in Chapter 4, several examples were discussed. In reference to the discussion above it seems that the distinctions between PA, PP, PM, and SG are trivial. What Sharkansky presents as a system model of the policy process is to Starling a system model of the management process. The labels they use are different, but the imaging as an input–throughput–output system model is similar. It seems that in broad outline most authors agree that there is a set of basic topics in the study. What that set looks like varies, but examples were given of how one can link the basic topics in a "wheel of public administration" (cf. Stillman, Raadschelders) or a multi-layered bookcase (Raadschelders) (Chapter 4). Neither the wheels nor the bookcase are intended as finite listings of public administration topics, but they do provide conceptual maps within which any topic can be situated.

The fourth element in the construction of public administration's identity is to consider its theories (Chapter 5). Instead of trying to categorize the study's theories into a sensible and complete overview, the study was presented as a dynamic arena that is dominated by the different desires of the two main audiences: academics and practitioners. Academics often adopt the specialist perspective and are then more interested in developing and testing theory. Practitioners more often come into the arena with a generalist perspective hoping for the usable knowledge required of the master craftsman. Obviously, both academics and practitioners can be artists in administration as well, reflecting upon the meaning and structure of their knowledge rather than upon theory and application. And, equally obvious, is that the arena in Chapter 5 shows that portraying academics as specialists and practitioners as generalists is too stereotypical and does not reflect the complexity of "forces" upon public administration research. Is it really possible to say that scientifically oriented research is of no consequence for, has no meaning to, and no influence upon the practitioner? Conversely, can one really maintain that tacit knowledge is irrelevant to scientific research?

In Chapter 6, yet another building block was offered in the construction of the study's identity: a characterization of its intellectual traditions and debates. It was argued that the American identity crisis debate (as discussed among academics but involving much more, see Chapter 1) is dominated by representatives of the scientific knowledge (i.e., the academic-research oriented group) and practical wisdom approaches (i.e., the academic-teaching oriented group). Scholars in the practical experience (i.e., the practitioner-research oriented group) approach are, with some exceptions, not actively involved. Those who work from a relativist perspective are generally somewhat disconnected from the other traditions.

The final building block is that of the various ways in which scholars in the study have tried to integrate knowledge. Different types of knowledge integration across the three branches of learning were distinguished, as were phases of knowledge integration (from multi- to interdisciplinarity) and types of knowledge integration in the study. Also, examples were provided of how the interdisciplinarity of the study can be mapped (Chapter 7).

The question whether this set of conceptualizations provides a satisfactory identity of the study cannot be answered. It is very likely that many will disagree with those offered in this book and either advocate a different set of conceptualizations (within the notion of conceptual mapping) or simply say that this study was based upon the wrong premise (that of interdisciplinarity) and then continue to advocate rigor in a positivist sense. Clearly, the argument in this book is that no approach to understanding government can be denounced, for the simple reason that no one can claim to have mastered the knowledge that has been acquired in all of the study's specializations and across the other sciences to make a convincing case that some type of knowledge is superior. No one can claim to be omniscient.[3] Developing public administration as a scientific enterprise in the narrow sense of science literally narrows our understanding of this most complex social phenomenon. Some can sacrifice breadth for depth. It will continue to be important to develop the study as a science in the narrow sense, as long as the arena within which this science is developed is explicitly laid out (which concepts, theories, etc., belong and which not?) and its proponents acknowledge that their approach is valid within established and acknowledged ceteris paribus conditions (as is

---

[3] Although, it seems that some authors expect omniscience from journal editors, especially when an editor's competence in a particular research area or a research method is questioned by authors. Fortunately, editors can rely on reviewers who have the expertise to gauge the quality of a particular submission.

any other approach). Others emphasize breadth over depth, but should acknowledge that the scientists' approach has its worth.

Meanwhile, there is one element to the identity of public administration that needs to be discussed separately and that is the question whether a global public administration is emerging and how this relates to the various national traditions.

8.5 Global and Local Public Administration

Few will argue with the statement that government is a global phenomenon. In fact, bar Antarctica, the continents of the world are divided into territorial jurisdictions most of which are represented in the United Nations. To varying degrees, governments have penetrated their societies, perhaps more so in highly developed than in lesser developed welfare states. What most governments face is the challenge to govern in such a manner that basic human rights are at least protected, if not advanced. There are various international public (e.g., United Nations) and private (e.g., Transparency International) forum organizations dedicated to this objective. Some scholars have suggested that since government has become a global phenomenon, the study of public administration is globalizing as well.

Caiden (1994) is one of those scholars who argues that globalization will lead to conceptual convergence in public administration, and that – as a consequence – unity of knowledge is coming within reach. It is true that scholars and practitioners in many governments, whether in the Western or in the non-Western world, conceptualize the challenges of administration and governance in terms similar to those developed in Western Europe and the United States (see for Africa, e.g., Adamolekun, 1999). That is to say, they use the same "words" (bureaucracy, accountability, civil service reform, corruption, management, efficiency, decentralization, welfare state reform, etc.) to identify contemporary challenges no matter how they vary in the real world of different cultural settings. By contrast, Hofstede (1991) argued that convergence would be hard to expect since at

> ...the national level cultural differences reside mostly in values, less in practices (as long as we compare otherwise similar people). At the organizational level, cultural differences reside mostly in practices, less in values. (Hofstede, 1991: 182)

Contrary to what Caiden believes, convergence toward a universal study of public administration is difficult if not impossible because of different national state and administrative cultures. These differences in national culture are not only apparent in how the study is conceptualized and perceived but also in how theory can be applied. Aldrich referred to this when recognizing that organizational " . . . innovations have failed when introduced into societies with non-supportive cultural and institutional traditions" (1979: 22). In other words, transplanting the experiences and/or the best practices of one country to another does not guarantee successful adoption and many development administration scholars and consultants will concur.

Thus, the study of public administration has global elements (i.e., structural features of administration in various countries) as well as local elements (i.e., how these structures function in a particular cultural setting). The national culture is not only visible, though, in how particular structures function, but also in how they are perceived. Do people think at the village market level, small scale, or do they perceive reality as a large whole, a grand design?

8.6 The Disciplined Interdisciplinary Identity and Some Last Thoughts

In the mystery novel *Belgrave Square* by Anne Perry, several of the main characters attend a performance of *Lohengrin*. One of them admits to prefer Gilbert and Sullivan whereupon another responds: "You are too English [. . .]. Wagner would say your imagination is pedestrian. We [the English] make fun of the grand design because we do not understand it, and cannot sustain an intellectual passion because at that level we are still children" (1992: 147). It is a leap from opera to the study of public administration, and whether this statement – intended to reflect a sentiment in the 1880s – fairly describes a difference today between English (and American) scholarship on the one hand and that of their continental neighbors on the other can be questioned. However, the Czech historian Krejčí notes that the British are more concerned with facts and that, by implication, continental-European scholars focus on theories (2004: xiv). Also, the sociologist MacIver observed in 1929 that Americans understood method as a research technique for collecting, recording, sorting, classifying, tabulating, and counting facts, while to Germans " . . . method is a principle in terms of which he arranges facts in categories, determines the relation of the categories to one another, analyses a social situation or a large-scale social movement into its essential factors, and offers a synthetic interpretation of the world" (quoted in Higham, 1979: 8). To be sure, American scholarship has not produced a Max Weber, while German scholarship has not been the breeding ground of a Herbert Simon.

The quote from Perry illustrates, though, very well the difference between Anglo-American and Continental-European scholars. The former generally approach the study of public administration inductively (Americans) and/or essayisticly (the English, certainly up to the 1980s) while the latter develop comprehensive frameworks or grand designs for the study (the Dutch, French,

Germans). This book neither has the features of a grand design in the traditional continental-European way of unifying the study around one central concept and then deriving a series of hierarchically organized sub-concepts, nor does it have the American features of organizing the study as a "string of specializations." A top-down approach to establishing a study's nature and identity does not work. In this book the less traditional bottom-up approach of conceptually mapping the study's building blocks, that is, topical areas, sources of knowledge, theory arena, schools of thought, and types of knowledge integration has been used.

Public administration is and ought to be a field of study that is organizationally independent, because that has allowed for the expansion of its substantive interests and, one must be practical too, for increases in student enrollments. As soon as the study is reduced to subfield status, such as in political science, it is reduced to being a toolbag for practitioners. As Wise has pointed out:

> ... Obviously, public administration is an inter-disciplinary field and political science-based investigations of the field of public administration do not capture the full range of activity. (1999: 150–1)

A technocratic approach to the study no longer reflects the range of interests that the study encompasses today. As an independent study it has become increasingly interdisciplinary.

From the perspective of public administration, political science is and always will be relevant, but as one of the administrative sciences. Keep in mind that the study of public administration cannot lay exclusive claim upon its object of knowledge; it can argue convincingly, though, that it is the only study that seeks to capture government and governance in all its manifestations. Hence, to suggest that the study lacks rigor and that it ought to develop a disciplinary identity by laying exclusive claims is impossible, because neither is there any theoretical coherence nor can its scholarly community claim exclusive control over its body of knowledge.

Rigor has not only been pursued through theoretical and/or methodological refinement, but also through the organization of research. With an eye on research programs in the natural sciences and in medicine, comparable research programs have emerged in the social sciences (especially in economics and psychology), where one or a few full professors, and several associate and assistant professors work with a batch of doctoral students, each of which tackling one piece of the larger puzzle. This type of program is not so common, yet (?), in public administration. This could be because the number of "scientists" is not as large.

The degree to which such programs may become more common is directly related to the number of scholars embracing scientific knowledge as defined in

Chapters 2 and 6. The more scholars believe in scientific knowledge narrowly defined, the more the advancement of knowledge will be channeled through the avenues carved out by the senior members of a research team. Naturally, aspiring scholars profit from the experience of seasoned scholars, but it may also stifle innovation. This is what *Lord of the Rings* author Tolkien had in mind when, in his Valedictory Address, he expressed concern about postgraduate research factories that focus on publishing and meeting grant requirements, rather than on being original and creative (see quote at the opening of this chapter). In the same spirit, Starbuck observed that social scientists prefer research methods (i.e., statistical analysis of databases created through mail surveys) that allow for the mass-production of publications, rather than for the production of knowledge (2006: 84). Tolkien's remark quoted at the opening of this chapter follows an observation several pages earlier that could be applicable to doctoral research: " ...one must feel grave disquiet, when the legitimate inspiration is not there; when the subject or topic of 'research' is imposed, or is 'found' for a candidate out of someone else's bag of curiosities ... " (2006: 227). So far, and only regarding the study of public administration, there is not much reason to believe Tolkien's concern has become reality, and that is because in the study of public administration the majority of scholars have shown great discipline in developing, protecting, and advancing the fundamental interdisciplinarity that makes the study so successful in capturing a reality that we all can recognize (see quote from Lasch at the beginning of this chapter).

Bibliography

Aaltonen, M. (2007). "The Return to Multi-Causality," *Journal of Future Studies*, 12(1), 81–6.

Abbott, A. (2001). *Chaos of Disciplines*. Chicago/London: The University of Chicago Press.

Aberbach, J.D., R.D. Putnam, and B.A. Rockman (1981). *Bureaucrats and Politicians in Western Democracies*. Cambridge, MA: Harvard University Press.

Adamolekun, L. (ed.) (1999). *Public Administration in Africa: Main Issues and Selected Country Studies*. Boulder, CO: Westview Press.

Adams, G.B. (1992). "Enthralled with Modernity: The Historical Context of Knowledge and Theory Development in Public Administration," *Public Administration Review*, 52(4), 363–73.

—— D.L. Balfour (1998). *Unmasking Administrative Evil*. London: Sage.

Aldrich, H.E. (1979). *Organizations and Environments*. Upper Saddle River, NJ: Prentice Hall.

—— M. Ruef (2006). *Organizations Evolving*. London/Thousand Oaks: Sage.

Alford, J.R., and J.R. Hibbing (2004). "The Origin of Politics: An Evolutionary Theory of Political Behavior," *Perspectives on Politics*, 2(4), 707–23.

Almond, G.A. (1988). "Separate Tables: Schools and Sects in Political Science," *PS: Political Science and Politics*, 21(4), 828–42.

—— S. Verba (1963). *The Civic Culture: Political Attitudes and Democracy in Five Nations*. Princeton: Princeton University Press.

Alt, J.E., M. Levi, and E. Ostrom (eds.) (1999). *Competition and Cooperation: Conversations with Nobelists about Economics and Political Science*. New York: Russell Sage Foundation.

—— K.A. Shepsle (eds.) (1990). *Perspectives on Positive Political Economy*. Cambridge: Cambridge University Press.

Amariglio, J., S. Resnick, and R.D. Wolff (1993). "Division and Difference in the "Discipline" of Economics," in E. Messer-Davidow, D.R. Shumway, and D.J. Sylvan (eds.), *Knowledges: Historical and Critical Studies in Disciplinarity*. Charlottesville: University Press of Virginia, 150–84.

Anderson, B. (2006). *Imagined Communities: Reflection on the Origin and Spread of Nationalism*. London/New York: Verso.

Andrews, R., G.A. Boyne, and R.M. Walker (2008). "Reconstructing Emprical Public Administration: Lutonism or Scientific Realism?," *Administration & Society*, 40(2), 324–30.

Argyris, C. (1973*a*). "Some Limits of Rational Man Organizational Theory," *Public Administration Review*, 33(3), 253–67.

—— (1973*b*). "Organizational Man: Rational and Self-Actualizing," *Public Administration Review*, 33(4), 354–7.

Aristotle (1976). *The Ethics of Aristotle. The Nicomachean Ethics*. London: Penguin Books (translated by J.A.K. Thomson).

Armstrong, D. (1993). "The Medical Division of Labor," in E. Messer-Davidow, D.R. Shumway, and D.J. Sylvan (eds.), *Knowledges: Historical and Critical Studies in Disciplinarity*. Charlottesville: University Press of Virginia, 232–42.

Armstrong, K. (2007). *The Bible. A Biography*. New York: Grove Press.

Arnold, P.E. (1995). "Reform's Changing Role," *Public Administration Review*, 55(5), 407–17.

Asch, S.E. (1955). "Opinions and Social Pressure," *Scientific American*, 193(5), 31–5.

Astley, W.G., and A.H. van de Ven (1983). "Central Perspectives and Debates in Organization Theory," *Administrative Science Quarterly*, 28(2), 245–73.

Auby, J.M. (1966). *Traité de science administrative*. Paris: Mouton.

Ausubel, D.P. (1963). *The Psychology of Meaningful Verbal Learning*. New York: Grune and Stratton.

—— (1968). *Educational Psychology: A Cognitive View*. New York: Holt, Rinehart and Winston.

Axelrod, R. (1976). *The Structure of Decision: The Cognitive Maps of Political Elites*. Princeton, NJ: Princeton University Press.

Babbie, E. (1998). *The Practice of Social Research*. Belmont, CA: Wadsworth Publishing Company.

Badie, B., P. Birnbaum (1983). *The Sociology of the State*. Chicago: University of Chicago Press (trans. A. Goldhammer).

Bailey, M.T. (1992). "Do Physicists Use Case Studies? Thoughts on Public Administration Research," *Public Administration Review*, (52)1, 47–54.

Bailey, W.G. (1995). *The Encyclopedia of Police Science*. New York: Garland.

Banfield, E.C. (1957). "A Criticism of the Decision Making Schema," *Public Administration Review*, 17(3), 278–85.

Barley, S.R., and G. Kunda (1992). "Design and Devotion: Surges of Rational and Normative Ideologies in Control in Managerial Discourse," *Administrative Science Quarterly*, 37(2), 363–99.

Barnard, C.I. (1968, 2nd ed.). *The Functions of the Executive*. Cambridge, MA/London: Harvard University Press (30th anniversary printing with introduction by Kenneth R. Andrews).

Barrow, C.W. (2008). "The Intellectual Origins of New Political Science," *New Political Science*, 30(2), 215–44.

Barth, T.J., and M.T. Green (1999). "Public Administration Handbooks: Why, How, and Who?," *Public Administration Review*, 59(6), 535–44.

Bartolini, S. (1993). "On Time and Comparative Research," *Journal of Theoretical Politics*, 5(1), 131–67.

Becher, T., and P.R. Trowler (2001). *Academic Tribes and Territories: Intellectual Inquiry and the Culture of Disciplines*. Buckingham/Philadelphia: Society for Research into Higher Education & Open University Press.

Bechtel, W. (ed.) (1986). *Integrating Scientific Disciplines*. Dordrecht: Martinus Nijhoff Publishers.

Beck Jörgenson, T. (1996). "From Continental Law to Anglo-Saxon Behaviorism: Scandinavian Public Administration," *Public Administration Review*, 56(1), 94–103.

Bekke, A.J.G.M., Th.A.J. Toonen, and J.L. Perry (eds.) (1996). *Civil Service Systems in Comparative Perspective*. Bloomington: Indiana University Press.

Bellah, R.N. (1999). "Freedom, Coercion, Authority," *Academe: Bulletin of the American Association of University Professors*, 85(1), 16–21.

—— R. Madsen, W.M. Sullican, A. Swidler, and S.M. Tipton (1996). *Habits of the Heart: Individualism and Commitment in American Life*. Berkeley: University of California Press.

Bendor, J. (1988). "Formal Models of Bureaucracy," *British Journal of Political Science*, 18(2), 353–95.

—— T.M. Moe (1985). "An Adaptive Model of Bureaucratic Politics," *American Political Science Review*, 79(3), 755–74.

—— K.W. Shotts (2001). "Recycling the Garbage Can: An Assessment of the Research Program," *American Political Science Review*, 95(1), 169–90.

Bennis, W.G., and H.J. O'Toole (2005). "How Business Schools Lost their Way," *Harvard Business Review*, 86(5), 96–104.

Benton, T., and I. Craib (2001). *Philosophy of Social Science: The Philosophical Foundations of Social Thought*. Houndmills: Palgrave.

Berlin, I. (1991). *The Crooked Timber of Humanity: Chapter in the History of Ideas*. New York: Alfred A. Knopf.

—— (1993). *The Magus of the North: J.G. Hamann and the Origins of Modern Irrationalism*. New York: Farrar, Straus and Giroux.

—— (1996). "Political Judgement," in ibid. (ed.), *The Sense of Reality. Studies in Ideas and their History*. New York: Farrar, Straus and Giroux, 40–53.

—— (1999). *The Roots of Romanticism*. Princeton: Princeton University Press.

—— (2000). *The Power of Ideas*. London: Chatto & Windus.

—— (2002 [1969]). *Liberty*. ed., H. Hardy Oxford/New York: Oxford University Press.

Berman, H.J. (1974). *The Interaction of Law and Religion*. Nashville/New York: Abingdon Press.

—— (1983). *Law and Revolution. The Formation of the Western Legal Tradition*. Cambridge, MA: Harvard University Press.

Bertelli, A.M. (2004). "Strategy and Accountability: Structural Reform Litigation and Public Management," *Public Administration Review*, 64(1), 28–42.

—— L.E. Lynn Jr. (2006). *Madison's Managers: Public Administration and the Constitution*. Baltimore: The Johns Hopkins University Press.

Bevir, M. (1999). *The Logic of the History of Ideas*. Cambridge: Cambridge University Press.

Bhat, G.N. (2007). "Recovering the Historical *Rechtsstaat*," *Review of Central and East European Law*, 32(1), 65–97.

Bingham, R.D., and W.M. Bowen (1994). "Mainstream Public Administration Over Time: A Topical Content Analysis of Public Administration Review," *Public Administration Review*, 54(2), 204–8.

Birnbaum, P. (1985). "Sur la Dé-différentation de l'État," *International Political Science Review*, 6(1), 57–63.

Björkman, J.W. (2003). "South Asian and Western Administrative Experience: The Past in the Present," in B.G. Peters, and J. Pierre (eds.), *Handbook of Public Administration*. Thousand Oaks: Sage, 192–203.

Blau, P.M., and R.A. Schoenherr (1971). *The Structure of Organizations*. New York: Basic Books.

Bloom, A.D. (1987). *The Closing of the American Mind*. New York: Simon & Schuster.

Bogason, P. (2000). *Public Policy and Local Governance: Institutions in Postmodern Society*. Cheltenham, UK/Northampton, MA: Edward Elgar.

—— (2008). "Book review of Stanford F. Schram, Brian Caterino (eds.), *Making Political Science Matter: Debating Knowledge, Research, and Method* (New York: New York University Press, 2006) and of Raymond D. Gordon (2007), *Power, Knowledge, and Domination* (Stockholm: Liber)," *Administrative Theory & Praxis*, 30(4), 530–7.

Bolton, M.J., and G.B. Stolcis (2003). "Ties That Do Not Bind: Musings on the Specious Relevance of Academic Research," *Public Administration Review*, 63(5), 626–30.

Bothamly, J. (2002). *Dictionary of Theories*. Detroit: Visible Ink.

Bouckaert, G., and W. Van den Donk (eds.) (2010). *The European Group for Public Administration (1975–2010). Perspectives for the Future*. Brussels: Bruylant.

Bougon, M.G. (1992). "Congregate Cognitive Maps: A Unified dynamic Theory of Organization and Strategy," *Journal of Management Studies*, 29(3), 369–89.

Bovaird, T. (2002). "Public Management and Governance: Emerging Trends and Potential Future Directions," in E. Vigoda (ed.), *Public Administration. An Interdiscplinary Critical Analysis*. New York: Marcel Dekker, 345–76.

Bowman, J.S., and S.G. Hajjar (1978). "English-Language Journals in Public Administration: An Analysis," *Public Administration (UK)*, 56(2), 203–25.

Box, R.C. (1992). "An Examination of the Debate Over Research in Public Administration," *Public Administration Review*, (52)1, 62–9.

—— (2005). *Critical Social Theory in Public Administration*. Armonk: M.E. Sharpe.

Bozeman, B. (1979). *Public Management and Policy Analysis*. New York: St. Martin's Press.

Braybrooke, D. (1987). *Philosophy of Social Science*. Engelwood Cliffs, NJ: Prentice-Hall Inc.

Brendel, D.H. (2006). *Healing Psychiatry: Bridging the Science/Humanities Divide*. Cambridge, MA: MIT Press.

Brower, R.S., M.Y. Abolafia, and J.B. Carr (2000). "On Improving Qualitative Methods in Public Administration Research," *Administration & Society*, 32(4), 363–97.

Brudney, J.L., L.J. O'Toole, and H.G. Rainey (eds.) (2000). *Advancing Public Management: New Developments in Theory, Methods, and Practice*. Washington, DC: Georgetown University Press.

Buchanan, C.D. (1933). "Substantivized Adjectives in Old Norse," *Language*, 9(2), Language Dissertations no. 15. Washington, DC: Linguistic Society of American, 5–62.

Buchanan, J.M., and G. Tullock (1962). *The Calculus of Consent. Logical Foundations of Constitutional Democracy*. Ann Arbor: The University of Michigan Press.

Buckley, M.R. (1998). "The Disconnect between the Science and Practice of Management," *Business Horizons*, 41(2), 1–10.

Burrell, G., and G. Morgan (1979). *Sociological Paradigms and Organisational Analysis*. London: Heinemann.

Cahill, T. (2008). *Masteries of the Middle Ages and the Beginning of the Modern World*. New York: Nan A. Talese Anchor Books.

Caiden, G.E. (1994). "Globalizing the Theory and the Practice of Public Administration," in J.C. Garcia-Zamor and R. Khator (eds.), *Public Administration in the Global Village*. Westport, CT: Praeger Publishers, 45–59.

Caldwell, L.K. (1965). "Public Administration and the Universities: A Half-Century of Development," *Public Administration Review*, 25(1), 52–60.

—— (1975). "Managing the Transition to Postmodern Society," *Public Administration Review*, 36(6), 567–72.

Campbell, D.T. (1969). "Ethnocentrism of Disciplines and the Fish-Scale Model of Omniscience," in M. Sherif, and C.W. Sherif (eds.), *Interdisciplinary Relationships in the Social Sciences*. Chicago: Aldine Publishing Company, 328–48.

Candler, G.G. (2006). "The Comparative Evolution of Public Administration in Australia, Brazil, and Canada," *Canadian Public Administration/Administration Publique du Canada*, 49(3), 334–49.

—— (2008). "Epistemic Community or Tower of Babel? Theoretical Diffusion in Public Administration," *The Australian Journal of Public Administration*, 67(3), 294–306.

Carpenter, D.P. (2001). *The Forging of Bureaucratic Autonomy. Reputations, Networks, and Policy Innovation in Executive Agencies, 1862–1928*. Princeton/Oxford: Princeton University Press.

Cassirer, E. (2006). "Science," in ibid. (ed.), *An Essay on Man*. Gesammelte Werke Hamburger Ausgabe. Hamburg: Felix Meiner Verlag, 207–21.

Catlaw, T.J. (2007). *Fabricating the People: Politics and Administration in the Biopolitical State*. Tuscaloosa: The University of Alabama Press.

Catton, W.R. (1966). *From Animistic to Naturalistic Sociology*. New York: McGraw-Hill.

Cavadino, M., and J. Dignan (1996). *The Penal System: An Introduction*. London: Sage.

Cawkell, T. (2000). "Visualizing Citation Connections," in B. Cronin and H.B. Atkins (eds.), *The Web of Knowledge. A Festschrift in Honor of Eugene Garfield*. Medford, NJ: Information Today, Inc., 177–94.

Chase, W.C. (1982). *The American Law School and the Rise of Administrative Government*. Madison: The University of Wisconsin Press.

Cheit, E.F. (1991). "The Shaping of Business Management Thought," in D. Easton, and C.S. Schelling (eds.) (1991). *Divided Knowledge. Across Disciplines, Across Cultures*. Newbury Park: Sage, 195–218.

Chevallier, J. (1996). "Public Administration in Statist France," *Public Administration Review*, 56(1), 67–74.

—— D. Loschak (1974). *Introduction à la Science Administrative*. Paris: Dalloz.

Cigler, B.A., and H.L. Neiswender (1991). "'Bureaucracy' in the Introductory American Government Textbook," *Public Administration Review*, 51(5), 442–50.

Clarke, S. (2007). "Against the Unification of the Behavioral Sciences." *Behavioral and Brain Sciences*, 30(1), 21–2.

Cleary, R.E. (1992). "Revisiting the Doctoral Dissertation in Public Administration: An Examination of the Dissertations of 1990," *Public Administration Review*, 52(1), 55–61.

Cohn, J. (1999). "Irrational Exuberance. When Did Political Science Forget about Politics?" *The New Republic*, October 25, 25–32.

Colomer, J.M. (2007). "What Other Sciences Look Like," *European Political Science*, 6(2), 134–42.

Comfort, L.K. (1994). "Self-Organization in Complex Systems," *Journal of Public Administration Research and Theory*, 4(3), 393–410.

Coontz, S. (1992). *The Way We Never Were: American Families and the Nostalgia Trap*. New York: Basic Books.

Corcoran, P.E. (1993). "Time and Purpose in the Language of Social Science," in H. Redner (ed.), *An Heretical Heir of the Enlightenment: Politics, Policy, and Science in the Work of Charles E. Lindblom*. Boulder, CO: Westview Press, 97–128.

Cossette, P. (2002). "Analysis of the Thinking of F.W. Taylor Using Cognitive Mapping," *Journal of Management History*, 40(2), 168–82.

—— M. Audet (1992). "Mapping of an Idiosyncratic Schema," *Journal of Management Studies*, 29(3), 325–47.

Cox, R. (1993). "Why is it Difficult to Teach Comparative Politics to American Students?," *Political Science & Politics*, 26(1), 68–72.

Crowther-Heyck, H. (2005). *Organization Man: The Life and Work of Herbert A. Simon*. Baltimore, MD: Johns Hopkins University Press.

Cunningham, R., and L. Weschler (2002). "Theory and the Public Administration Student/Practitioner," *Public Administration Review*, 62(1), 104–9.

Cutting, B., and A. Kouzmin (2005). "Governance in U.S. Public Administration: Revisiting the Blacksburg Manifesto and Beyond." Paper presented at the 18th Annual Meeting of the Public Administration Theory Network, Krakow, Poland, 9–11 June.

Dahl, R.A. (1947). "The Science of Public Administration: Three Problems," *Public Administration Review*, 7(1), 1–11.

—— (1961). "The Behavioral Approach in Political Science: Epitaph for a Monument to a Successful Protest," *American Political Science Review*, 55(4), 763–72.

—— (1970). *After the Revolution? Authority in a Good Society*. New Haven: Yale University Press.

Dahl, R.A., and C.E. Lindblom (1953). *Politics, Economics, and Welfare: Planning and Politico-Economic Systems Resolved into Basic Social Processes*. New York: Harper & Row.

D'Andrade, R. (1986). "Three Scientific World Views and the Covering Law Model," in D.W. Fiske and R. Shweder (eds.), *Metatheory in Social Science: Pluralism and Subjectivities*. Chicago/London: The University of Chicago Press, 19–41.

Daneke, G.A. (1990). "A Science of Public Administration?," *Public Administration Review*, 50(3), 383–92.

Darden, L., and N. Maull (1977). "Interfield Theories," *Philosophy of Science*, 44(1), 43–64.

Davidson, J.F. (1961). "Political Science and Political Action," *American Political Science Review*, 55(4), 851–60.

Davidson, B. (1992). *The Black Man's Burden: Africa and the Curse of the Nation-State*. New York: Times Books.

Davy, T.J. (1962). "Public Administration as a Field of Study in the United States," *International Review of Administrative Sciences*, 28(1), 64–9.

Dawkins, R. (2006), *The Selfish Gene*, 30th anniversary edition. Oxford: Oxford University Press.

Debbasch, C. (1989). *Science Administrative; Administration Publique*. Paris: Dalloz.

Denhardt, R.B. (2001). "The Big Questions of Public Administration Education," *Public Administration Review*, 61(5), 526–34.

—— (2004). *Theories of Public Organization*. Belmont, CA: Wadsworth/Thomson Learning.

Dewey, J. (1927). *The Public and its Problems*. New York: Henry Holt and Company.

De Zwart, F. (2002). "Administrative Practice and Rational Inquiry in Postmodern Public Administration Theory," *Administration & Society*, 34(5), 482–98.

Diamond, J. (2005). *Collapse: How Societies Choose to Fail or Succeed*. New York: Viking.

Diggins, J.P. (1996). *Max Weber: Politics and the Spirit of Tragedy*. New York: Basic Books.

Dimock, M.E. (1936). "The Criteria and Objectives of Public Administration," in J.M. Gaus, L.D. White, and M.E. Dimock (eds.), *The Frontiers of Public Administration*. Chicago: The University of Chicago Press, 116–29.

—— (1958). *A Philosophy of Administration: Toward Creative Growth*. New York: Harper & Row.

Dishman, R.B. (1971). *Burke and Paine: On Revolution and the Rights of Man*. New York: Charles Scribner.

Dogan, M. (1996). "Political Science and the Other Social Sciences," in R.E. Goodin and H-D. Klingemann (eds.), *A New Handbook of Political Science*. Oxford: Oxford University Press, 97–130.

Donovan, C. (2005). "The Governance of Social Science and Everyday Epistemology," *Public Administration (UK)*, 83(3), 597–615.

Downs, A. (1967). *Inside Bureaucracy*. Boston: Little, Brown.

Dreschler, W. (2000). "On the Possibility of Quantitative-Mathematical Social Science, Chiefly Economics: Some Preliminary Considerations," *Journal of Economic Studies*, 27(4/5), 246–59.

Dreyfus, H., and S. Dreyfus (1986). *Mind over Machine: The Power of Human Intuition and Expertise in the Era of the Computer*. New York: Free Press.

Dror, Y. (2001). *The Capacity to Govern*. A Report to the Club of Rome. London: Frank Cass.

Dubnick, M.J. (1999). "Demons, Spirits, and Elephants: Reflections on the Failure of Public Administration Theory." Paper delivered at the 1999 Annual Meeting of the American Political Science Association, Atlanta, GA.

Dunleavy, P. (1991). *Democracy, Bureaucracy and Public Choice. Economic Explanations in Political Science*. New York: Harvester Wheatsheaf.

Durham, G. H. (1940). "Politics and Administration in Intergovernmental Relations," *Annals*, 207 (1), 1–60.

Dyson, K.H.F. (1980). *The State Tradition in Western Europe: A Study of an Idea and Institution*. New York: Oxford University Press.

Easton, D. (1969). "The New Revolution in Political Science," *American Political Science Review*, 63(4), 1051–61.

—— (1985). "Political Science in the United States: Past and Present," *International Political Science Review*, 6(1), 133–52.

—— (1991a). "The Division, Integration, and Transfer of Knowledge," in D. Easton, and C.S. Schelling (eds.), *Divided Knowledge: Across Disciplines, Across Cultures*. Newbury Park: Sage, 7–36.

—— (1991b). "Political Science in the United States," in D. Easton, and C.S. Schelling (eds.), *Divided Knowledge: Across Disciplines, Across Cultures*. Newbury Park: Sage, 37–58.

Eden, C. (1992). "On the Nature of Cognitive Maps," *Journal of Management Studies*, 29(3), 261–5.

—— F. Ackerman, and S. Cropper (1992). "The Analysis of Cause Maps," *Journal of Management Studies*, 29(3), 309–24.

Ellwood, J.W. (1996). "Political Science," in D.F. Kettl and H.B. Milward (eds.), *The State of Public Management*. Baltimore/London: The Johns Hopkins University Press, 51–74.

—— (2000). "Prospects for the Study of the Governance of Public Organizations and Policies," in C.J. Heinrich, and L.E. Lynn Jr. (eds.), *Governance and Performance. New Perspectives*. Washington, DC: Georgetown University Press, 319–35.

Elmore, R. (1986). "Graduate Education in Public management: Working the Seams of Government," *Journal of Policy Analysis and Management*, 6(1), 69–83.

Encarta Online Encyclopedia (2009). http:///Encarta.msn.com/text_761590313__ 0/International_Organization.html downloaded January 12.

Englehart, J.K. (2001). "The Marriage between Theory and Practice," *Public Administration Review*, 61(3), 371–4.

Erikson, E.H. (1968). *Identity: Youth and Crisis*. New York: W.W. Norton & Company.

Etzioni, A. (1988). *The Moral Dimension: Toward a New Economics*. New York: The Free Press.

Farmer, D.J. (1995). *The Language of Public Administration: Bureaucracy, Modernity, and Postmodernity*. Tuscaloosa, AL: University of Alabama Press.

—— (1999). Public Administration Discourse: A Matter of Style? *Administration & Society*, 31(3), 299–320.

—— (2005). *To Kill the King: Post-Traditional Governance and Bureaucracy*. Armonk, NY: M.E. Sharpe.

—— (2010). *Public Administration in Perspective: Theory and Practice Through Multiple Lenses*. Armonk, NY: M.E. Sharpe.

Farr, J. (1988). "The History of Political Science," *American Journal of Political Science*, 32(4), 1175–95.

Fay, B.C. (1975/80). *Social Theory and Political Practice*. London: George Allen & Unwin.

—— (1996). *Contemporary Philosophy of Social Science*. Cambridge, MA: Blackwell Publishers.

—— J.D. Moon (1998 [1977]). "What Would an Adequate Philosophy of Social Science Look Like," in E.D. Klemke, R. Hollinger, and D.W. Rudge (eds.), *Introductory Readings in the Philosophy of Science*. Amherst, NY: Prometheus Books, 171–89.

Ferlie, E., L.E. Lynn Jr, and C. Pollitt (2007). "Afterword," in ibid. (eds.), *The Oxford Handbook of Public Management*. Oxford, Oxford University Press, 720–9.

Fernandes, R., and H.A. Simon (1999). "A Study of How Individuals Solve Complex and Ill-Structured Problems," *Policy Sciences*, 32(3), 225–45.

Fesler, J.T. (1982). "The Presence of the Administrative Past," *American Public Administration: Patterns of the Past*. Washington, DC: American Society for Public Administration.

Fesler, J.W. (1988). "The State and its Study. The Whole and the Parts," *PS: Political Science and Politics*, 21(4), 891–901.

Finer, S.E. (1997). *The History of Government from the Earliest Times*. Oxford: Oxford University Press.

Finkenthal, M. (2001). *Interdisciplinarity: Toward the Definition of a Metadiscipline?* New York: Peter Lang.

Fiol, C.M., and A.S. Huff (1992). "Maps for Managers: Where Are We? Where Do We Go from Here?," *Journal of Management Studies*, 29(3), 267–85.

Fischer, F. (2000). *Citizens, Experts, and the Environment: The Politics of Local Knowledge*. Durham, NC: Duke University Press.

Fiske, D.W. (1986). "Specificity of Method and Knowledge in Social Science," in D.W. Fiske and R. Shweder (eds.), *Metathoery in Social Science: Pluralism and Subjectivities*. Chicago/London: The University of Chicago Press, 61–82.

Fleishmann, J.L. (1991). "A New Framework for Integration: Policy Analysis and Public Management," in D. Easton, and C.S. Schelling (eds.), *Divided Knowledge. Across Disciplines, Across Cultures*. Newbury Park: Sage, 219–43.

Flora, P., and A. Heidenheimer (1990). *The Development of Welfare States in Europe and America*. New Brunswick, NJ: Transaction.

Flyvbjerg, B. (2001). *Making Social Science Matter: Why Social Inquiry Fails and How it can Succeed Again*. Cambridge: Cambridge University Press.

Frederickson, H.G. (1980). *New Public Administration*. University: University of Alabama Press.

—— (1997). *The Spirit of Public Administration*. San Francisco: Jossey-Bass.

—— (2003). "Look, Public Administration Ain't Rocket Science," *PA-Times*, 26, 11.

—— R.R. Mayer (symposium eds.) (1989). "Minnowbrook II: Changing Epochs of Public Administration," *Public Administration Review*, 49(2), 95–227.

—— K.B. Smith (2003). *The Public Administration Theory Primer*. Boulder, CO: Westview.

Frissen, P.H.A. (1999). *Politics, Governance, and Technology: A Postmodern Narrative on the Virtual State*. Cheltenham, UK/Northampton, MA: Edward Elgar.

Fry, B.C., and J.C.N. Raadschelders (2008). *Mastering Public Administration*. Washington, DC: CQ Press.

Fuller, S. (1993). "Disciplinary Boundaries and the Rhetoric of the Social Sciences," in E. Messer-Davidow, D.R. Shumway, and D.J. Sylvan (eds.), *Knowledges: Historical and*

Critical Studies in Disciplinarity. Charlottesville/London: University Press of Virginia, 125–49.

Gadamer, H.-G. (1975). *Truth and Method*. New York: The Seabury Press.

Gans, J.S., and G.B. Shepherd (1994). "How are the Mightly Fallen: Rejected Classic Articles by Leading Economists," *Journal of Economic Perspectives*, 8(1), 165–79.

Garfield, E. (1993). "Co-Citation Analysis of the Scientific Literature: Henry Small on Mapping the Collective Mind of Science," *Current Contents*, 19 (May), 293–4.

—— (1998). "Mapping the World of Science," Presentation at the 150 Anniversary Meeting of the American Association for the Advancement of Science, February 14, at www.garfield.library.upenn.edu/papers/mapsciworld accessed January 26, 2009.

—— A.I. Pudovkin, and V.I. Istomin (2003). "Mapping the Output of Topical Searches in the *Web of Knowledge* and the Case of Watson-Crick," *Information Technology and Libraries*, 22(4) 183–7.

Garnett, J.L. (1980). *Reorganizing State Government: The Executive Branch*. Boulder, CO: Westview.

—— A. Kouzmin (1997). *Handbook of Administrative Communication*. New York: Marcel Dekker.

Gaus, J.M. (1950). "Trends in the Theory of Public Administration," *Public Administration Review*, 10(3), 161–8.

Gibson, W.R.B. (1908). *The Problem of Logic*. London: Adam and Charles Black.

Gieryn, T.F. (1983). "Boundary-Work and the Demarcation of Science from Non-science: Strains and Interests in Professional Interests of Scientists," *American Sociological Review*, 48(6), 781–95.

Gill, J., and K.J. Meier (2000). "Public Administration Research and Practice: A Methodological Manifesto," *Journal of Public Administration Research and Theory*, 10(1), 157–99.

Gintis, H. (2007). "A Framework for the Unification of the Behavioral Sciences," *Behavioral and Brain Sciences*, 30(1), 1–61.

—— (2009). *The Bounds of Reason: Game Theory and the Unification of the Behavioral Sciences*. Princeton, NJ: Princeton University Press.

Gökalp, I. (2000). "On Complexity and Interdisciplinarity: Or how to Bridge Disciplinary Cultures," accessed at http://ieeexplore.ieee.org/stamp/stamp.jsp?arnumber=00915575 November 13, 2008.

Golembiewski, R.T. (1977). *Public Administration as a Developing Discipline: Part 2, Organization Development as a One of a Future Family of Miniparadigms*. New York: Marcel Dekker.

—— (1996). "The Future of Public Administration: End of a Short Stay in the Sun? Or a New Day A-Dawning?," *Public Administration Review*, 56(2), 139–48.

Good, J.M.M. (2000). "Disciplining Social Psychology: A Case Study of Boundary Relations in the History of the Human Sciences," *Journal of the History of the Behavioral Sciences*, 36(4), 383–403.

Goodin, R.E., and H-D. Klingemann (1996). "Political Science: The Discipline," in ibid. (eds.), *A New Handbook of Political Science*. Oxford: Oxford University Press, 3–49.

Goodnow, F.J. (1893). *Comparative Administrative Law, an Analysis of the Administrative Systems, National and Local, of the United States, England, France and Germany*. New York/London: G.P. Putnam's Sons.

—— (1990). *Politics and Administration: A Study in Government*. New York: MacMillan.

Goodsell, C.T. (1990). "Emerging Issues in Public Administration," in N.B. Lynn, A. Wildavsky (eds.), *Public Administration: The State of the Discipline*. Chatham, NJ: Chatham House, 491–502.

—— (1997). "Bureaucracy's House in the Polis: Seeking an Appropriate Presence," *Journal of Public Administration Research and Theory*, 7(3), 393–417.

—— (2001). *The American Statehouse: Interpreting Democracy's Temples*. Lawrence: University Press of Kansas.

—— (2006). "A New Vision for Public Administration," *Public Administration Review*, 66(4), 623–35.

Gorski, Ph.S. (2001). "Beyond Marx and Hintze? Third-Wave Theories of Early Modern State Formation," *Comparative Studies of Society and History*, 43(4) 851–61.

Gortner, H.F., K.L. Nichols, and C. Ball (2007). *Organization Theory: A Public and Nonprofit Perspective*. Belmont, CA: Wadsworth/Thomson Learning.

Grofman, B. (2007). "Toward a Science of Politics?," *European Political Science*, 6(2), 143–55.

Grote, R. (1999). "Rule of Law, Rechtsstaat, and 'État de droit," in C. Stark (ed.), *Constitutionalism, Universalism, and Democracy – A Comparative Analysis*. Baden-Baden: Nomos, 269–306.

Gulick, L. (1937). "Notes on the Theory of Organization," in L. Gulick and L.F. Urwick (eds.), *Papers on the Science of Administration*. New York: Institute of Public Administration.

Gunnell, J.G. (2002). "Handbooks and History: Is It Still the American Science of Politics?," *International Political Science Review*, 23(4), 339–54.

—— (2006). "The Founding of the American Political Science Association: Discipline, Profession, Political Theory, and Politics," *American Political Science Review*, 100(4), 479–86.

Guy, M.E. (2003). "Ties that Bind: The Link between Public Administration and Political Science," *The Journal of Politics*, 65(3), 641–55.

Hacking, I. (1993). "Working in a New World: The Taxonomic Solution," in P. Horwich (ed.), *World Changes: Thomas Kuhn and the Nature of Science*. Cambridge, MA: MIT Press, 275–309.

—— (1996). "The Disunities of the Sciences," in P. Gallison, and D. Stump (eds.), *The Disunity of Science*. Stanford, CA: Stanford University Press, 37–74.

Haddow, A. (1969). *Political Science in American Colleges and Universities, 1636–1900*. New York: Octagon (reprint of 1939 edition).

Halder, A. (1975). "Knowledge," in Karl Rahner (ed.), *Encyclopedia of Theology: A Concise Sacramentum Mundi*. New York: Seabury Press, 800–13.

Hall, E.T. (1983). *The Dance of Life. The Other Dimension of Time*. Garden City, NY: Anchor Press/Doubleday.

—— (1989). *Beyond Culture*. New York: Anchor Books.

Hammond, T.H. (1993). "Toward a General Theory of Hierarchy: Books, Bureaucrats, Basketball Tournaments, and the Administrative Structure of the National-State," *Journal of Public Administration Research and Theory*, 1(1), 120–45.

Hannan, M.T., and J.H. Freeman (1978). "The Population Ecology of Organizations," in M.W. Meyer and Associates, *Environments and Organizations*. San Francisco: Jossey-Bass, 131–71.

Haque, M.S. (1996). "The Intellectual Crisis in Public Administration in the Current Epoch of Privatization," *Administration & Society*, 27(4), 510–36.

Hardin, G. (1968). "The Tragedy of the Commons," *Science*, 162(3859), 1243–8.

Harmon, M.M. (1995). *Responsibility as Paradox: A Critique of Rational Discourse on Government*. Thousand Oaks: Sage.

—— (2006). *Public Administration's Final Exam: A Pragmatist Restructuring of the Profession and the Discipline*. Tuscaloosa: The University of Alabama Press.

Hartmann, J., and A.M. Khademian (2010). "Culture Change Refined and Revitalized: The Road Show and Guides for Pragmatic Action," *Public Administration Review*, 70(6), 845–56.

Hays, S.W., and R.W. Kearney (1995). *Public Personnel Administration: Problems and Prospects*. Englewood Cliffs, NJ: Prentice-Hall.

Heater, D. (1990). *Citizenship: The Civic Ideal in World History, Politics, and Education*. London: Longman.

Heckelman, J.C., and R. Whaples (2003). "Are Public Choice Scholars Different?," *PS: Political Science & Politics*, 46(4), 797–9.

Heclo, H. (1978). "Issue networks and the Executive Establishment," in A. King (ed.), *The New Political System*. Washington, DC: American Enterprise Institute.

Heinrich, C.J., and L.E. Lynn (eds.) (2000). *Governance and Performance: New Perspectives*. Washington, DC: Georgetown University Press.

Hendriks, F. (2010). *Vital Democracy: A Theory of Democracy in Action*. Oxford: Oxford University Press.

Henriques, G.R. (2003). "The Tree of Knowledge System and the Theoretical Unification of Psychology," *Review of General Psychology*, 7(2), 150–82.

—— (2004). "Psychology Defined," *Journal of Clinical Psychology*, 60(12), 1207–21.

Henry, N. (1975). "Paradigms of Public Administration," *Public Administration Review*, 35(4), 378–86.

——(1999). *Public Administration and Public Affairs*. Upper Saddle River, NJ: Prentice Hall.

—— (2010, 11th ed.). *Public Administration and Public Affairs*. New York: Longman.

—— C.T. Goodsell, L.E. Lynn Jr., C. Stivers, and G.L. Wamsley (2008). "Understanding Excellence in the Master of Public Administration Degree." Washington, DC: American Society for Public Administration, February 19 (this report has been reprinted in three consecutive issues of the *PA-Times* (May, pp. 15 and 21; June pp. 21 and 23; July, p. 21).

Herz, J.H. (1976 [1957]). "Rise and Demise of the Territorial State," in ibid. (ed.), *The Nation-State and the Crisis of World Politics*. New York: David McKay Company, Inc.

Hesse, J.J. (ed.) (1982). *Politikwissenschaft und Verwaltungswissenschaft*. Opladen: Nomos Verlaggesellschaft.

Heyen, E.V. (1994). *Images of Government. Memoirs, Caricatures, Novels, Architecture.* Yearbook of European Administrative History, vol.6. Baden-Baden: Nomos Verlagsgesellschaft.

Higham, J. (1979). "The Matrix of Specialization," in A. Oleson, and J. Voss (eds.), *The Organization of Knowledge in Modern America, 1860–1920.* Baltimore: The Johns Hopkins University Press, 3–18.

Hill, L.B. (1992). "Taking Bureaucracy Seriously," in ibid. (ed.), *The State of Public Bureaucracy.* Armonk: M.E. Sharpe, 15–58.

Hodgkinson, C. (1978). *Towards a Philosophy of Administration.* Oxford: Oxford University Press.

Hodgson, G.M. (2001). *How Economics Forgot History: The Problem of Historical Specificity in Social Science.* London: Routledge.

—— (2004). *The Evolution of Institutional Economics: Agency, Structure and Darwinism in American Institutionalism.* London: Routledge.

Hoffman, M.C. (2002). "Paradigm Lost: Public Administration at Johns Hopkins University, 1884–96," *Public Administration Review,* 62(1), 12–23.

Hofstede, G. (1997 [1991]). *Cultures and Organizations: Software of the Mind.* New York: McGraw-Hill.

—— G.J. Hofstede (2005). *Cultures and Organizations: Software of the Mind.* New York: McGraw & Hill.

Hood, C.C. (1986). *The Tools of Government.* Chatham, NJ: Chatham House Publihsers, Inc.

—— (1990). "Public Administration: Lost an Empire, Not Yet Found a Role?," in A. Leftwich (ed.), *New Developments in Political Science: An International Review of Achievements and Prospects.* Aldershot: Edward Elgar, 107–25.

—— (1998). *The Art of the State: Culture, Rhetoric, and Public Management.* Oxford: Clarendon Press.

—— (2007). "Public Management: The Word, the Movement, The Science," in E. Ferlie, L.E. Lynn Jr, and C. Pollitt (eds.), *The Oxford Handbook of Public Management.* Oxford, Oxford University Press, 7–26.

—— M. Jackson (1991). *Administrative Argument.* Aldershot: Dartmouth Publishing Company Limited.

Houston, D.J., and S.M. Delevan (1990). "Public Administration Research: An Assessment of Journal Publications," *Public Administration Review,* 50(6), 674–81.

—— S.M. Delevan (1994). "A Comparative Assessment of Public Administration Journal Publications," *Administration & Society,* 26(2), 252–71.

Hummel, R.P. (1977). *The Bureaucratic Experience.* New York: St. Martin's Press.

—— (2007). "Toward Bindlestiff Science: Let's All Get Off the 3:10 to Yuma," *Administration & Society,* 39(8), 1013–20.

Hurst, J.W. (1977). *Law and Social Order in the United States.* Ithaca, NY: Cornell University Press.

Imperial, M.T., J.L. Perry, and M.C. Katula (2007). "Incorporating Service Learning into Public Affairs Programs: Lessons for the Literature," *Journal of Public Affairs Education,* 13(2), 243–64.

Infeld, D.L. (2002). *Disciplinary Approaches to Aging*, general ed., New York/London: Routledge.

Jaynes, J. (1990 [1976]). *The Origins of Consciousness in the Break of the Bicameral Mind*. Boston/New York: Houghton Mifflin.

Jones, B.D. (2003). "Bounded Rationality and Political Science: Lessons from Public Administration and Public Policy," *Journal of Public Administration Research and Theory*, 13(4), 395–412.

Jun, J.S. (2006). *The Social Construction of Public Administration. Interpretive and Critical Perspectives*. Albany: State University of New York Press.

Kaboolian, L. (1996). "Sociology," in D.F. Kettl and H. Brinton Milward (eds.), *The State of Public Management*. Baltimore: The Johns Hopkins University Press, 75–91.

Kandel, E.R. (2006). *In Search of Memory: The Emergence of a new Science of Mind*. New York: W.W. Norton & Company, Ltd.

Kant, I. (1988). *Logic*. New York: Dover Publications, Inc. (trans. with intro. Robert S. Hartman and Wolfgang Schwartz).

—— (1996). *Critique of Pure Reason*. Indianapolis/Cambrdige: Hackett Publishing Company, Inc. (trans. Werner S. Pluhar; intro. Patricia Kitcher).

Kaplan, A. (1964). *The Conduct of Inquiry. Methodology for Behavioral Science*. San Francisco, CA: Chandler Publishing.

Kapucu, N. (2003). "Coordinating without Hierarchy: Public – Non-Profit Partnerships." Paper presented at the Annual Conference of the International Association of Schools and Institutes of Administration, Miami, September 14–18.

Karl, B.D. (1983). *The Uneasy State: The United States from 1915 to 1945*. Chicago: University of Chicago Press.

Kass, H.D., and B.L. Catron (1990). *Images and Identities in Public Administration*. Newbury Park: Sage Publications.

Katz, R., and Kahn, R.L. (1966). *The Social Psychology of Organizations*. New York. Wiley.

Katznelson, I., and H.V. Milner (2002). "American Political Science: The Discipline's State and the State of the Discipline," in ibid. (eds.), *Political Science: The State of the Discipline*. New York: W.W. Norton, 1–26.

Kay, A. (2006). *The Dynamics of Public Policy*. Cheltenham: Edward Elgar.

Keller, L., and M. Spicer (1997). "Political Science and Public Administration: A Necessary Cleft?," *Public Administration Review*, 57(3), 270–1.

Kelman, S. (2007). "Public Administration and Organization Studies," in J.P. Walsh, and A. Brief (eds.), *Academy of Management Annals*, vol.1, New York: Erlbaum, 225–67.

Kettl, D.F. (1993). "Public Administration: The State of the Field," in A.W. Finifter (ed.), *Political Science: The State of the Discipline II*. Washington, DC: The American Political Science Association, 407–28.

—— (1999). "The Future of Public Administration," *Journal of Public Affairs Education*, 5 (2), 127–33.

—— H.B. Milward (eds.) (1996). *The State of Public Management*. Baltimore: The Johns Hopkins University Press.

Khodr, H. (2005). "Public Administration and Political Science: An Historical Analysis of the Relation between the Two Academic Disciplines." Unpublished Ph.D. dissertation, Florida State University.

Khurana, R. (2007). *From Higher Aims to Hired Hands: The Social Transformation of American Business Schools and the Unfulfilled Promise of Management as a Profession.* Princeton: Princeton University Press.

Kickert, W.J.M. (1996). "Expansion and Diversification of Public Administration in the Postwar Welfare State: The Case of the Netherlands," *Public Administration Review*, 56(1), 88–94.

—— (2008). "Distinctiveness in the Study of Public Management in Europe," in ibid. (ed.), *The Study of Public Management in Europe and the US: A Comparative Analysis of National Distinctiveness.* London: Taylor & Francis, 1–13.

—— R.J. Stillman II (eds.) (1999). *The Modern State and its Study: New Administrative Sciences in a Changing Europe and United States.* Cheltenham, UK/Northampton, MA: Edward Elgar.

Kincaid, H. (1996). *Philosophical Foundations of the Social Sciences: Analyzing Controversies in Social Research.* Cambridge: Cambridge University Press.

Kiser, L. (1999). "Democracy and the University Curriculum." Paper presented at the Workshop in Political Theory and Policy Analysis. Bloomington: Indiana University.

—— E. Ostrom (1982). "The Three Worlds of Action: A Metatheoretical Synthesis of Institutional Approaches," in E. Ostrom (ed.), *Strategies of Public Inquiry.* Beverly Hills, CA: Sage, 179–222.

Klein, J.T. (1985). "The Interdisciplinary Concept: Past, Present, and Future," in L. Levin, and I.O. Lind (eds.), *Re-Assessing the Concept in Light of Institutional Experience.* Stockholm: OECD, 104–36.

—— (1990). *Interdisciplinarity. History, Theory, and Practice.* Detroit: Wayne State University Press.

—— (1993). "Blurring, Cracking, and Crossing: Permeation and the Fracturing of Discipline," in E. Messer-Davidow, D.R. Shumway, and D.J. Sylvan (eds.), *Knowledges: Historical and Critical Studies in Disciplinarity.* Charlottesville: University Press of Virginia, 185–211.

—— (1996). *Crossing Boundaries: Knowledge, Disciplinarities, and Interdisciplinarities.* Charlottesville: University Press of Virginia.

Kline, S.J. (1995). *Conceptual Foundations for Multidisciplinary Thinking.* Stanford, CA: Stanford University Press.

Knights, D., and H. Willmott (1997). "The Hype and Hope of Interdisciplinary Management Studies," *British Journal of Management*, 8(1), 9–22.

Knoflacher, H. (2004). "Roles of Measures in Changing Transport and Other Behavior." Presentation accessed at www.ivv.tuwien.ac.at/fileadmin/mediapool_Knoflacher/ 2004 December 17, 2008.

Koestler, A. (1986 [1959]). *The Sleepwalkers: A History of Man's Changing Vision of the Universe.* London: Penguin Books.

König, K. (1970). *Erkenntnissen der Verwaltungswissenschaft.* Berlin: Duncker & Humblot.

—— (1980). "Les tendances Intégrationnistes dans la science administrative," in G. Langrod (ed.), *Science et Action Administratives*. Paris: Éditions d'Organisation, 25–47.

Koppenjan, J., and E.-H. Klijn (2004). *Managing Uncertainties in Networks: A Network Approach to Problem Solving and Decision Making*. London/New York: Routledge.

Krause, G.A. (2001). "Coping with Uncertainty: Analyzing Risk Propensities of SEC Budgetary Decisions, 1949–97," *American Political Science Review*, 97(1), 171–88.

—— K.J. Meier (eds.) (2003). *Politics, Policy, and Organizations: Frontiers in the Scientific Study of Bureaucracy*. Ann Arbor: University of Michigan Press.

Krejčí, J. (2004). *The Paths of Civilization: Understanding the Currents of History*. Houndmills: Palgrave MacMillan.

Kritzer, H.M. (1996). "The Data Puzzle: The Nature of Interpretation in Quantitative Research," *American Journal of Political Science*, 40(1), 1–32.

Kuhn, T.S. (1970*a*). *The Structure of Scientific Revolutions*. Chicago/London: The University of Chicago Press (second, enlarged edition).

—— (1970*b*). "Reflections on My Critics," in I. Lakatos and A. Musgrave (eds.), *Criticism and the Growth of Knowledge*. London: Cambridge University Press, 231–78.

—— (1973 [1962]). *The Structure of Scientific Revolutions*. Chicago: The University of Chicago Press.

Kukla, A. (1992). "Unification as Goal for Psychology?," *American Psychologist*, 47(9), 1054–5.

Kunkel, J.H. (1992). "The Units of Unification: Theories or Propositions?," *American Psychologist*, 47(9), 1058–9.

Kurki, M. (2008). *Causation in International Relations: Reclaiming Causal Analysis*. Cambridge: Cambridge University Press.

Lakatos, I. (1970). "Falsification and the Methodology of Scientific Research Programmes," in I. Lakatos, and A. Musgrave (eds.), *Criticism and the Growth of Knowledge*. London: Cambridge University Press, 91–196.

Lalman, D., J. Oppenheimer, and P. Swistak (1993). "Formal Rational Choice Theory: A Cumulative Science of Politics," in A.W. Finifter (ed.), *Political Science: The State of the Discipline II*. Washington, DC: The American Political Science Association, 77–104.

Lammers, C.J. (1974). "Mono- and Poly-Paradigmatic Developments in Natural and Social Sciences," in R. Whitley (ed.) (1974). *Social Processes of Scientific Development*. London: Routledge & Kegan Paul, 123–47.

Lamont, M. (2009). *How Professors Think: Inside the Curious World of Academic Judgment*. Cambridge, MA: Harvard University Press.

—— V. Molnár (2002). "The Study of Boundaries in the Social Sciences," *Annual Review of Sociology*, 28, 167–95.

Lan, Z., and K.K. Anders (2000). "A Paradigmatic View of Contemporary Public Administration Research: An Empirical Test," *Administration & Society*, 32(2), 138–65.

Landau, M. (1969). "Redundancy, Rationality, and the Problem of Duplication and Overlap," *Public Administration Review*, 29(4), 346–58.

—— (1972). *Political Theory and Political Science: Studies in the Methodology of Political Inquiry*. New York/The MacMillan Company.

Lane, J.-E. (1996). *Constitutions and Political Theory*. Manchester: Manchester University Press.

Lasch, C. (1977). *Haven in a Heartless World*. New York/London: W.W. Norton & Company.

Lennox, J.G. (1999). "Philosophy of Biology," in M.H. Salmon, J. Earman, J.G. Glymour, J.G. Lennox, P. Machamer, J.E. McGuire, J.D. Norton, W.C. Salmon, and K.F. Schaffner (eds.), *Introduction to the Philosophy of Science*. Indianopolis: Hackett Publishing, 269–309.

Lenoir, T. (1993). "The Discipline of Nature and the Nature of Disciplines," in E. Messer-Davidow, D.R. Shumway, and D.J. Sylvan (eds.), *Knowledges: Historical and Critical Studies in Disciplinarity*. Charlottesville: University Press of Virginia, 70–102.

Levine, D.N. (1995). *Visions of the Sociological Tradition*. Chicago: The University of Chicago Press.

Lichbach, M.I., and A.S. Zuckerman (1997). *Comparative Politics. Rationality, Culture, and Structure*. Cambridge: Cambridge University Press.

Lindblom, C.E. (1959). "The Science of Muddling Through," *Public Administration Review*, 19(1), 79–88.

—— (1990). *Inquiry and Change: The Troubled Attempt to Understand and Shape Society*. New Haven: Yale University Press.

—— (1997). "Political Science in the 1940s and 1950s," *Dædalus*, 126(1), 225–52.

—— D.K. Cohen (1979). *Usable Knowledge: Social Science and Social Problem Solving*. New Haven: Yale University Press.

Lindenfeld, D.F. (1997). *The Practical Imagination: The German Sciences of State in the Nineteenth Century*. Chicago: The University of Chicago Press.

Lowi, T.J. (1992a). "Lowi and Simon on Political Science, Public Administration, Rationality and Public Choice," *Journal of Public Administration Research and Theory*, 2(2):105–12.

—— (1992b). "The State in Political Science: How We Become What We Study," *American Political Science Review*, 86(1), 1–7.

Luhman, N. (1966). *Theorie der Verwaltungswissenschaft: Bestandaufnahme und Entwurf*. Cologne/Berlin: Grote.

—— (1985). "The Theory of Social Systems and its Epistemology: Reply to Danilo Zolo's Critical Comments," *Philosophy of the Social Sciences*, 16(1), 129–34.

Luhrmann, T. (2000). *Of Two Minds: The Growing Disorder in American Psychiatry*. New York: Alfred A. Knopf.

Luton, L.S. (1999). "History and American Public Administration," *Administration & Society*, 31(2), 205–21.

—— (2007). "Deconstructing Public Administration Empiricism," *Administration & Society*, 39(4), 527–44.

—— (2008). "Beyond Empiricists versus Postmodernists," *Administration & Society*, 40(2), 211–19.

Lynn, L.E. (1996a). "Knowledge for Practice: Of What Use are the Disciplines?," in D.F. Kettl and H.B. Milward (eds.), *The State of Public Management*. Baltimore: The Johns Hopkins University Press, 47–50.

—— (1996*b*). *Public Management as Art, Science, and Profession*. Chatham, NJ: Chatham House.

—— (2001). "The Myth of the Bureaucratic Paradigm: What Traditional Public Administration Really Stood For," *Public Administration Review*, 61(2), 144–60.

—— C.J. Heinrich and C.J. Hill (2000). "Studying Governance and Public Management: Why? How?," in C.J. Heinrich and L.E. Lynn (eds.), *Governance and Performance. New Perspectives*. Washington, DC: Georgetown University Press, 1–33.

—— —— —— (2008). "The Empiricist Goose has not been Cooked!," *Administration & Society*, 40(1), 104–9.

MacDonald, G., and P. Pettit (1981). *Semantics and Social Science*, London/Boston: Routledge & Kegan Paul.

MacDonald, P.K. (2003). "Useful Fiction or Miracle Maker: The Competing Epistemological Foundations of Rational Choice Theory," *American Political Science Review*, 97(4), 551–65.

Machlup, F. (1961). "Are the Social Sciences Really Inferior?," *Southern Economic Journal*, 17(2), 173–84.

MacIntyre, A. (1979). "Social Science Methodology as the Ideology of Bureaucratic Authority," in K. Knight (ed.), *Through the Looking Glass: Epistemology and the Conduct of Enquiry*. Cambridge: Polity Press, 53–69.

——(1998). "Social Science Methodology as the Ideology of Bureaucratic Authority," *The MacIntyre Reader* (ed. K. Knight). Notre Dame, IN: University of Notre Dame Press.

Mainzer, L.C. (1994). "Public Administration in Search of a Theory: The Interdisciplinary Illusion," *Administration & Society*, 26(3), 359–94.

Mäki, U. (1999). "Explanatory Unification: Double and Doubtful," *Philosophy of the Social Sciences*, 31(4), 488–506.

—— C. Marchionni (2009). "On the Structure of Explanatory Unification: The Case of Geographical Economics," *Studies in History and Philosophy of Science*, 40(2), 185–95.

Mann, M. (1986). *The Sources of Social Power: Volume I. A History of Power from the Beginning to A.D. 1760*. Cambridge: Cambridge University Press.

Mansilla, V.B. (2006). "Interdisciplinary Work at the Frontier: An Empirical Examination of Expert Interdisciplinary Epistemologies," *Issues in Integrative Studies*, 24, 1–31.

Maranto, M. (2005). *Beyond a Government of Strangers: How Career Executives and Political Appointees can Turn Conflict into Cooperation*. Lanham, ND: Lexington Books.

March, J.G. (2009). "Public Administration, Organizations and Democracy," in P.G. Roness and H. Sætren (eds.), *Change and Continuity in Public Sector Organizations*. Bergen: Fagbokforlaget, 23–44.

—— J.P. Olsen (1982). "The New Institutionalism: Organizational Factors in Political Life," *American Political Science Review*, 78(3), 738–49.

—— —— (1989). *Rediscovering Institutions*. New York: Free Press.

Marini, F. (ed.) (1971). *Toward a New Public Administration: The Minnowbrook Perspective*. Scranton, PA: Chandler.

Maritain, J. (1979). *An Introduction to Philosophy*. London: Sheed and Ward (trans. E.I. Watkin).

Martin, R.C. (1952). "Political Science and Public Administration: A Note on the State of the Union," *American Political Science Review*, 46(3), 660–76.

Martin, J. (1992). *Cultures in Organizations. Three Perspectives*. New York/Oxford: Oxford University Press.

Masterman, M. (1970). "The Nature of a Paradigm," in I. Lakatos and A. Musgrave (eds.), *Criticism and the Growth of Knowledge*. London: Cambridge University Press, 51–89.

Matheson, C. (2009). "Understanding the Policy Process: The Work of Henry Mintzberg," *Public Administration Review*, 69(6), 1148–71.

Mayntz, R. (1978). *Soziologie der öffentliche Verwaltung*. Heidelberg/Karlsruhe: C.F. Müller Juristischer Verlag.

Mazlish, B. (1998). *The Uncertain Sciences*. New Haven/London: Yale University Press.

McCurdy, H.E. (1986). *Public Administration: A Bibliographical Guide to the Literature*. New York/Basel: Marcel Dekker, Inc.

—— R.E. Cleary (1984). "Why Can't We Resolve the Research Issue in Public Administration?," *Public Administration Review*, 44(1), 49–55.

McDermott, R. (2004). "The Feeling of Rationality: The Meaning of Neuroscientific Advances for Political Science," *Perspectives in Politics*, 2(4), 691–706.

McDonald, L. (1993). *The Early Origins of the Social Sciences*. Montreal: McGill-Queen's University Press.

McGovern, P.J. (ed.) (2010). "Perestroika in Political Science: Past, Present, and Future," *PS: Perspectives on Politics*, 8(3), 725–54.

McKenzie, E. C. (1994). *Privatopia: Homeowner Associations and the Rise of Residential Private Government*. New Haven, CT: Yale University Press.

—— (2005). "Planning Through Residential Clubs: Homeowners' Associations," *Economic Affiars*. Oxford: Institute of Economic Affairs, Blackwell Publishing, 28–31.

McNally, R.J. (1992). "Disunity in Psychology: Chaos or Speciation?," *American Psychologist*, 47(9), 1054.

McSwite, O.C. (1997). *Legitimacy in Public Administration: A Discourse Analysis*. Thousand Oaks: Sage.

—— (2002). *Invitation to Public Administration*. New York/London: M.E. Sharpe.

Mead, L.M. (2010). "Scholasticism in Political Science," *Perspectives on Politics* 8(2), 453–64.

Medicus, G. (2005). "Mapping Transdisciplinarity in Human Sciences," in Janis W. Lee (ed.), *Focus on Gender Identity*. New York: Nova Science Publishers, 95–114.

—— (2008). "Basic Theory of Human Sciences: Block 1 (Fundamental Theory of Human Sciences)." No. 6, in the university course on *Einführung in die Humanethologie* (i.e., Introduction to Human Ethology), University of Innsbruck, Austria. Accessed at http://www.homepage.uibk.ac.at/~c720126/humanethologie/ws/medicus/block1 December 17, 2008.

Meier, K.J. (2005). "Public Administration and the Myth of Positivism: The AntiChrist's View," *Administrative Theory & Praxis*, 27(4), 650–68.

—— (2007a). "The Public Administration of Politics, or, What Political Science Could Learn from Public Administration," *PS: Political Science & Politics*, 60(1), 3–9.

—— (2007b). "The Public Administration of Politics, or What Political Science Could Learn from Public Administration," *PS: Political Science and Politics*, 40(1), 3–9.

—— G.A. Krause (2003*a*). "The Scientific Study of Bureaucracy: An Overview," in ibid. (eds.), *Politics, Policy, and Organizations. Frontiers in the Scientific Study of Bureaucracy*. Ann Arbor: The University of Michigan Press, 1–19.

—— —— (2003*b*). "Conclusion: An Agenda for the Scientific Study of Bureaucracy," in ibid. (eds.), *Politics, Policy, and Organizations. Frontiers in the Scientific Study of Bureaucracy*. Ann Arbor: The University of Michigan Press, 292–307.

—— L.J. O'Toole (2006). *Bureaucracy in a Democratic State; A Governance Perspective*. Baltimore: Johns Hopkins University Press.

—— —— (2007). "Deconstructing Larry Luton, or What Time is the Next Train to Reality Junction?," *Administration & Society*, 39(6), 786–96.

—— —— (2009). "The Proverbs of New Public Management. Lessons From an Evidence-Based Research Agenda," *American Review of Public Administration*, 39(1), 4–22.

—— —— H.T. Goerdel (2006). "Management Activity and Program Performance: Gender as Management Capital," *Public Administration Review*, 66(1), 24–36.

Meinecke, F. (1957). *Macchiavellism. The Doctrine of Raison d'État and Its Place in Modern History*. New Haven: Yale University Press.

Melzer, A.M., J. Weinberger, and M.R. Zinman (2003). *The Public Intellectual: Between Philosophy and Politics*. Lanham, MD: Rowman & Littlefield.

Merriam, C.E. (1934). *Civic Education in the United States*. New York: Charles Scribner's Sons.

Merton, R.K. (1967). *On Theoretical Sociology: Five Essays, Old and New*. New York/ London: The Free Press/Collier McMillan.

Meyer, M.W. (1979). *Change in Public Bureaucracies*. Cambridge: Cambridge University Press.

Mikesell, J.L. (2007). *Fiscal Administration. Analysis and Application in the Public Sector*, 7th ed. Belmont, CA: Thomson Wadsworth.

Miller, T.C. (ed.) (1984). *Public Sector Performance. A Conceptual Turning Point*. Baltimore/ London: The Johns Hopkins University Press.

Miller, H.T. (2002). *Postmodern Public Policy*. Albany: State University of New York Press.

—— (2003). "The Empirical Discourse of Positivism." Paper presented at the 16th annual conference of the Public Administration Theory Network, Anchorage, Alaska, June 19–21.

—— C.J. Fox (2000). "The Epistemic Community," *Administration & Society*, 32(6), 668–85.

—— —— (2007 [1995]). *Postmodern Public Administration*. Armonk, NY: M.E. Sharpe.

—— R. Islam (2003). "Pat-Net as Mainstream: A Bibliographic Hypothesis." Paper presented at the Annual Conference of the Public Administration Theory Network, June 19–21, 2003, Anchorage, Alaska.

Mills, C.W. (1959). *The Sociological Imagination*. New York: Oxford University Press.

Mitchell, W.C. (1988). "Virginia, Rochester, and Bloomington: Twenty-Five Years of Public Choice and Political Science," *Public Choice*, 56(1) 101–19.

—— (1999). "Political Science and Public Choice: 1950–1970," *Public Choice*, 98(2), 237–49.

Mitchell, D., and M.R. Dietrich (2006). "Integration without Unification: An Argument for Pluralism in the Biological Sciences." *The American Naturalist*, 168(S6), 73–9.

Moe, T.M. (1980). *The Organization of Interests*. Chicago: Chicago University Press.

—— (1990). "The Politics of Structural Choice: Toward a Theory of Public Bureaucracy," in O.E. Williamson (ed.), *Organization Theory. From Chester Barnard to the Present and Beyond*. New York: Oxford University Press, 116–53.

—— (2001). Comments at ASPA Panel on The State of Research about Bureaucracy. Phoenix, August 31.

Monroe, K., G. Almond, J. Gunnell, I. Shapiro, G. Graham, B. Barber, K. Shepsle, and J. Cropsey (1990). "The Nature of Political Science: A Roundtable Discussion," *PS: Political Science and Politics*, 23(1), 34–43.

Monroe, K.R., R. Hardin, R. Jervis, E. Ostrom, S. Rudolph, M. Smiley, and R. Smith (2002). "Shaking Things Up? Thoughts about the Future of Political Science: An Introduction," *PS: Perspectives on Politics*, 35(2), 181–205.

Montuschi, E. (2003). *The Objects of Social Science*. London/New York: Continuum.

Morçöl, G., and L.F. Dennard (2000). *New Sciences for Public Administration and Policy: Connections and Reflections*. Burke, VA: Chatelaine Press.

Morgan, G. (1983). *Beyond Method: Strategies for Social Research*. Beverly Hills: Sage.

Morgan, D.F. (1990). "Administrative Phronesis: Discretion and the Problem of Administrative Legitimacy in Our Constitutional System," in H.D. Kass and B.L. Catron (eds.), *Images and Identities in Public Administration*. Newbury Park: Sage, 67–86.

Mosher, F.C. (1956). "Research in Public Administration: Some Notes and Suggestions," *Public Administration Review*, 16(2), 169–78.

—— (1968). *Democracy and the Public Service*. New York: Oxford University Press.

Mouzelis, N.P. (1967). *Organisation and Bureaucracy: An Analysis of Modern Theories*. Chicago: Aldine Publishing Company.

—— (1991). *Back to Sociological Theory: The Construction of Social Orders*. New York: St. Martin's Press.

—— (2008). *Modern and Postmodern Social Thinking: Bridging the Divide*. Cambridge: Cambridge University Press.

Munro, W.B. (1928). "Physics and Politics – An Old Analogy Revised," *American Political Science Review*, 22(1), 1–11.

Murphy, W.T. (1997). *The Oldest Social Science? Configurations of Law and Modernity*. Oxford: Clarendon Press.

Nelson, R.R., and S.G. Winter (1982). *An Evolutionary Theory of Economic Change*. Cambridge, MA/London: The Belknap Press of Harvard University Press.

Newell, W.H. (2006). "Decision Making in Interdisciplinary Studies," in G. Morçöl (ed.), *Handbook on Decision Making*. New York: Marcel Dekker, 245–64.

Nisbet, R. (1975). *The Twilight of Authority*. New York: Oxford University Press.

—— (1986). *The Making of Modern Society*. Brighton: Wheatsheaf Books Ltd.

Norton, A. (2004). *95 Theses on Politics, Culture, and Method*. New Haven: Yale University Press.

Novak, W.J. (2008). "The Myth of the 'Weak' American State," *American Historical Review*, 113(3), 752–72.

Novak, J.D., and A.J. Cañas (2008). "The Theory Underlying Concept Maps and How to Construct and Use Them." Technical Report Tools 2006-01, revised 01-2008, Florida Institute of Human and Machine Cognition. Accessed at http://cmap.ihmc.us/Publications/ResearchPapers/TheoryUnderlyingConceptMaps.pdf August 27, 2008.

Oleson, A., and J. Voss (eds.) (1979). *The Organization of Knowledge in Modern America, 1860–1920*. Baltimore: The Johns Hopkins University Press.

Olsen, J.P. (2001). "Garbage Cans, New Institutionalism, and the Study of Politics," *American Political Science Review*, 95(1), 191–8.

Olson, M. (1965). *The Logic of Collective Action: Public Goods and the Theory of Groups*. Cambridge, MA: Harvard University Press.

Orchard, L., and H. Stretton (1997). "Public Choice," *Cambridge Political Economy Society*, 21(3), 409–30.

Ostrom, V. (1974). *The Intellectual Crisis in American Public Administration*. University, AL: The University of Alabama Press.

—— (1977). "The Undisciplinary Discipline of Public Administration: A Response to Stillman's Critique," *Midwest Review of Public Administration*, 11(4), 304–8.

—— (1997). *The Meaning of Democracy and the Vulnerability of Democracies*. Ann Arbor: University of Michigan Press.

Ostrom, E. (1990). *Governing the Commons: The Evolution of Institutions for Collective Action*. Cambridge: Cambridge University Press.

—— (1992). *Crafting Institutions for Self-Governing Irrigation Systems*. San Francisco: ICS Press.

—— (1997). *The Comparative Study of Public Economies*. Acceptance speech as recipient of the Frank E. Seidman Distinguished Award in Political Economy.

—— (2007). "Institutional Rational Choice: An Assessment of the Institutional Analysis and Development Framework," in P.A. Sabatier (ed.), *Theories of the Policy Process*. Boulder, CO: Westview Press, 21–64.

Oswick, D.E., (2008). "It's All about Commensurability – Isn't it?," *Administration & Society*, 40(3), 423–6.

O'Toole, L.J. (1977). "Lineage, Continuity, Frederickson, and the 'New Public Administration.'" *Administration & Society*, 9(2), 233–52.

—— (1995). "Diversity or Cacophony? The Research Enterprise in Public Administration," *Public Administration Review*, 55(3), 293–7.

—— K.J. Meier (1999). "Modeling the Impact of Public Managment: Implications of Structural Context," *Journal of Public Administration Research and Theory*, 9(4), 505–26.

Overman, E.S. (1989). "Response to R.F. Shangraw and M.M. Crow," *Public Administration Review*, 49(2), 159–60.

—— (1996). "The New Sciences of Administration: Chaos and Quantum Theory," *Public Administration Review*, 56(5), 487–91.

Page, E.C. (1992). *Political Authority and Bureaucratic Power: A Comparative Analysis*. New York: Harvester Wheatsheaf.

—— (2003). "Wine, Taxes, and Prison: A Premodernist View of Thick Description," in M.R. Rutgers (ed.), *Retracing Public Administration*. Amsterdam: JAI Press, 153–60.

—— B. Jenkins (2005). *Policy Bureaucracy. Government with a Cast of Thousands*. Oxford: Oxford University Press.

Painter, M., and B.G. Peters (2010). *Tradition and Public Administration*. New York: Palgrave Macmillan.

Pantin, C.F.A. (1968). *The Relation between the Sciences*. Cambridge: Cambridge University Press.

Perry, J.L. (1991). "Strategies for Building Public Administration Theory," in J.L. Perry (ed.), *Research in Public Administration*, vol.1. Stamford, CT: JAI Press, 1–18.

—— K.L. Kraemer (1986). "Research Methodology in the Public Administration Review, 1975–1984," *Public Administration Review*, 46(3), 215–26.

—— —— (1990). "Research Methodology in Public Administration: Issues and Patterns," in N.B. Lynn, and A. Wildavsky (eds.), *Public Administration. The State of the Discipline*. Chatham, NJ: Chatham House, 347–72.

Perry, A. (1992). *Belgrave Square*. New York: Fawcett Columbine.

Peters, B.G. (1989). *The Politics of Bureaucracy*. New York: Longman.

—— (1991). *The Politics of Taxation. A Comparative Perspective*. Cambridge, MA: Blackwell.

Pfiffner, J.M. (1946 [1935]). *Public Administration*. New York: The Ronald Press Company.

—— R. Presthus (1967 [1935]). *Public Administration*. New York: The Ronald Press Company.

Phillips, D.C. (1987). *Philosophy, Science and Social Inquiry. Contemporary Methodological Controversies in Social and Related Applied Fields of Research*. Oxford: Pergamom Press.

Poggi, G. (1978). *The Development of the Modern State. A Sociological Introduction*. Stanford: Stanford University Press.

—— (1990). *The State: Its Nature, Development, and Prospects*. Stanford: Stanford University Press.

Polanyi, K. (1944). *The Great Transformation*. New York/Toronto: Rinehart & Company.

Polanyi, M. (1958). *Personal Knowledge: Towards a Post-Critical Philosophy*. Chicago: University of Chicago Press.

—— (1962). *Personal Knowledge: Towards a Post-Critical Philosophy*. New York: Harper Torch.

—— (1964 [1946]). *Science, Faith and Society: A Searching Examination of the Meaning and Nature of Scientific Inquiry*. Chicago: The University of Chicago Press.

—— (1966). *The Tacit Dimension*. Garden City, NY: Doubleday & Company, Inc.

Popper, K. (1963). *Conjectures and Refutations: The Growth of Scientific Knowledge*. London: Routledge.

Posner, R.A. (2001). *Public Intellectuals: A Study of Decline*. Cambridge, MA: Harvard University Press.

Pressman, J., and A. Wildavsky (1973). *Implementation: How Great Expectations in Washington Are Dashed in Oakland: Or, Why It's Amazing that Federal Programs Work at All*. Berkeley: University of California Press.

Presthus, R. (1964). "Decline of the Generalist Myth," *Public Administration Review*, 35(4), 211–16.

Preziosi, D. (1993). "Seeing Through Art History," in E. Messer-Davidow, D.R. Shumway, and D.J. Sylvan (eds.), *Knowledges: Historical and Critical Studies in Disciplinarity*. Charlottesville: University Press of Virginia, 215–31.

Price, D.K. (1965). *The Scientific Estate*. Cambridge, MA: The Belknap Press of Harvard University Press.

Putnam, R.D., R. Leonardi, and R.Y. Nanetti (1993). *Making Democracy Work: Civic Traditions in Modern Italy*. Princeton: Princeton University Press.

Raadschelders, J.C.N. (1997). "Size and Organizational Differentiation in Historical Perspective," *Journal of Public Administration Research and Theory*, (7)3, 419–41.

—— (1998*a*). "Vijftig Jaar Bestuurswetenschappen, 1947–1996," in H.M. de Jong (ed.), *Bestuurswetenschappen. Een analyse van 50 Jaar Bestuurswetenschappen*. Den Haag: VNG, 4–39.

—— (1998*b*). *Handbook of Administrative History*. New Brunswick, NJ: Transaction Publishers.

—— (1999). "A Coherent Framework for the Study of Public Administration," *Journal of Public Administration Research and Theory*, 9(2), 281–303.

—— (2000*a*). "Understanding Government in Society: We See the Trees, but Could We See the Forest?," *Administrative Theory & Praxis*, 22(2), 192–225.

—— (2000*b*). "Administrative History of the United States: Development and State of the Art," *Administration & Society*, 32(5), 499–528.

—— (2002). "Woodrow Wilson on the History of Government: Passing Fad or Constitutive Framework for His Philosophy of Governance?," *Administration & Society*, (35)5, 579–98.

—— (2003*a*). "Understanding Government Through Differentiated Integration," in M.R. Rutgers (ed.), *Retracing Public Administration*. Amsterdam: JAI Press, 329–56.

—— (2003*b*). *Government: A Public Administration Perspective*. Armonk, NY: M.E. Sharpe.

—— (2004). "A Model of the Arena of PA-Theory: Bogey Man, Doctor's Bag and/or Artist's Medium," *Administrative Theory & Praxis*, 26(1), 46–78.

—— (2005). "Government and Public Administration: Challenges to and Need for Connecting Knowledge," *Administrative Theory & Praxis*, 27(4), 602–27.

—— (2008). "Understanding Government: Four Intellectual Traditions in the Study of Public Administration," *Public Administration (UK)*, 86(4), 925–49.

—— (2009*a*). "Is American Public Administration Dissociating from Historical Context? On the Nature of time and the Need to Understand it in Government and Its Study," *American Review of Public Administration*, 40(3), 236–60.

—— (2009*b*). "Trends in the American Study of Public Administration: What do they Mean for Korean Public Administration?," *The Korean Journal of Policy Studies*, 23(2), 1–24.

—— (2010*a*). "Did Max Weber's Agony and Ecstacy Influence his Scholarship," *Public Administration Review*, 70(2), 304–16.

—— (2010*b*). "Identity Without Boundaries: Public Administration's Canon(s) of Integration," *Administration & Society* 42(2), 131–59.

—— (2011). "The Study of Public Administration in the United States," *Public Administration*, 89(1).

—— K-H. Lee (2011). "Trends in the Study of Public Administration: Empirical and Qualitative Observations from *Public Administration Review*, 2000–2009," *Public Administration Review*, 71(1), 19–33.

—— M.R. Rutgers (1989*a*). "Grondslagen en grondvragen van de bestuurskunde. Over de methodologische fundamenten van de bestuurskunde," *Bestuurswetenschappen*, 43(2), 72–81.

—— —— (1989*b*). "Verklaring en bureaucratie. Verklaren als methodologisch problem voor de bestuurskunde geïllustreerd aan de hand van bureaucratie-onderzoek," *Beleidsanalyse*, 89(2), 22–9.

—— M.R. Rutgers (1999). "The Waxing and Waning of the State and its Study: Changes and Challenges in the Study of Public Administration," in W.J.M. Kickert and R.J. Stillmann (eds.), *Administrative Sciences in Europe and the United States*. Cheltenham, UK/Northampton, MA: Edward Elgar, 17–35.

—— M.R. Rutgers (2001). "Developments and Trends in the Study of Public Administration, 1945–Present." Paper presented at meeting of Research Committee 32 of the International Political Science Association, March 29, 2001.

Raadschelders, J.C.N., and F.M. van der Meer (eds.) (1998). *L'entourage administratif du pouvoir exécutif*. Cahier d'Histoire de l'Administration no.5. Brussels: Ets. Bruylant.

—— T.A.J. Toonen, and F.M. Van der Meer (eds.) (2007). *The Civil Service in the 21st Century. Comparative Perspectives*. Houndmills: Palgrave MacMillan.

Radin, B. (2002). *The Accountable Juggler: The Art of Leadership in a Federal Agency*. Washington, DC: CQ Press.

—— (2010). "Brenda Bryant: There is Nothing More Practical than a Good Theory," *Public Administration Review*, 70(2), 289–94.

Radkau, J. (2009). *Max Weber: A Biography*. Cambridge: Polity Press.

Rainey, H.G. (1997). *Understanding and Managing Public Organizations*. San Francisco: Jossey Bass.

Rawls, J. (1971). *A Theory of Justice*. Cambridge, MA: Belknap.

Redford, E.S. (1961). "Reflections on a Discipline," *American Political Science Review*, 55(4), 755–62.

Redhead, M.L.G. (1984). "Unification in Science," *British Journal for the Philosophy of Science*, 35(3), 274–9.

Reeves, J.S. (1929). "Perspectives in Political Science, 1903–1928," *American Political Science Review*, 23(1), 1–15.

Reeves, R. (2007). *John Stuart Mill: Victorian Firebrand*. London: Atlantic Books.

Reiner, R. (1992). *The Politics of the Police*. New York: Harvester Wheatsheaf.

Reschke, C.H. (2005). "Strategy: The Path of History and Social Evolution," Paper for the Critical Management Studies Conference, Judge Institute, Cambridge.

Rhodes, R.A.W. (1979). *Public Administration and Policy Analysis*. Farnborough: Saxon House.

—— (1991). "Theory and Methods in British Public Administration: The View from Political Science," *Political Studies*, 39(3), 533–54.

—— (1996). "From Institutions to Dogma: Tradition, Eclecticism, and Ideology in the Study of British Public Administration," *Public Administration Review*, 56(1), 507–16.

—— C. Dargie, A. Melville, and B. Tutt (1995). "The State of Public Administration: A Professional History, 1970–1995," *Public Administration (UK)*, 73(1), 1–15.

Riccucci, N. (2010). *Public Administration: Traditions of Inquiry and Philosophies of Knowledge*. Washington, DC: Georgetown University Press.

Richter, M. (1968/69). "Comparative Political Analysis in Montesquieu and Tocqueville," *Comparative Politics*, 1(2), 129–60.

Rickert, H. (1962 [1899]). *Science and History: A Critique of Positivist Epistemology*. Princeton, NJ: D. van Nostrand.

Ridley, F.F. (1972). "Public Administration: Cause for Discontent," *Public Administration (UK)*, 50(1), 65–78.

Riedl, R. (1978/79). "Über die Biologie des Ursachen-Denkens: Ein evolutionistischer, systemtheoretischer Versuch," in H. von Ditfurth (ed.), *Mannheimer Forum – Ein Panorama der Naturwissenschaften*. Mannheim: Boehringer, 9–70.

—— (1984*a*). *Biology of Knowledge: The Evolutionary Basis of Reason*. Chichester: John Wiley & Sons.

—— (1984*b*). "Evolution and Evolutionary Knowledge: On the Correspondence between Cognitive Order and Nature," in F.M. Wuketits (ed.), *Concepts and Approaches in Evolutionary Epistemology: Towards and Evolutionary Theory of Knowledge*. Dordrecht: Kluwer, 35–50.

Ringer, F. (2004). *Max Weber: An Intellectual Biography*. Chicago/London: The University of Chicago Press.

Ritter, M. (2003). "Discovery of Double Helix Hits 50th Anniversary: Cardboard Cutouts, Flash of Insight Ignited Biological Revolution," *Norman Transcript*, February 26.

Rittel, H., and M. Webber (1973). "Dilemmas in a General Theory of Planning," *Policy Sciences*, 4(1), 155–69.

Rockman, B.A. (2000). "Fifty Years of Hard Labor: Working in the (Barren?) Vineyards of Public Administration." Paper for the World Congress of the International Political Science Association, Quebec City, Quebec, Canada, July 31 – August 6.

Rodgers, R., and N. Rodgers (2000). "Defining the boundaries of Public Administration: Undisciplined Mongrels versus Disciplined Purists," *Public Administration Review*, 60(5), 435–43.

Rohr, J.A. (1986). *To Run a Constitution: Legitimacy and the Administrative State*. Lawrence, KS: University Press of Kansas.

—— (1995). *Founding Republic in France and America: A study in Constitutional Governance*. Lawrence, KS: University Press of Kansas.

Rohrbaugh, J., and D.F. Andersen (1997). "Letter to the Editor," *Public Administration Review*, 57(2), 186.

Rose, R. (1976). "Disciplined Research and Undisciplined Problems," *International Social Science Journal*, 28(1), 99–121.

—— P.L. Davies (1994). *Inheritance in Public Policy: Change Without Choice in Britain*. London: Yale University Press.

Rosenau, P.M. (1992). *Postmodernism and the Social Sciences: Insights, Inroads, and Intrusions*. Princeton, NJ: Princeton University Press.

Rosenbloom, D.H., and R. Kravchuk (2005 [1983]). *Public Administration: Understanding Management, Politics and Law in the Public Sector*. New York: McGraw-Hill.

Ross, D. (1991). *The Origins of American Social Science*. Cambridge: Cambridge University Press.

Rouban, L. (2008). "Reform without Doctrine: Public Management in France," *International Journal of Public Sector Management*, 21(2), 133–49.

Rudolph, L.I., and S.H. Rudolph (2010). "Economics' Fall from Grace," *PS: Perspectives on Politics*, 8(3):747–8.

Rutgers, M.R. (1987). "Bestuurskunde: onderdelen en hulpwetenschappen," in A. Van Braam, M.-L. Bemelmans-Videc (eds.), *Leerboek Bestuurskunde*. Muiderberg: Coutinho, 303–7.

—— (1993). *Tussen Fragmentatie en Integratie. De bestuurskunde als kennisintegrerende wetenschap*. Delft: Eburon.

—— (1994). "Can the Study of Public Administration do Without a Concept of the State? Reflections on the Work of Lorenz von Stein," *Administration & Society*, 26(3), 395–412.

—— (1995). "Seven Sins in Thinking About the Study of Public Administration," *Administrative Theory & Praxis*, 17(1), 67–85.

Rutgers, M.R. (1996). "The Meaning of Administration. Translating Across Boundaries," *Journal of Management Inquiry*, 5(1), 14–20.

—— (1997). "Beyond Woodrow Wilson: The Identity of the Study of Public Administration in Historical Perspective," *Administration & Society*, 29(3), 276–300.

—— (1998). "Paradigm Lost: Crisis as Identity of the Study of Public Administration," *International Review of Administrative Sciences*, 64(4), 553–64.

—— (2001). "The Prince, His Welfare State, and its Administration: Christiaan Von Wolff's Administrative Philosophy," *Public Voices*, 4(3), 29–45.

—— (2004). *Grondslagen van de Bestuurskunde. Historie, Begripsvorming en Kennisintegratie*. Bussum: Coutinho.

—— (2009). "The Oath of Office as Public Value Guardian," *The American Review of Public Administration*, 40(4), 428–44.

Sanderson, S.K. (2001). *The Evolution of Human Sociality. A Darwinian Conflict Perspective*. Lanham: Rowman & Littlefield.

Sandford, J. (2010). "Nonprofits within Policy Fields," *Journal of Policy Analysis and Management*, 29(3), 637–44.

Sarin, R. (1999). "Book Review of Jennifer Halpern and Robert Stern, *Debating Rationality: Nonrational Aspects of Organizational Decision Making*. Ithaca/London: Cornell University Press," *Journal of Economic Literature*, 37(3), 1182–4.

Sartori, G. (2004). "Where is Political Science Going?" *PS: Political Science and Politics*, 37(4), 785–7.

Saunders, R.M. (1998). *In Search of Woodrow Wilson: Beliefs and Behavior*. Westport, CT/London: Greenwood Press.

Saunier, P.-Y. (2003). "Les voyages municipaux américains en Europe 1900–1940. Une piste d'histoire transnationale," *Yearbook of European Administrative History*, 15, 267–88.

Sayre, W. (1951). "Trends of a Decade in Administrative Values," *Public Administration Review*, 11(1), 1–9.

Sayre, W.S. (1958). "Premises of Public Administration: Past and Emerging," *Public Administration Review*, 18(2), 102–5.

Schaar, J.H., and S.S. Wolin (1963). "Review Essay: Essays on the Scientific Study of Politics: A Critique," *American Political Science Review*, 57(1), 125–50.

Schein, E.H. (1985). *Organizational Culture and Leadership: A Dynamic View*. San Francisco: Jossey-Bass.

Schön, D.A. (1983). *The Reflective Practitioner: How Professionals Think in Action*. New York: Basic Books.

Scott, J. (2000). "Rational Choice Theory," in G. Browning, A. Halcli, and F. Webster (eds.), *Understanding Contemporary Society: Theories of the Present*. Thousand Oaks, CA: Sage.

Secord, P.F. (1986). "Explanation in the Social Sciences and in Life Situations," in D.W. Fiske and R.A. Shweder (eds.), *Metatheory in Social Science: Pluralism and Subjectivities*. Chicago: The University of Chicago Press, 197–222.

Seibel, W. (1996). "Administrative Science as Reform: German Public Administration," *Public Administration Review*, 56(1), 74–81.

Self, P. (1979). *Administrative Theories and Politics: An Enquiry into the Structure and Processes of Modern Government*. London: George Allen & Unwin.

Shafritz, J.M., E.W. Russell, and C. P. Borick (2007). *Introducing Public Administration*, 5th ed. New York: Pearson Longman.

Shangraw, R.F., and M.M. Crow (1989). "Public Administration as Design Science," *Public Administration Review*, 49(2), 153–8.

Shapiro, I. (2005). *The Flight from Reality in the Human Sciences*. Princeton: Princeton University Press.

Sharkansky, I. (1978). *Public Administration: Policy-Making in Government Agencies*, 4th ed.: Chicago: Rand McNally.

Sherwood, F.P. (ed.) (2008). *Doctoral Education at the Washington Public Affairs Center: 28 Years (1973–2001) as a Public Service Outpost of the University of Southern California*. New York: iUniverse, Inc.

Shields, P.M. (2008). "Rediscovering the Taproot: Is Classical Pragmatism the Route to Renew Public Administration?," *Public Administration Review*, 68(2), 205–21.

Siffin, W.J. (1956). "The New Public Administration: Its Study in the United States," *Public Administration (UK)*, 34(4), 365–76.

Sil, R., and P.J. Katzenstein (2010). "Analytic Eclecticism in the Study of World Politics: Reconfiguring Problems and Mechanisms across Research Traditions," *Perspectives on Politics*, 8(2), 411–31.

Simon, H.A. (1948). "Review of The Administrative State," *Journal of Politics*, 10(6), 843–5.

—— (1952). "Development of Theory of Democratic Administration: Replies and Comments," *American Political Science Review*, 46(2), 494–6.

—— (1958). "The Decision-Making Schema: A Reply," *Public Administration Review*, 18(1), 60–3.

—— (1960). *The New Science of Management Decision*. New York: Harper & Row.

—— (1966 [1947]). "A Comment on The Science of Administration: Comment on article by Robert Dahl," in C.E. Hawley and R.G. Weintraub (eds.), *Administrative Questions and Political Answers*. New York: D. van Nostrand, 34–7.

—— (1969 [1946]). "The Proverbs of Administration," in A. Etzioni (ed.), *Readings on Modern Organizations*. Englewood Cliffs, NJ: Prentice-Hall., 32–49.

—— (1973*a*). "Applying Organization Technology to Organization Design," *Public Administration Review*, 33(3), 268–78.

—— (1973*b*). "Organizational Man: Rational or Self-Actualizing?," *Public Administration Review*, 33(4), 346–53.

—— (1981 [1969]). *The Sciences of the Artificial*. Cambridge, MA: The MIT Press.

—— (1985). "Human Nature in Politics: The Dialogue of Psychology with Political Science," *American Political Science Review*, 79(2), 293–304.

—— (1991). *Models of My Life*. New York: Basic Books.

——(1992). "Herbert Simon Responds," *Journal of Public Administration Research and Theory*, 2(2), 110–12.

—— (1995). "Guest Editorial," *Public Administration Review*, 55(5), 404–5.

—— (1957–1997a). *Administrative Behavior: A Study of Decision-Making Processes in Administrative Organization*, 4th ed. New York: The Free Press.

—— (1997b). *An Empirically Based Microeconomics*. Cambridge: Cambridge University Press.

—— D.W. Smithburg, and V.A. Thompson (1964 [1950]). *Public Administration*. New York: Alfred A. Knopf.

Skocpol, T. (2003). *Diminished Democracy: From Membership to Management in American Civic Life*. Norman, OK: Oklahoma University Press.

—— M. Ganz, and Z. Munson (2000). "A Nation of Organizers: The Institutional Origins of Civic Voluntarism in the United States," *American Political Science Review*, 94(3), 527–46.

Small, H. (1973). "Co-Citation in Scientific Literature: A New Measure of the Relationship between Two Documents," *Journal of the American Society for Information Science*, 24(4), 265–9.

—— (1993). "Macro-Level Changes in the Structure of Co-Citation Clusters: 1983–1989," *Scientometrics*, 26(2), 5–20.

—— (1997). "Update on Science Mapping: Creating Large Document Spaces," *Scientometrics*, 38(2), 275–93.

—— E. Garfield (1985). "The Geography of Science: Disciplinary and National Mappings," *Journal of Information Science*, 1(1), 147–59.

Smith, C.L. (1992). *In the Spirit of the Earth: Rethinking History and Time*. Baltimore: The Johns Hopkins University Press.

Snell, D.C. (2007). "The Invention of the Individual," in ibid. (ed.), *A Companion to the Ancient Near East*. Malden, MA: Blackwell, 379–91.

Snow, C.P. (1971). *Public Affairs*. New York: Charles Scribner's Sons.

Sober, E., and D.S. Wilson (1998). *Unto Others: The Evolution and Psychology of Unselfish Behavior*. Cambridge, MA: Harvard University Press.

Somit, A., and J. Tanenhaus (1967). *The Development of American Political Science: From Burgess to Behavioralism*. Boston: Allen and Bacon, Inc.

Sorauf, F.J. (1965). *Political Science: An Informal Overview*. Columbus, OH: Charles E. Merrill.

Sowa, J.F. (2006). "The Challenge of Knowledge Soup," in J. Ramadas and S. Chunawala (eds.), *Research Trends in Science, Technology and Mathematics Education*. Mumbai: Homi Bhabha Centre, 55–90.

Spicer, M.W. (2001). *Public Administration and the State: A Postmodern Perspective*. Tuscaloosa, AL: University of Alabama Press.

Staats, A.W. (1991). "Unified Positivism and Unification Psychology: Fad or New Field?," *American Psychologist*, 46(9), 899–912.

Stallings, R.A., and J.M. Ferris (1988). "Public Administration Research: Work in PAR, 1940–1984," *Public Administration Review*, 48(1), 580–7.

Starbuck, W.H. (2006). *The Production of Knowledge: The Challenge of Social Science Research*. Oxford: Oxford University Press.

Stark, A. (2002). "Why Political Scientists aren't Public Intellectuals," *PS: Perspectives on Politics*, 35(3), 577–9.

Starling, G. (2008). *Managing the Public Sector*, 8th ed. Boston: Thomson Wadsworth.

Stene, E.O. (1940). "An Approach to a Science of Administration," *American Political Science Review*, 35(6), 1124–37.

Sternberg, R.J., E.L. Grigorenko, and D.A. Kalmar (2001). "The Role of Theory in Unified Psychology," *Journal of Theoretical and Philosophical Psychology*, 21(2), 99–117.

Stever, J.E. (1988). *The End of Public Administration: Problems of the Profession in the Post-Progressive Era*. Dobbs Ferry, NY: Transnational Publishers.

Stillman, II, R.J. (1976). "Professor Ostrom'n New Paradigm for American Public Administration – Adequate or Antique?," *Midwest Review of Public Administration*, 10(4), 179–92.

—— (1978). "A Reply to Professor Ostrom," *Midwest Review of Public Administration*, 12(1), 41–4.

—— (1997). "American vs. European Public Administration: Does Public Administration Make the Modern State, or Does the State Make Public Administration?," *Public Administration Review*, 57(4), 332–8.

—— (1998). *Creating the American State: The Moral Reformers and the Modern Administrative World They Made*. Tuscaloosa/London: The University of Alabama Press.

—— (1991, 1999a). *Preface to Public Administration: A Search for Themes and Direction*. Burke, VA: Chatelaine Press.

—— (1999b). "American versus European Public Administration: Does Public Administration Make the Modern State, or does the State Make Public Administration," in W.J.M. Kickert and R.J. Stillman II (eds.), *The Modern States and its Study: New Administrative Sciences in a Changing Europe and the United States*. Cheltenham: Elgar, 247–60.

—— (2010). *Public Administration: Concepts and Cases*, 8th ed. Boston: Houghton Mifflin.

Stivers, C. (2000). *Bureau Men, Settlement Women: Constructing Public Administration in the Progressive Era*. Lawrence, KA: University Press of Kansas.

—— (2007). "Public Administration's Myth of Sisyphus," *Administration & Society*, 39(8), 1008–12.

Stojkovic, S., D. Kalinich, and J. Klofas (1996). *Criminal Justice Organizations: Administration and Management*. Belmont, CA: Wadsworth.

Stone, D.C. (1975). "Birth of ASPA – A Collective Effort in Institution Building," *Public Administration Review*, 35(1), 83–93.

Storing, H.J. (ed.) (1962). *Essays on the Scientific Study of Politics*. New York: Holt, Rinehart and Winston.

Streib, G., B.J. Slotkin, and M. Rivera (2001). "Public Administration Research from a Practitioner Perspective," *Public Administration Review*, 61(5), 515–25.

Stump, E. (2003). *Aquinas*. London: Routledge.

Taagepera, R. (2007). "Why Political Science is not Scientific Enough: A Symposium," *European Political Science*, 6(2), 111–13.

—— (2008). *Making Social Sciences More Scientific: The Need for Predictive Models*. Oxford: Oxford University Press.

Taylor, C. (1998 [1971]). "Interpretation and the Sciences of Man," in E.D. Klemke, R. Hollinger, and D.W. Rudge (eds.), *Introductory Readings in the Philosophy of Science*. Amherst, NY: Prometheus Books, 110–27.

Tead, O. (1935). "Amateurs Versus Experts in Administration," *Annals*, 189(1), 42–7.

—— H.C. Metcalf (1926 [1920]). *Personnel Administration: Its Principles and Practice*. New York: McGraw-Hill.

Thieme, W. (1984). *Verwaltungslehre*. Cologne: Carl Heymanss.

Thompson, F.J. (1999). "Symposium on the Advancement of Public Administration," *Journal of Public Affairs Education*, 5(2), 119–25.

Thompson, F.J. (2007). "The Political Economy of Public Administration," in J. Rabin, W.B. Hildreth, and G.J. Miller (eds.), *Handbook of Public Administration*. Boca Raton: Taylor & Francis, 1063–99.

Thompson, J.D., R.W. Hawkes, and R.W. Avery (1969). "Truth Strategies and University Organizations," *Education Administration Quarterly*, 5(2), 4–25.

Thomson, M.E., and D.E. Brewster (1978). "Faculty Behavior in Low Paradigm versus High Paradigm Disciplines: A Case-Study," *Research in Higher Education*, 8(2), 169–75.

Tilly, C. (ed.) (1975). "Reflections on the History of European State Making," in ibid. (ed.), *The Formation of National States in Western Europe*. Princeton: Princeton University Press, 17–46.

—— (1990). *Coercion, Capital, and European States AD 990–1990*. Cambridge, MA: Basil Blackwell.

—— (1991). "How (and What?) are Historians Doing?," in D. Easton and C.S. Schelling (eds.) (1991). *Divided Knowledge: Across Disciplines, Across Cultures*. Newbury Park: Sage Publications, 86–117.

Tinbergen, N. (1963). "On the Aims and Methods of Ethology," *Zeitschrift für Tierpsychologie*, 20(3), 410–63.

Tocqueville, A. de (1969). *Democracy in America*. New York: Harper Perennial.

Tolkien, J.R.R. (2006). "Valedictory Address," in ibid (ed.), *The Monsters and the Critics*. London: Harper Collins, 224–40.

Tolman, E.C. (1948). "Cognitive Maps in Rats and Men," *Psychological Review*, 55(4), 189–208.

Toonen, T.A.J., and T.J.G. Verheyen (1999). "Public Administration Education in Europe: In Need of Convergence and Europeanisation?," in T.J.G. Verheijen and B. Connaughton (eds.), *Higher Education Programmes in Public Administration: Ready for the Challenge of Europeanisation?* Limerick, Ireland: Center for European Studies, University of Limerick, 395–413.

Toulmin, S. (1972). "The Variety of Rational Enterprises," in ibid. (ed.), *Human Understanding*. Princeton: Princeton University Press.

Trigger, B.G. (2003). *Understanding Early Civilizations: A Comparative Study*. Cambridge: Cambridge University Press.

Trochim, W.M.K. (1989). "Concept Mapping: Soft Science or Hard Art?," *Evaluation and Program Planning*, 12(1), 87–110.

Tucker, R.C. (ed.) (1978). *The Marx-Engels Reader*. New York: Norton.

Turner, R. (1991). "The Many Faces of American Sociology: A Discipline in Search of Identity," in D. Easton and C.S. Schelling (eds.), *Divided Knowledge: Across Disciplines, Across Cultures*. Newbury Park: Sage Publications, 59–85.

Van Baalen, P., and L. Karsten (2007). "Is Management Interdisciplinary? The Evolution of Management as an Interdisciplinary Field of Research and Education in the Netherlands," *Erim Report Series "Research in Management."* Rotterdam: Erasmus University, School of Economics.

Van Braam, A. (1989). *Filosofie van de Bestuurswetenschappen*. Leiden: Martinus Nijhoff.
—— (1998). "Het kenobject van de Nederlandse bestuurskunde in beweging," in H.M. de Jong (ed.), *Bestuurswetenschappen. Een analyse van vijftig jaar bestuurswetenschappen*. Den Haag: VNG, 40–53.
—— with M.L. Bemelmans-Videc (1986). *Leerboek Bestuurskunde*. Muiderberg: Coutinho.
Van Dale (1984). *Groot Woordenboek der Nederlandse Taal*. Utrecht/Antwerpen: Van Dale Lexicografie bv.
Van Gigch, J.P. (1997). "The Design of an Epistemology for the Management Discipline Which Resolves Dilemmas Among Ethical and Other Imperatives," *Systems Practice*, 10(4), 381–94.
—— (2001*a*). "Comparing the Epistemologies of Scientific Disciplines in Two Distinct Domains: Modern Physics versus Social Sciences. I The Epistemology and Knowledge Characteristics of the Physical Sciences," *Systems Research and Behavioral Science*, 19(2), 199–209.
—— (2001*b*). "Comparing the Epistemologies of Scientific Disciplines in Two Distinct Domains: Modern Physics versus Social Sciences. II The Epistemology and Knowledge Characteristics of the Physical Sciences," *Systems Research and Behavioral Science*, 19(6), 551–62.
Van Porijs, P. (1981). *Evolutionary Explanation in the Social Sciences: An Emerging Paradigm*. Totowa, NJ: Rowman and Littlefield.
Van Riper, P. (1967). "Hit 'Em Harder, John, Hit 'Em Harder," *Public Administration Review*, 27(4), 339–42.
Van de Ven, A.H., and M.S. Poole (1995). "Explaining Development and Change in Organizations," *The Academy of Management Review*, 20(3), 510–40.
Van der Eyden, T. (2003). *Public Management of Society: Rediscovering French Institutional Engineering in the European Context*. Amsterdam: IOS Press.
Vanelli, R. (2001). *Evolutionary Theory and Human Nature*. Boston: Kluwer Academic Publishers.
Ventriss, C. (1987). "Two Critical Issues of American Public Administration: Reflections of a Sympathetic Participant," *Administration & Society*, 19(1) 25–47.
Verheijen, T., and B. Connaughton (eds.) (1999). *Higher Education Programmes in Public Administration: Ready for the Challenge of Europeanisation?* Limerick, Ireland: Center for European Studies, University of Limerick.
Vigoda, E. (2002). "The Legacy of Public Administration," in ibid. (ed.), *Public Administration: An Interdiscplinary Critical Analysis*. New York: Marcel Dekker, 1–18.
Von Borch, H. (1954). *Obrigkeit und Widerstand: Zur politischen Soziologie des Beamtentums*. Tübingen: J.C.B. Mohr.
Von Hayek, F.A. (1974). "The Pretence of Knowledge," Nobel Memorial Prize Lecture. December 11, Stockholm http://At werdet.atspace.com/bin/hayek_lecture accessed May 6, 2008.
Von Mises, L. (1990). "Social Science and Natural Science," in R. Ebeling (ed.), *Money, Method, and Market Process: Essays by Ludwig von Mises*. Auburn: Kluwer (originally in *Journal of Social Philosophy & Jurisprudence* (1942) 7(3), 240–53).
Von Seckendorf, V.L. (1976 [1656]. *Teutscher Fürstenstaat*. Glashütten im Taunus: Verlag Detlev Auvermann.

Von Stein, L. (1865/66). *Die Verwaltunglehre: Die Lehre von der volziehende Gewalt, ihr Recht und Organismus* (Part I), *Die Verwaltungslehre: Die Lehre von der Innern Verwaltung* (Part II). Stuttgart: Verlag der J.G. Gotta'schen Buchhandlung.

—— (1887/88). *Handbuch der Verwaltungslehre. Der Begriff der Verwaltung und das System der politischen Staatswissenschaften* (Part I), *Handbuch der Verwaltungslehre. Die Verwaltung und das Gesellschaftlichen Leben* (Part III). Stuttgart: Verlag der J.G. Gotta'schen Buchhandlung.

Wachhaus, A. (2009). "Networks in Contemporary Public Administration: A Discourse Analysis," *Administrative Theory & Praxis*, 31(1), 59–77.

Wade, N. (2006). *Before the Dawn: Recovering the Lost History of Our Ancestors*. London: Penguin.

Wald, E. (1973). "Toward a Paradigm of Future Public Administration," *Public Administration Review*, 33(4), 366–72.

Waldo, D. (1952a). "Development of Theory of Democratic Administration," *American Political Science Review*, 46(1), 81–103.

—— (1952b). "Development of Theory of Democratic Administration: Replies and Comments," *American Political Science Review*, 46(2), 500–3.

—— (1961). "Organization Theory: An Elephantine Problem," *Public Administration Review*, 21(2), 210–15.

—— (1965 [1955]). *The Study of Public Administration*. New York: Random House.

—— (1968a). "Public Administration," *The Journal of Politics*, 30(2), 443–79.

—— (1968b). "Scope and Theory of Public Administration," in J.C. Charlesworth (ed.), *Theory and Practice of Public Administration: Scope, Objectives, and Methods*. Philadelphia: American Academy of Political and Social Science, 1–26.

—— (ed.) (1971). *Public Administration in a Time of Turbulence*. New York: Chandler.

—— (1975). "Political Science: Tradition, Discipline, Profession, Science, Enterprise," in F.I. Greenstein, and N.W. Polsby (eds.), *Political Science: Scope and Theory*. Vol. I of *Handbook of Political Science*. Reading, MA: Addison-Wesley Publishing Co., 1–130.

—— (1978). "Organization Theory: Revisiting the Elephant," *Public Administration Review*, 38(6), 589–97.

—— (1984 [1948]). *The Administrative State: A Study of the Political Theory of American Public Administration*. New York: Holmes & Meier.

—— (1987 [1968]). "Public Administration in a Time of Revolution," in J.M. White and A.C. Hyde (eds.), *Classics of Public Administration*. Chicago: The Dorsey Press, 361–9.

—— (1996 [1980]). "Public Administration and Ethics: A Prologue to a Preface," in R.J. Stillman II (ed.), *Public Administration: Concepts and Cases*. Boston: Houghton Mifflin, 460–71.

Walker, H. (1937). *Public Administration in the United States*. New York: Farrar & Rinehart.

Walker, L.S. (1990). "Woodrow Wilson, Progressive Reform and Public Administration," in P. van Riper (ed.), *The Wilson Influence on Public Administration: From Theory to Practice*. Washington, DC: American Society for Public Administration, 83–98.

Walker, T.C. (2010). "The Perils of Paradigm Mentalities: Revisiting Kuhn, Lakatos, and Popper," *Perspectives on Politics*, 8(2), 433–51.

Wamsley, G.L. (1996). "A Public Philosophy and Ontological Disclosure as the Basis for Normatively Grounded Theorizing in Public Administration?," in G.L. Wamsley and

J.F. Wolf (eds.), *Refounding Democratic Public Administration: Modern Paradoxes, Postmodern Challenges*. Thousand Oaks, CA: Sage, 351–401.

—— J.F. Wolf (1996). "Introduction: Can A High-Modern Project Find Happiness in a Postmodern Era?," in G.L. Wamsley and J.F. Wolf (eds.), *Refounding Democratic Public Administration: Modern Paradoxes, Postmodern Challenges*. Thousand Oaks, CA: Sage, 1–37.1

—— M.N. Zald (1973). *The Political Economy of Public Organizations: A Critique and Approach to the Study of Public Administration*. Lexington, MA: Lexington Books.

—— R.N. Bacher, C.T. Goodsell, P.S. Kronenberg, J.A. Rohr, C.M. Stivers, O.F. White, and J.F. Wolf (1990). *Refounding Public Administration*. Newbury Park: Sage.

Weaver, W. (1958). *A Quarter Century in the Natural Sciences*. Annual Report. New York: The Rockefeller Foundation.

Webber, C., and A. Wildavsky (1986). *A History of Taxation and Expenditure in the Western World*. New York: Simon & Schuster.

Weber, M. (1946). "Science as a Vocation," in H.H. Gerth and C. Wright Mills (trans. and eds.), *From Max Weber: Essays in Sociology*. New York: Oxford University Press, 129–56.

—— (1949). *The Methodology of the Social Sciences* (trans. and ed. E.A. Shils and H.A. Finch). New York: The Free Press.

—— (1980). *Wirtschaft und Gesellschaft. Grundriss der Verstehenden Soziologie*, 5th ed. (ed. J. Winckelman). Tübingen: J.C.B. Mohr.

—— (1985). "Objektive Möglichkeit und adequate Verursachung in der historischen kausalbetrachtung," in ibid. (ed.), *Gesammelte Aufsätze zur Wissenschaftslehre* , 6th ed. (edited J. Winckelman). Tübingen: J.C.B. Mohr, 146–214.

Weinberg, S. (2001). *Facing Up: Science and Its Cultural Adversaries*. Cambridge, MA/ London: Harvard University Press.

Weinsheimer, J.C. (1985). *Gadamer's Hermeneutics: A Reading of Truth and Method*. New Haven: Yale University Prsess.

Wenke, R.J., and D.I. Olszewski (2007). *Patterns in Prehistory: Humankind's First Three Million Years*. New York: Oxford University Press.

Weschler, L.F. (1982). "Public Choice: Methodological Individualism in Politics," *Public Administration Review*, 42(3), 288–94.

Westney, D.E. (1987). *Imitation and Innovation: The Transfer of Western Organizational Patterns to Meiji Japan*. Cambridge, MA/London: Harvard University Press.

Whicker, M.L., R.A. Strickland, and D. Olshfiski (1993). "The Troublesome Cleft: Public Administration and Political Science," *Public Administration Review*, 53(6), 531–41.

—— —— —— (1997). "Rejoinder to Keller and Spicer," *Public Administration Review*, 57(3), 271–2.

White, L.D. (1926). *Introduction to the Study of Public Administration*. New York: The MacMillan Co.

White, J.D. (1986*a*). "On the Growth of Knowledge in Public Administration," *Public Administration Review*, 46(1), 15–24.

—— (1986*b*). "Dissertations and Public in Public Administration," *Public Administration Review*, 46(3), 227–34.

—— G.B. Adams, and J.P. Forrester (1996). "Knowledge and Theory Development in Public Administration: The Role of Doctoral Education and Research," *Public Administration Review*, 56(5), 441–52.

Bibliography

White, O.F., and C. McSwain (1990). "The Phoenix Project: Raising a New Image of Public Administration from the Ashes of the Past," *Administration & Society*, 22(1), 3–38.

Whitley, R.D. (1976). "Umbrella and Polytheistic Scientific Disciplines and Their Elites," *Social Studies of Science*, 6(3–4), 471–97.

—— (1978). "The Organization of Scientific Work in 'Configurational' and 'Restricted' Sciences," *International Journal of Sociology*, 8(1–2), 95–112.

Wight, C. (2002). "Philosophy of Social Science and International Relations," in W. Carlsnaes, T. Risse, and B. Simmons (eds.), *Handbook of International Relations*. London: Sage, 23–51.

Williams, M. (2000). *Science and Social Science: An Introduction*. London: Routledge.

Williamson, O.E. (1996). *The Mechanisms of Governance*. Oxford: Oxford University Press.

Willoughby, W.F. (1927). *Principles of Public Administration*. Washington, DC: The Brookings Institution.

Wilson, W. (1889–1918). *The State: Elements of Historical and Practical Politics*. Boston: D.C. Heath & Company.

—— (1970). *The Papers of Woodrow Wilson* (ed. A.S. Link et al.), vol.8. Princeton: Princeton University Press.

——(1887–1992)., "The Study of Administration. R. J. Stillman," *Public Administration Concepts and Cases*. Boston: Houghton Mifflin, 6–17.

Wilson, E.O. (1998). *Consilience: The Unity of Knowledge*. New York: Alfred A. Knopf.

Winch, P. (1986 [1958]). *The Idea of a Social Science and its Relation to Philosophy*. London: Routledge & Kegan Paul.

Wise, L.R. (1999). "Taking Stock: Evidence about the Standing of Public Administration in America," *Journal of Public Affairs Education*, 5(2), 145–55.

Wolin, S.S. (1969). "Political Theory as a Vocation," *American Political Science Review*, 63(4), 1062–82.

Wren, D.A. (1972). *The Evolution of Management Thought*. New York: Ronald Press.

Wright, B. (2011). "Public Administration as an Interdisciplinary Field: Assessing Its Relationship with the Fields of Law, Management, and Political Science," *Public Administration Review*, 71(1), 96–101.

Wuketits, F.M. (1990). *Evolutionary Epistemology and Its Implications for Humankind*. Albany, NY: State University of New York Press.

Wylie, A. (1999). "Rethinking Unity as a "Working Hypothesis" for Philosophy of Science: How Archaeologists Exploit the Disunities of Science," *Perspectives on Science*, 7(3), 293–317.

Yankelovich, D. (1991). *Coming to Public Judgment: Making Democracy Work in a Complex World*. Syracuse, NY: Syracuse University Press.

Zorn, K. (1989). "The Economic Perspective on Public Administration," *Public Administration Review*, 49(2), 213–14.

Zukav, G. (1979). *The Dancing Wu-Li Masters: An Overview of the New Physics*. New York: William Morris.

Author Index

Author Index

Trochim, W.M.K. 38
Trowler, P.R. 62
Tucker, R.C. 43
Tullock, G. 122
Turner, R. 32

Van Baalen, P. 191
Van Braam, A. 21, 23, 153, 160, 207, 211–12
Van de Ven, A.H. 197
Van den Donk, W. 70, 155
Van der Eyden, T. 210
Van der Meer, F.M. 120
Vanelli, R. 54, 190
Van Gigch, J.P. 63–4 68
Van Parijs, Ph. 64
Van Riper, P.P. 27
Ventriss, C. 20
Verba, S. 119
Verheyen, T.J.G. 39, 210
Vigoda, E. 20
Von Borch, H. 14
Von Hayek, F.A. 62, 64, 66
Von Mises, L. 139
Von Seckendorf, V.L. 158, 209
Von Stein, L. 156
Voss, J. 212

Wachhaus, A. 106
Wade, N. 12
Wald, E. 138
Waldo, D.2, 8, 19–20, 24, 27, 38, 40, 75, 81, 83, 103, 127, 136, 143, 150–3, 156, 167, 176–7, 192, 198, 211–12
Walker, H. 106
Walker, L.S. 105
Walker, T.C. 6
Wamsley, G.L. 5, 23, 94, 111, 127, 131, 133, 1155, 157, 165, 168, 188, 195
Weaver, W. 62
Webber, M. 179

Weber, M. 10, 14, 65, 217
Weinberg, S. 137, 166–7
Weinsheimer, J.C. 66
Wenke, R.J. 33
Weschler, L.F. 173
Westney, D.E. 159
Whaples, R. 163
Whicker, M.L. 133
White, J.D. 21, 132, 151, 197
White, L.D. 106, 126
White, O.F. 150, 155
Whitley, R.D. 62, 70
Wight, C. 32, 42, 205
Wildavsky, A. 118
Williams, M. 33, 48
Williamson, O.E. 163
Willmott, H. 32, 193
Willoughby, W.F. 106
Wilson, D.S. 105, 183
Wilson, E.O. 43, 46, 64–5, 71, 182, 194
Wilson, W. 81
Winch, P. 40, 65
Windelband, W. 61
Winter, S.G. 138, 158
Wise, L.R. 127, 218
Wolf, J.F. 23, 133, 157
Wolin, S. 27, 164
Wren, D.A. 119
Wright, B. 202
Wuketits, F.M. 11, 52, 64
Wylie, A. 204, 206

Yankelovich, D. 28, 45, 83, 160, 165

Zald, M.N. 94, 111, 195
Zimbardo, P.G. 52, 67
Zorn, K. 198
Zuckerman, A.S. 32
Zukav, G. 47, 67

Subject Index